EDMUND SPENSER

EDMUND SPENSER

A Critical Study

BY

B. E. C. DAVIS

M.A. Oxon., Reader in English and Head of the
English Department at Westfield College,
University of London

NEW YORK

RUSSELL & RUSSELL · INC

1962

PUBLISHED 1933 BY CAMBRIDGE UNIVERSITY PRESS, LONDON
PUBLISHED 1962 BY RUSSELL & RUSSELL, INC. NEW YORK
BY ARRANGEMENT WITH CAMBRIDGE UNIVERSITY PRESS
L. C. CATALOG CARD NO: 62—10228

PRINTED IN THE UNITED STATES OF AMERICA

CONTENTS

PREFACE

Notwithstanding the attention devoted to Spenser in recent periodicals, for the general reader he still remains an "admired but neglected poet" as Thomas Warton described him in 1754. Since Dean Church's *Life* (1879) and Grosart's Edition (1882–4), the only works of importance devoted exclusively to the study of his writings and published in England have been the Oxford Editions (1909–10, 1912), Professor W. L. Renwick's *Edmund Spenser* (1925), together with his edition of Spenser now in progress, and various editions of separate works, among which priority must be given to C. H. Herford's *Shepheardes Calender* (1895). The defect has been partially made good through the diligence of American scholars, particularly through the researches of F. I. Carpenter, C. G. Osgood, E. A. Greenlaw, R. E. N. Dodge, P. W. Long and J. B. Fletcher; but most of their material remains within the confines of periodicals, whilst many of the problems at issue call for further investigation. It can hardly be disputed that, during the last half-century, Spenser has received less attention, apart from detached articles or cursory notices, than any other English poet of equal rank. Nor is it difficult to account for this neglect of a subject so riddled with pitfalls or of a writer whose tastes and interests seem so far removed from those of to-day.

The poetry of Spenser represents the meeting between the old world and the new, between the traditions of the Middle Ages and those of the Renaissance. The raw material of so eclectic an artist needs classification. For this reason, in the present work I have considered my author first as the New Poet of that English Renaissance which sprang from the

Preface

union of classical and mediæval culture, secondly as the Poet's Poet, prescribing by example to his successors a grammar of poetry that has withstood the test of time. If, as I believe, Spenser deserves recognition not merely as a weaver of fine phrases and fantasies but as a thinker and an interpreter of his age, this was because the New Poet was also the Poet's Poet, or, in other words, through the creative influence of Humanism upon an individual poetic genius. The last chapter, therefore, is intended to follow in logical sequence from the two sections preceding it (chapters III–V and VI–VIII). As this is not a biographical study, chapters I and II are to be regarded merely as introductory. I make no claim to have discovered fresh biographical material, and question whether many more particulars of importance are now obtainable. But the story of Spenser's life will bear re-telling, if only for the rejection of unauthorised hypotheses tacitly accepted as proven facts. Moreover, it appeared unsatisfactory to attempt to examine different aspects of a poet's work without preliminary consideration of the man, his circle and environment in the light of the most recent researches.

Among numerous authorities consulted first place must be given to Professor F. I. Carpenter's *Reference Guide to Edmund Spenser*, with the supplement of Miss Alice Parrott (*Studies in Philology*, Oct. 1928, xxv, 468 ff.), which have proved invaluable and to which every student of Spenser must feel himself deeply indebted. Another work of which I have gladly availed myself is Professor C. G. Osgood's *Concordance to the Poems of Edmund Spenser*. Useful suggestions concerning sources and analogues have been supplied by the earlier Spenserians, including Warton and the various collaborators with Todd, whose monumental edition of

Preface

1805 has yet to be superseded. Lastly I would acknowledge my obligations to Professor Greenlaw's articles on Spenser's use of ancient philosophy, to Miss P. Henley's *Spenser in Ireland*, which has supplied a few historical details previously unnoticed, and to the various authorities cited in the notes. Carpenter's *Guide* has spared me the labour of compiling a complete bibliography; but for the convenience of the reader I have appended a summary list of editions and of books for further reference.

BERNARD E. C. DAVIS

October 1932

CHAPTER I

Life and Works

I

I T was a material misfortune for Spenser, born in or about the year 1552,[1] that the span of his life should have been roughly cotemporaneous with an interregnum between two aristocracies of letters. A generation later the son of a reputable London citizen—identified, on slender evidence, with John Spenser, free journeyman to the Merchant Taylors,—and of the even more obscure Elizabeth Spenser might have found his level with Shakespeare, Dekker, Jonson and the throng of middle-class wits then holding the boards within a mile of East Smithfield, his supposed birthplace.[2] Under their genial influence his melancholic disposition might have been tempered by the saving grace of humour, and the potential capacity for satire, even for drama, displayed at intervals in his writings might have reached fruition. But from a worldly aspect Spenser's time and circumstance were out of joint, debarring him, on the one hand, from the "mob of gentlemen that wrote at ease" and, on the other, from the widening ranks of a democratic intelligentsia which he could regard only with suspicion and contempt. The violent fluctuation of his temper between extremes of enthusiasm and disillusion betray the restlessness of the thwarted idealist who found love more bitter than sweet, the seats of learning hotbeds of dissension and the carpet knighthood of Kenilworth but a travesty of ancient chivalry. He turned to poetry as a refuge from actuality, consorting in a world of make-believe with a society whose living counterpart he could only admire and envy from a distance. Under the flattering unction of poetic licence the newly rich

Edmund Spenser

Spencers of Althorpe, who had won their coat of arms within living memory and who could trace their descent over little more than a century,[3] are magnified into "a house of ancient fame" of which he boasts himself the meanest, proud to salute his three noble cousins, "Phyllis, Charillis and sweet Amaryllis", if only in the graceless rôle of poor relation.

The cultural influences affecting his childhood and youth were such as may well have fired that ambition towards social advancement which he was destined never to satisfy. As "pore scholler" of the Merchant Taylors' School he must have come under the tutelage of Richard Mulcaster, one of the most enlightened pedagogues of his day, appointed headmaster in 1561. The curriculum prescribed in Mulcaster's *Positions for the training up of children*, and presumably followed, as far as practicable, in his school, includes vocational training, the study of music and dramatic art, physical exercise for children of both sexes, a sifting process for dividing the intelligent from the unteachable, with many other innovations which must have startled his readers. In his *Elementarie* (1582), writing primarily for the benefit of middle-class educators and scholars, he stresses the importance of an early grounding in vernacular grammar as opposed to the exclusive cult of the classics: "I love Rome, but London better; I favour Italie, but England more; I honour the Latin, but I worship the English". His views upon this subject at least are in substantial agreement with E.K.'s defence of the "New Poet", whose tribute to "Wrenock" in "December", notwithstanding close dependence upon his original, Marot's *Eglogue au Roy*, may bear reference to his old schoolmaster:

> And for I was in thilke same looser yeares,
> (Whether the Muse so wrought me from my byrth,
> Or I to much beleeved my shepherd peeres,)
> Somedele ybent to song and musicks mirth,
> A good old shephearde, Wrenock was his name,
> Made me by arte more cunning in the same.[4]

Life and Works

On May 20, 1569, Spenser matriculated as sizar of Pembroke Hall, Cambridge, where he remained for the next seven years with the support of the Nowells, a wealthy Lancashire family who had already contributed towards his maintenance at school. At intervals throughout this period he was recommended for extra commons on grounds of ill-health, which may possibly have been aggravated through the performance of various menial duties required of him as a sizar. Concerning his intellectual activities we can only conjecture. The English universities, as corporate institutions, were still in the throes of Scholasticism and in retard of many academies abroad; but Cambridge could boast of several distinguished scholars who by individual effort had given unmistakable proof of their zeal for humane studies. Sir John Cheke (1514-57), "a man of men, supernaturally traded in all tongues", born in Cambridge and elected Professor of Greek in 1540, was the pioneer to a school of humanists whose main object was the advancement of English letters upon a surer classical foundation. His pupil, Roger Ascham (1515-68), Fellow of St John's and famed as a teacher of ancient tongues, had given practical demonstration of his principles in *Toxophilus* and *The Scholemaster*, composed of "English matter in the Englishe tongue for Englishe men". Thomas Wilson (1525-81), another pupil of Cheke and a friend of Ascham, had written text-books on the arts of logic and rhetoric which remained as standard authorities throughout the century. Two of the most celebrated English philosophers, Everard Digby, the Aristotelian, and his opponent, William Temple, the Ramist, were contemporaries of Spenser, the former at St John's, the latter at King's. Thus the representation of "my Mother Cambridge" as adorning "plenteous Ouse"

> With many a gentle Muse and many a learned Wit[5]

is no mere figure of speech but an undeniable statement of fact.

Among the earlier alumni of Pembroke Hall were several stalwart Protestants, including Nicholas Ridley, John Brad-

Edmund Spenser

ford—both victims of the Marian persecution—Edmund Grindal, subsequently Archbishop of Canterbury, and other like "singular men, the late ornaments of Cambridge". The Master in Spenser's time was John Young, afterwards Bishop of Rochester. His contemporaries included Lancelot Andrewes, also of the Merchant Taylors' School, Edward Kirke—probably the "E.K." of the *Calender*—and last, but not least, the notorious Gabriel Harvey, elected Fellow of Pembroke in 1570. The customary abuse of Harvey as a pernicious influence upon Spenser dates back to Marprelate times when Thomas Nashe directed against him a barrage of vituperation upon this and other grounds. He was unquestionably a pedant, a coxcomb and a bounder, though in these respects no worse than many a university don in every age. His academic successes tended to accentuate his innate vulgarity and an inferiority complex which found its outlet in aggressive self-assertion. But though his enemies might taunt him with the unfortunate fact that his father was a ropemaker no one could justly call in question the sincerity of his enthusiasm for scholarship. The mutual affection between "Colin" and "Hobbinol" is sufficiently profound to evoke from E.K. a lengthy defence of "paederastic" love, though with an eye to possible traducers he is at pains to exonerate his two friends from the charge of "execrable and horrible sinnes of forbidden and unlawful fleshlinesse". Their correspondence during the years 1579 and 1580 shows that at this critical period Harvey, to his credit, was not simply misdirecting Spenser's talents but seeking to stimulate his interest in practical affairs as an antidote to morbid introspection. That Spenser was fully conscious of their differences both in temper and genius may be gathered from the playful sonnet addressed from Dublin, on July 18, 1586, to "Harvey, the happy above happiest men", and especially from its conclusion:

> For Life, and Death, is in thy doomefull writing!
> So thy renowme lives ever by endighting;

4

yet long after he had far outshone his eccentric acquaintance he could still accord "Hobbinol" honourable place in *Colin Clouts Come Home Againe*.

If the "Edmund Spenser" cited in a document of October 18, 1569, as the bearer of letters from Sir Henry Norris, ambassador in France, to the Queen[6] be identical with our poet he must have entered Cambridge as a freshman of considerable prestige. Even at this early date he appears to have given evidence of his poetic talent, for there is good reason for assigning to him a group of sonnets embodied in Theodore Roest's *Theatre of Worldlings* (1569), a religious tract translated from the original French of St John Vander Noodt, a Dutch Protestant refugee.[7] Six of these sonnets are translations from Marot's French version of Petrarch, eleven from Du Bellay's *Songe* and the remaining four from the Apocalypse. The sonnets from Petrarch are practically identical with the "formerly translated" *Visions of Petrarch* as printed in Spenser's *Complaints*. Those from Du Bellay are rendered in blank verse; otherwise they would closely resemble the corresponding numbers in *The Visions of Bellay*. Towards the end of 1579 Spenser was preparing a collection of poems, with illustrations, entitled "Dreames", from which the three sets of "Visions" afterwards included in *Complaints* are probably extracts or recensions. It is unlikely that he would have wasted his energies in refurbishing another's translation of such trifles or have permitted spurious pieces to appear under his name in *Complaints*; and the only alternative is to admit the sonnets of the *Theatre* within the canon of his works.[8]

But his interests at Cambridge were not confined to scholarship and letters, for the seven years which he spent there coincided with a period of storm and stress within the university which left its mark upon much of his earlier writing. Incessant bickering between orthodox Anglicans and disaffected Puritans came to a head in 1571, when Thomas Cartwright, Lady Margaret Professor from 1569 to 1570 and champion of the Puritan cause, was expelled from his fellowship at Trinity by Whitgift, the Master. The issue rent the university in twain, most of the senior officials conforming with the dictates of authority, their subordinates and juniors embracing the cause of the oppressed Puritans. Spenser's part in the affair can only be deduced through indirect evidence. His intimate, Harvey, stoutly supported the Puritans and, probably on this account, some years later got himself in evil odour with Perne, the Vice-Chancellor, a notorious turncoat, who appears to have opposed Harvey's case for election as University Orator. Writing to Spenser in 1580, amid a deal of innuendo and balderdash respecting present conditions in Cambridge, Harvey notes: "No more adoe aboute Cappes and Surplesses; Maister *Cartwright* nighe forgotten . . . Caetera faerè, ut olim: Bellum inter Capita, & membra continuatum".[9] In the meantime Spenser had taken his stand with Harvey and the Puritans. The outcome was the satiric section of the *Calender*, composed after he had gone down but while the burning question at issue in Cambridge and the polemic idiom of the combatants were still green in memory.

Of his activities between 1576, when he commenced M.A., and the autumn of 1579, when he had become attached to the household of the Earl of Leicester, little is known, though much has been conjectured. Two books which he presented to Harvey in 1578—Turler's *Travailer* and the *Howleglas*—are still extant. The inscription upon the former—"Ex Dono Edmundi Spenseri, Episcopi Roffensis Secretarii",—proves that at this time Spenser was acting as secretary to Young, now Bishop of Rochester,[10] a fact that would account for his tribute to "Roffy" and for touches of Kentish local colour in the *Calender*. In the following summer Harvey addressed to him a letter complaining that, without permission, Spenser had published some of his correspondent's English "Verlayes" and demanding as compensation "the clippings of your thris honorable mustachyoes and subboscoes", a sum of one hundred and two hairs, paid by instalments. In another letter, undated but probably belonging to the

6

same period, Harvey, appointed to deliver an Encænia Oration, implores Spenser to lend him "on tolerable oration, and twoe or three reasonable argumentes".[11]

Slight and insignificant as these records may appear, they are by no means valueless. In the gloss to "June" E.K. states that, on the advice of Hobbinol (Harvey), Colin "came into the South" from the "Northparts", which have been taken to mean either Althorpe, the seat of his rich relatives, or Lancashire, supposed, by a not too credible tradition, to have been the native county of his father. But the evidence of his continued intimacy with Harvey and of his interest in university affairs which is afforded by Harvey's Letter-Book, the published Spenser-Harvey correspondence and the *Calender* strongly favours the presumption that for a time he continued to reside near Cambridge, perhaps at Audley End, Harvey's home. His attacks upon the ignorance, idleness and avarice of the Anglican clergy, identified, by approved Puritan tactic, with "Papists", are all in the manner of Cartwright and his adherents. In June, 1577, Archbishop Grindal, formerly visitor to the Merchant Taylors' School, had been sequestrated from his official functions in consequence of his disinclination to suppress Puritan "prophesyings". So in contrast with the "proud and ambitious Morrell"—the High Church Bishop of London, John Aylmer—"Algrind" figures as "a shepheard great in gree", bruised by the shell fish (Puritans) which the eagle (Elizabeth) would have broken upon his "bared scalpe". The designation of Colin as "Roffy's boy", with the story of "Roffy" and "Lowder"—John Young and possibly his Chancellor, Hugh Lloyd,—clearly refers to the period during which Spenser was in Young's employment. Other allusions, no less specific but veiled by the discreet silence or prevarication of E.K., would doubtless have been duly recognised and appreciated by the limited public for which they were primarily intended.[12]

Meanwhile the New Poet was rapidly accumulating fresh

resources. From the outset his interest appears to have been aroused by the moral writings of Cicero, Seneca, Plutarch and the author of *Ecclesiastes*, whose influence is reflected throughout all his work. His earliest pieces consist of translations or adaptations from the foreign poets of the Pléiade or Petrarchan schools, and the contempt for popular poetry evinced throughout *The Teares of the Muses*, which probably dates from this period, is in complete accord with the same tradition. *The Shepheardes Calender* shows a wider and more thorough acquaintance with bucolic poetry, both ancient and modern, than any previous English work of the same type; and since, by the end of 1579, he had already begun to compose *The Faerie Queene*, he must have been collecting material from contemporary chronicles, mediæval allegory and popular romance.

The seeds of poetry gathered from these diverse origins first reached fruition in the wonderful year of project and achievement, 1579. But the most memorable experience of these salad days was the affair with "Rosalind", that mysterious "Widdowes daughter of the Glenne" who remained for more than a dozen years, if not to the end, the object of his desire. Making due allowance for the borrowed plumes of the *Calender* as of most Elizabethan love poetry, the reader is cautious of accepting Colin's expostulations at face value; and doubtless Rosalind would long since have gone the way of many others into the limbo of "convention" but for the foresight of E.K., whose statements are too specific to be overridden: "*Rosalinde*, is also a feigned name, which, being wel ordered, wil bewray the very name of hys love and mistresse, whom by that name he coloureth"; "he calleth Rosalind the Widowes daughter of the glenne, that is, of a country Hamlet or borough, which I think is rather sayde to coloure and concele the person, then simply spoken. For it is well knowen, even in spighte of Colin and Hobbinoll, that shee is a Gentlewoman of no meane house, nor endewed with anye vulgare and common gifts, both of nature and

8

manners: but suche indeede, as neede nether Colin be ashamed to have her made knowne by his verses, nor Hobbinol be greved, that so she should be commended to immortalitie for her rare and singular vertues".[13] One could hardly imagine the ambitious and fastidious Colin capable of so gross an indiscretion as to fall in love with the daughter of a "meane" house, despite her bucolic setting, which, as E.K. reminds his readers, is in strict conformity with authority from Theocritus downwards. Aubrey states that Rosalind was a "kinswoman of Sir Erasmus Dryden's lady", and that in his time a room at Canons Ashby, Northants, the home of Sir Erasmus Dryden, was still known as "Spenser's chamber".[14] But the identification of Rosalind with "Eliza Nord", daughter of Sir Thomas North, is purely conjectural, since the *Calender* affords no means of determining whether she hailed from Kent or from those "Northern parts" whence Colin has retreated.[15] It is possible, however, to trace the bare outlines of the story by piecing together allusions in the *Calender* and in the Spenser-Harvey correspondence. At first Rosalind was pleased to accept Colin's advances, styling him her "Signor Pegaso" and acknowledging that he had "all the intelligences at his commandment". But she succumbed to the wiles of one "Menalcas", who turned her "faultlesse fayth" to "faithlesse fere", leaving the hapless Colin with nothing but his Muse to console him.

The poetry inspired by memories of Rosalind in the course of the next fifteen years soared higher and higher beyond its first object. Renaissance Platonists recognise six progressive grades of love. In the first the lover sees only the physical beauty of the beloved; in the second he discerns spiritual beauty symbolised in outward form; in the third he apprehends the principle of universal beauty; in the fourth he recognises the image of heavenly beauty within himself; in the fifth he advances to the contemplation of heavenly beauty; in the sixth he enters into union with it. Each of these stages is represented in the erotic poetry of Spenser. The *Calender* tells a tale of jealousy and disillusion, of the woes that beset the lover as gall embittering honey. But even in the first two *Hymnes*, offsprings of greener youth, the note has changed with the transfiguration of material form into an idea more permanent and satisfying:

> But they, which love indeede, looke otherwise,
> With pure regard and spotlesse true intent,
> Drawing out of the object of their eyes
> A more refyned forme, which they present
> Unto their mind, voide of all blemishment;
> Which it reducing to her first perfection,
> Beholdeth free of fleshes frayle infection.
>
> Such is the powre of that sweet passion,
> That it all sordid basenesse doth expell,
> And the refyned mynd doth newly fashion
> Unto a fairer forme, which now doth dwell
> In his high thought, that would it selfe excell,
> Which he beholding still with constant sight,
> Admires the mirrour of so heavenly light.

An Hymne of Heavenly Beautie represents the lover in the final stage of ecstasy:

> And looke at last up to that Soveraine Light,
> From whose pure beams al perfect beauty springs,
> That kindleth love in every godly spright
> Even the love of God; which loathing brings
> Of this vile world and these gay-seeming things;
> With whose sweete pleasures being so possest,
> Thy straying thoughts henceforth for ever rest.[16]

In the later poems, largely, no doubt, as the result of Spenser's subsequent love-affairs, Rosalind becomes more and more ethereal. Perhaps she had to submit to the mortification of reading *Amoretti*, some of which may have been originally addressed to her, and of taking to heart the lamentable history of Mirabella, the despiser of love, published at about the same time. But if so, for charity let us hope that she did not miss the glowing tribute to her memory given to the world but a year since:

> For she is not like as the other crew
> Of shepheards daughters which emongst you bee,
> But of divine regard and heavenly hew,
> Excelling all that ever ye did see.
> Not then to her that scorned thing so base,
> But to my selfe the blame that lookt so hie:
> So hie her thoughts as she her selfe have place,
> And loath each lowly thing with loftie eie.[17]

Nor, perhaps, is this the last that we hear of her. The delectable picture of Calidore, Colin and the Graces dancing around

> Another Damzell, as a precious gemme
> Amidst a ring most richly well enchaced,
> That with her goodly presence all the rest much graced,[18]

ostensibly refers to the heroine of *Epithalamion*. But the appearance of Colin with his tale of constancy unrequited and of the country lass now numbered among the graces suggests the *double entendre* of a eulogy to the new mistress that is at the same time a swan song to the first.

Rosalind's obduracy rendered her the more desirable. But sympathising friends were unwilling to allow so bright a wit as Colin to waste in despair at such provocation, and it was Hobbinol who at length persuaded him to leave the melancholy scenes of his discomfiture for brighter prospects in the south:

> Then, if by me thou list advised be,
> Forsake the soyle that so doth thee bewitch:
> Leave me those hilles where harbrough nis to see,
> Nor holy-bush, nor brere, nor winding witche:
> And to the dales resort, where shepheards ritch,
> And fruictful flocks, bene every where to see:
> Here no night-ravenes lodge, more black then pitche,
> Nor elvish ghosts, nor gastly owles doe flee.[19]

Though Rosalind may have been partly responsible for this change of front E.K. doubtless hit near the mark in bluntly stating that Colin came south, not only "for speciall occasion of private affaires" but also "for his more preferment". In the *View* Irenæus states that he was present at the execution of Murrogh O'Brien, which took place on July 1, 1577; and the gruesome detail recorded in connection with the incident reads as a personal reminiscence. It is therefore possible, though unproven, that at the time Spenser was serving under Sir Henry Sidney, the Lord Deputy. In any case, perhaps through Harvey's good offices, he obtained an introduction to the Sidneys and by October 5, 1579, was installed at Leicester House in the Strand, which appears to have been his headquarters until his appointment as secretary to Lord Grey in the following summer. The two letters addressed to Harvey in the course of the next few months and published, together with his replies, by that born self-advertiser in 1580 supply details of the greatest interest respecting Spenser's opinions and projects at this critical point of his career.

An introduction to "that miracle of the age", Philip Sidney, and to Leicester, the hope of the Puritans and the most powerful minister in the realm, offered golden opportunity for advancement. But at first it was necessary to walk warily. The rebuff that Stephen Gosson had recently sustained in return for dedicating to Sidney *A School of Abuse* was sufficient warning to "Master Immerito", "leaste by overmuch cloying their noble eares, I should gather a contempt of myself". The *Calender* was written "in honour of a private Personage unknowne, which of some yl-willers might be upraided, not to be so worthie, as you knowe she is";[20] and the absence of direct allusion to Sidney implies that the dedication was decided upon only at the eleventh hour, presumably at Harvey's instigation. Sidney's return for the compliment was confined to a guarded note in the *Apologie*, and it is doubtful whether his intimacy with Spenser extended beyond the normal familiarity between a young nobleman and a confidential secretary of kindred tastes within his uncle's household. The "Areopagus", in which Spenser proudly associates himself with "the twoo worthy Gentlemen, Master *Sidney* and Master *Dyer*", was probably little more than a figure of speech. On the other hand, and notwithstanding the frigidity of *Astrophel*, there is no reason to question the sincerity of Spenser's admiration for "the patron of my young Muses", himself a "true poem" and a pattern of brave courtier, whose lofty views of his art tallied in all essentials with those of the New Poet.[21]

Self-interest and the snobbery of an age which did not recognise letters as a polite occupation instilled within Spenser a reluctance to publish that continued throughout his life. After his first success ten years were to elapse before he again claimed the attention of the public. Most of the *Complaints* were written long before publication but deliberately withheld. The cantos of Mutability were published posthumously, while a considerable number of pieces known only by their titles never passed beyond the author's circle and still "sleep in silence". The *Calender* might have been long delayed but for Harvey's encouragement; and when finally it appeared Spenser took care to safeguard himself under a double cloak of anonymity and innuendo. But for all this discreet affection of modesty he was fully alive to the main chance, as may be gathered from the letter which he addressed to Harvey in October, 1579.

The letter, which may have been edited by Harvey before publication, falls into two parts.[22] Evidently Harvey has been urging Spenser to seize his opportunity by striking while the iron is hot; and now the latter confesses himself "determined to alter mine owne former purpose, and subscribe to your advizement . . . for that, in all things I attribute so muche to your judgement, that I am evermore content to annihilate mine owne determinations, in respecte thereof". He has recently "been with" the Queen and declines to satisfy his correspondent's curiosity with any details respecting this experience. But he makes no secret of his gratification at finding himself held "in some use of familiarity" by Sidney and Dyer; and with the assurance as of a newly fledged "Areopagite" he proceeds to criticise Harvey's hexameters, offering in exchange a specimen of his own "unhappie verse". To this is appended a portion of a letter dated October 5, but "thorough one mans negligence quite forgotten". He expects to be sent abroad upon some weighty business, "which will be (I hope, I feare, I thinke), the next weeke, if I can be dispatched of my Lorde, I goe thither, as sent by him, and maintained most what of him: and there am to employ my time, my body, my minde, to his Honours service". Accordingly he offers his correspondent a Latin poem of farewell as from "Immerito sui, mox in Gallias navigaturi". The proposed itinerary, extending from Gaul to the Pyrenees, the Caucasus and Babylon—a mere literary flourish—cannot be taken seriously; but the autobiographical material which composes the greater part of the poem is of the greatest interest. Still in the toils of love, Spenser would defend himself against Harvey, its despiser; "Quam levis est Amor, et tamen haud levis est Amor omnis". Unconvinced by the Stoic creed of indifference to sensual pleasures and the things of this world, he yet realises that he cannot waste his youth and genius in drudgery or idleness and therefore welcomes the opportunity of seeking his fortune through travel. That the defence went home is evident from Harvey's reply, dated October 23, in which he declares his complete scepticism as to Immerito's immediate departure and reverts to his former line of attack: "Credite me, I will never linne baityng at you, til I have rid you quite of this yonkerly, and womanly humor".[23]

By the following April, however, the situation had evidently changed. At the conclusion of a letter sent by Spenser to Harvey on April 2 his sweetheart sends cordial greetings wondering why she has received no response to her letters;

and Harvey, no longer the kill-joy of the previous autumn, in two subsequent letters dated April 7 and April 23, duly pays his addresses first to "your sweet Harte" and subsequently, at greater length, to "altera Rosalindula", "Domina Immerito, mea bellissima Collina Clouta".[24] The presumption that, in the interval, Spenser had been married appears, at first sight, to be strengthened by the recent discovery of the marriage register of "Edmounde Spenser to Machabyas Chylde" at St Margaret's, Westminster, on October 27, 1579. But it can only remain a presumption in view of the ascertained existence of other "Edmund Spensers" at this date and in default of any corroborative evidence, external or internal, connecting our poet with the said "Machabyas". The tone of Spenser's correspondence with Harvey in October, 1579, is certainly not suggestive of impending marriage, and *The Shepheardes Calender*, "made in honour" of Rosalind, was scarcely a fitting tribute to a recently espoused bride. In the absence of further proof the theory of Spenser's early marriage must be left as an open question only of passing interest; for whether "Rosalindula" refers to wife or to mistress, she drops forthwith out of the picture.[25]

In the letter of April 2, after further discussion on hexameters, Spenser proceeds to describe some of his pieces in process of composition. "Dreams"—perhaps identical with "My Slomber" which he proposed to offer Dyer—has grown to the same dimension as the *Calender* by reason of E.K.'s gloss, "running continually in maner of a Paraphrase" and of "the pictures so singularly set forth", possibly reproduced from *A Theatre for Worldlings*. Of "The Dying Pellicane" nothing is known; but eleven years later, in the preface to *Complaints*, Ponsonbie listed it as no longer obtainable. The "Stemmata Dudleiana" was composed of "sundry apostrophes" to the Dudleys, destined ultimately to be commemorated not in eulogy but in the elegiac *Ruines of Time*. Perhaps the most ambitious of these juvenilia was "Epithalamion Thamesis", a poem in hexameters which evidently embodied material subsequently utilised in *The Faerie Queene*, IV, xi:

For in setting forth the marriage of the Thames: I shewe his first beginning, and offspring, and all the Countrey, that he passeth thorough, and also describe all the Rivers throughout Englande, whyche came to this Wedding, and their righte names, and right passage, &c. A worke, beleeve me, of much labour, wherein notwithstanding Master *Holinshed* hath much furthered and advantaged me, who therein hath bestowed singular paines, in searching oute their first heades and sources: and also in tracing and dogging oute all their Course, til they fall into the Sea.[26]

William Vallans, in the preface to his *Tale of Two Swannes* (1590), mentions the "Epithalamion Thamesis" as a work which he has seen and which deserves to be published, adding further that an English version, "though long since it was promised, yet it is not perfourmed". He may, however, be referring to a piece by another author on the same subject, which was not uncommon and upon which Camden based his *Epithalamion Isidis et Thamesis*. If Spenser's lost poem covered the same ground as the canto describing the marriage of the rivers in *The Faerie Queene* its source was William Haryson's description of England, prefixed to the historical portion of Holinshed's *Chronicle*.[27]

Harvey was not too well pleased at these independent flights of his pupil; and his replies betray the pique and apprehension of the cicerone whose victim is determined at all costs to go his own gait. To the criticism of his verses he retorts with characteristic violence; he has never seen or heard of "your gorbellyed Master's rules", nor will he plead guilty to any infringement of the law of accent. At the same time he throws considerable light upon the evil influence which he was vainly endeavouring to wield over his pupil. The "Dreames" "savour of that singular extraordinarie veine and invention, which I have ever fancied moste, and in a manner admired onelye in *Lucian, Petrarche, Aretine*,

Pasquill, and all the most delicate, and fine conceited Grecians and Italians:. . . whose chiefest endevour, and drifte was, to have nothing vulgare, but in some respecte or other, and especially in *lively Hyperbolicall Amplifications,* rare, queint, and odde in every pointe, and as a man would saye, a degree or two at the leaste, above the reache, and compasse of a common Schollers capacitie". So the poet is to cultivate extravagance, a widespread heresy and the worst possible advice to offer to so decorative a poet as Spenser. But it is enough for Harvey that the "Dreames" conform with authority, and for the same reason he proceeds to extol the "Nine Comedies, whereunto in imitation of Herodotus you give the names of the *Nine Muses",* comparing them with the comedies of Ariosto and placing their author on a plane with *"Bibiena, Machiavel* and *Aretine",* who chose "rather to advaunce themselves that way than any other".[28] This is at once the most interesting and most puzzling of allusions to Spenser's lost works. That a poet educated under Richard Mulcaster should try his hand at writing comedies is understandable. Many of the word pageants embodied in *The Faerie Queene* reflect the influence of the theatre, and a passage in "October" suggests that the writer may have seriously aspired to drama:

> O! if my temples were distaind with wine,
> And girt in girlonds of wild Yvie twine,
> How could I reare the Muse on stately stage,
> And teache her tread aloft in buskin fine,
> With queint Bellona in her equipage.[29]

Harvey may be using the word "comedies" as a synonym for satires; otherwise, if they were ever completed, it is extraordinary that they should have disappeared, leaving no trace. He had evidently seen sufficient of them to be in a position to praise their "finenesse of plausible Elocution" and "rarenesse of Poetical invention"; but this may have amounted to no more than a draft of choric prologues subsequently re-assembled to form the declamatory speeches of *The Teares of the Muses.*

But the "Dreames" and "Comedies" were not the only works submitted to Harvey; and another fragment, more highly esteemed by its author than either of these, met with his unqualified disapproval. He was "voyde of al judgement" if the "Nine Comedies" came not nearer those of Ariosto than did the *Elvish Queene* to the *Orlando Furioso*. The drift of Harvey's censure is unmistakable. He realises that he is losing hold of the brilliant young pupil whom he had hoped to win to the service of his own crabbed muse but who has been beguiled by the toys of romance. "But I will not stand greatly with you in your owne matters. If so be the *Faerye Queene* be fairer in your eie than the *Nine Muses*, and *Hobgoblin* runne away with the Garland from *Apollo*: Marke what I saye, and yet I will not say that I thought, but there an End for this once, and fare you well, till God or some good Aungell putte you in a better minde."[40]

He could scarcely say otherwise; for by this time Spenser had given open proof of his intention to wing his own flight. *The Shepheardes Calender*, registered under the date December 5, 1579, was published before the end of the year 1579–80 as a small quarto volume, dedicated to Sir Philip Sidney, with preface and gloss by E.K. Since E.K. displays ignorance of facts upon which Spenser must have been better informed the supposition that the poet was his own annotator is untenable; and it is generally agreed that the initials stand for Edward Kirke, a contemporary at Pembroke mentioned as an acquaintance in the correspondence with Harvey. It is clear, however, that through his editor Spenser took occasion to offer his public not only explanations of difficulties but an apology for his own position as New Poet, consciously abandoning the dry rut of English custom to cleave virgin soil for himself. His literary co-mates, differing widely in temper and genius, were united in their contempt for the "rakehellye route of our ragged rymers" and in their devotion to the common object of founding a school of polite vernacular poetry. Harvey imagined the problem to turn

mainly on verse. Sidney could only deplore his contemporaries' "want of desert", and confess his inability to find
a remedy. It was left for Spenser to show, by example rather
than precept, that the fruits of Greece and Rome must be not
simply plucked and exported but transplanted anew upon
English soil.

"He hath laboured", says E.K., "to restore, as to theyr
rightfull heritage, such good and naturall English words, as
have ben long time out of use, and almost cleane disherited";
and this revival of "good and naturall words" carried with it
a wholesale process of naturalisation. In a mosaic of patterns from the bucolic poets of all ages—Theocritus, Bion,
Moschus, Virgil, Mantuan and Marot—the one acknowledged
master is "Tityrus", or Chaucer, esteemed not as a venerable
antique but as "the God of Shepheardes . . . . who taught me
homely, as I can, to make". English verse forms—rime
couée, ballad measure and "Chaucerian" couplets—predom-
inate over those of foreign extraction like the *sestina* of
"August" or the "ditties" of "April" and "November".
The subject-matter likewise bespeaks a muse of native
origin. The scenery and local colour is that of the Kentish
Weald. The principal characters bear homely English names
like Colin Clout (from Skelton), Willye, Cuddie, Piers,
Hobbinol, and their customs and beliefs betray their English
upbringing. The superstitious Morrell, standing by the
source of

> salt Medway, that trickling stremis
> Adowne the dales of Kent,
> Till with his elder brother Themis
> His brackish waves be meynt,

recalls other spots no less hallowed by tradition:

> St Michels Mount who does not know,
> That wardes the Westerne coste?
> And of St Brigets bowre, I trow,
> All Kent can rightly boaste.[31]

Edmund Spenser

Palinode describes the gathering of "May-buskets and smelling brere", the decking of Church pillars ere daylight

> With Hawthorne buds, and swete Eglantine,
> And girlonds of roses, and Sopps in wine,

the country dances to pipe and tabor welcoming the May King with Flora his Queen, the nymphs and fairies accompanying her, "pierlesse pleasures" that

> chace the lingring Night
> With Heydeguyes, and trimly trodden traces.[32]

True, Palinode is worsted in the argument, which turns on the old *L'Allegro-Il Penseroso* issue treated centuries before in *The Owl and the Nightingale*; but he puts up a strong defence with which his author has obviously a good deal of sympathy. The pastoral, then at its prime, had as yet lost none of its vitality and what Spenser has borrowed he has made his own. For all its foreign trappings the *Calender* is more thoroughly English than any polite poetry since Chaucer; and it glistens with the dew of youth.

A second edition, transferred from the original publisher to John Harrison the younger, appeared in 1581; others followed in 1586, 1591 and 1597. In *An Apologie for Poetrie* Sidney condescended to note that "*The Shepheards Kalender* hath much poetrie in his Eglogues; indeed worthy the reading, if I be not deceived", though he "dared not allow" its archaic diction. William Webbe, in his *Discourse of English Poetrie* (1586), associating the *Calender* with the name of Spenser, describes its author as "the rightest English poet that ever I read"; but this unexceptionable criticism did not prevent him from perverting some of Spenser's verses to "English hexameters". While there is no evidence to show that the *Calender* was a best seller its success was certainly sufficient to establish its author's footing in the world of letters and to secure in advance a public favourably disposed towards his bolder venture ten years later.

But his immediate object, from his own confession, was to

advance his fortunes by striking while the iron was hot. The
expectations entertained by his circle as to the result of this
first enterprise are plainly indicated in a letter of Harvey, who
contrasts his own poverty with the prospective opulence of
Colin:

> But Master *Collin Cloute* is not every body, and albeit his olde
> Companions, Master Cuddy and Master Hobbinoll be as little
> beholding to their Mistresse Poetrie, as ever you wist: yet he
> peradventure, by the meanes of hir special favour, and some
> personall priviledge, may happely live by *dying Pellicanes*, and
> purchase great landes, and Lordshippes, with the money, which
> his *Calendar* and *Dreames* have and will affourde him.

Harvey, for his part, will for the future employ his time upon
those studies that carry "meate in their mouth, having evermore their eye uppon the Title *De pane lucrando*, and their
hand upon their halfpenny"; and in this spirit he readily en-
dorses the complaint of Cuddie to Piers in "October". But
unless these remarks are to be taken as pure banter he has
miscalculated the prospects of the New Poet, whose own
disappointment at the reception of his work may be gathered
from numerous hints in the Spenser-Harvey correspondence
summed up in the suggestive tag,

> O Tite, siquid, ego,
> Ecquid erit pretii?[33]

It would appear that by seeking to gratify his new patrons
with the anti-clericalism of his Cambridge associates the
headstrong young adventurer found himself hoist with his
own petard. Leicester, who had no love for Grindal and only
a political interest in the Puritan party, might well have
applied to himself trenchant allusions to wolves that devour
God's fold, to "lovers of Lordships and troublers of state".
Meanwhile the whole situation had been complicated by the
proposed marriage between the Queen and the Duke of
Alençon. Leicester's opposition to this scheme was occasioned partly by self-interest, partly by his rivalry to Burleigh, one of its supporters; and it is not unlikely that his

intrigues on this account gave rise to Spenser's anticipation of a journey abroad in October, 1579. A few weeks earlier, Simier, Alençon's Master of Robes, had informed the Queen of Leicester's secret marriage with the Countess of Essex, as the result of which Leicester was out of favour and even threatened with imprisonment. In January, 1579–80, his nephew, Philip Sidney, added fuel to the flames by protesting against the Alençon match in a letter to the Queen, which led to his temporary banishment from court and retirement to Wilton. With misguided zeal, perhaps with the object of retrieving some of the favour which he may have forfeited through the *Calender*, Spenser seized the opportunity of attacking the foes of his patrons; and in so doing he seems to have blocked the way to his own advancement.[34]

Such was the occasion of *Mother Hubberds Tale*, drafted in 1579 or early in 1580, though not published until 1591, when it appeared with additions in *Complaints*. The Queen's habit of nicknaming her courtiers after the various beasts suggested the adaptation of mediæval fable, particularly of *Reynard the Fox*, to the present political crisis; and further hints may have been drawn from the history of the fox turned courtier as set forth in the more recent *Speculum Vitæ Aulicæ* of Hartman Schopper. Spenser's positive defence of his patrons does not extend beyond a passing allusion to Leicester's marriage as the lion's "late chayne" and a purple patch of eulogy to the brave courtier, inspired by Castiglione, but plainly glancing at Sidney. All his main effort is directed to the satiric delineation of Leicester's opponents, with Burleigh as chief butt for attack. So the fox, representing Burleigh, figures as the foe of learning, arch-deceiver and conspirator against the commonwealth, backed by his curdog, the ape, or Simier whom the Queen had styled her "monkey". After an adventurous career as bogus soldiers, husbandmen and parsons, the two impostors at length succeed in gaining admission to the court, where their quick wits soon procure their advancement. The ape's "fine feates and Courtly complement" enable him to hoodwink everyone around him, to abuse sacred poetry, to mock God's holy ministers; but the prime mover of all his plots is Reynard, skilled in every practice "of coosinage and cleanly knaverie", ready to assume any disguise—of merchant, lawyer, broker or farmer—in order to reap profits from them all. Finally the two deceivers steal from the lion the royal insignia, which enable the ape to reign as mountebank king with the fox as chief minister; and thus, for a time, they maintain a rule of oppression and injustice, supported by

> a warlike equipage
> Of forreine beasts, not in the forest bred,
> But part by land and part by water fed,[35]

in other words, Burleigh's foreign mercenaries.

As a specimen of polemic satire touching the most vital issues in religion, politics and social organisation *Mother Hubberds Tale* has few rivals and with justice Dryden places it in the forefront of its kind. The nature of the fable allows far bolder and more effective attack upon the vices of court, the ignorance and simony of the Protestant clergy, the cant of the leveller than the gentle thrusts and innuendoes admitted in the *Calender*. In its present form the poem has clearly undergone revision, for the narrative is broken at line 942, the lion changes his rôle of chief courtier for that of monarch, while the bitter plea for "pore suters" must have been added after the failure of Spenser's suits in 1590–1. But such lack of coherence constitutes no serious defect in a work avowedly modelled upon the rambling, vituperative satires of the Middle Ages. Notwithstanding the distance that divides Spenser's vehement special pleading from Chaucer's genial impartiality, *Mother Hubberds Tale*, in respect of both matter and form, is the most Chaucerian of his pieces. His graphic representation of the dress, speech and conduct in vogue among the several grades of society shows the hand of an eye-witness in close touch with the life that he describes. Vested interests, stimulated perhaps by genuine apprehension of alien influence in the court, have for once aroused the visionary from his dream, recalling him to the sterner and more sordid affairs of the material world. Given the opportunity he can wield his bludgeon with the best.

But his zeal had outrun discretion, apparently gaining little favour from the individuals in whose interests it had been spent. Only a month or two before the publication of the *Calender* the printer, Hugh Singleton, had been prosecuted for printing an attack, by John Stubbes, upon the Alençon marriage and narrowly escaped losing his right hand. Perhaps Singleton obtained a contract for printing *Mother Hubberds Tale* when favourable opportunity should arise; and his associations with the anti-Alençon party may account for the choice of so inferior a craftsman as printer of the *Calender* which is, nevertheless, admirably produced, probably under the personal supervision of its author. Subsequently the *Calender* passed into the hands of another printer—Singleton, after his terrible warning, being probably glad to shake off so dangerous a responsibility. But compared with *Mother Hubberds Tale* the *Calender* was innocuous. Had Singleton or any other printer dared to publish the former in 1579 or 1580 he might have expected short shrift; and had Burleigh seen it, even in manuscript, he would probably have taken steps to suppress it, in which case neither Spenser, nor his publisher, Ponsonbie, would have cared to issue it in 1591. Leicester himself may have forbidden publication, anticipating the storm that might be aroused by so outspoken an attack upon his rivals. At the same time he probably determined to rid himself of so dangerous a henchman as this New Poet, whose *Calender* could not have been all to his liking and whose further importunities were calculated to do him more harm than good.

By the spring of 1580, when Spenser addressed the second of his extant letters to Harvey, it seems more than likely that he was becoming estranged from his employer, to whom he refers only in the most formal terms. His "Stemmata

Dudleiana" of which "must more advisement be had, than so lightly to send them abroade" never saw the light in its original shape. Had Leicester chosen he might have again befriended Spenser, for by March, 1580, he was restored to favour and had recovered much of his former influence. But the unfortunate poet was now to suffer the penalty of elevation to a social status which his means could not sustain. It was probably sheer necessity that compelled him, in the summer of 1580, to accept the office of secretary to a strong opponent of Leicester, Arthur, Lord Grey of Wilton, newly appointed Deputy of Ireland.

The post was a disappointment, and for many years after Spenser chafed at the lot which had doomed him to pass his days as an exile in a barbarous land. His natural despondency must assuredly have reached its lowest depths during the later months of 1580, and it is perhaps to this period that we should assign an undated letter addressed to him by Harvey in response to a "bill of complaynte" against the iron age in which they are living. The letter purports to convey a joint answer from "a company of honest good fellows" gathered together at Harvey's fireside, Harvey taking upon himself the office of "secretary", doubtless as a ruse for airing his own opinions; and beneath the farrago of jest and pedantry of which it is largely composed lies an invaluable commentary upon the tastes and tenets of the plaintiff:

Sir, yower newe complaynte of the newe world is nye as owlde as Adam and Eve, and full as stale as the stalist fasshion that hath bene in fasshion since Noes fludd. You crie oute of a false and trecherous worlde, and therein ar passing eloquent and pathetical in a degree above the highest. Nowe I beseeche you, Syr, did not Abell live in a false and trecherous worlde, that was so villanouslye and cruelly murtherid of his owne very brother? Na, did not ould Grandsier himselfe live in a false and trecherous worlde, that was so suttelye and fraudently putt beside so incomparablely ritche and goodlye possession as Paradise was?... You suppose that the first age was the goulde age. It is nothinge soe. Bodin defendith the goulde age to flourishe nowe, and owr first grandfathers to have rubbid thorowghe in the iron and brasen age at the beginninge when all thinges were rude and unperfitt in comparison of the exquisite finesse and delicacye, that we ar growen unto at these dayes. You suppose it a foolish madd worlde, wherein all thinges ar overrulid by fansye. What greater error? All thinges else ar but troble of minde and vexation of spiritt. Untill a mans fansye be satisfied, he wantith his most soveraigne contentement, and cannot never be at quiet in himselfe. You suppose most of these bodily and sensual pleasures are to be abandonid as unlawfull and the inwarde contemplative delightes of the minde more zelously to be imbracid as most commendable. Good Lord, you a gentleman, a courtier, an yuthe, and go aboute to revive so owlde and stale a bookishe opinion, deade and buried many hundrid yeares before you or I knewe whether ther were any worlde or noe!....You suppose us students happye, and thinke the aire praeferrid that breathithe on thes same greate lernid philosophers and profonde clarkes. Would to God you were on of these men but a sennighte. I dowbte not but you would sweare ere Sundaye nexte, that there were not the like wofull and miserable creaturs to be fownde within the cumpas of the whole world agayne...Your greatist and most erronious suppose is that Reason should be mistrisse and Appetite attend on her ladiships person as a pore servante and handmayden of hers...There is a variable course and revolution of all thinges. Summer gettith the upperhande of wynter, and wynter agayne of summer. Nature herselfe is changeable, and most of all delightid with vanitye; and arte, after a sorte her ape, conformith herselfe to the like mutabilitye...So it standith with mens opinions and judgmentes in matters of doctrine and religion.[36]

The similarity, both in thought and illustration, between the arguments which Harvey would here refute and the posthumous cantos of Mutability is so close as to have persuaded some readers that the "Bill of Complaint" was an early draft of these cantos, subsequently laid aside.[37] But this theory, at first sight plausible, is difficult to sustain. Even if the "Bill of Complaint" was in verse it must have been completely transformed before it could have remotely resembled the cantos of Mutability, completed after Spenser's settlement at Kilcolman and representing the fruits of his maturest thought and workmanship. But this consideration in no way detracts from the historical importance of Harvey's letter. The hard-headed materialist, of the earth earthy, who in another letter compares lovers to alchemists dreaming of gold but blinded and suffocated by fumes from their charcoal, would dispel the sentimental whims of the melancholic youth to whom this goodly frame, the earth, seems but a sterile promontory. Obviously the "complaint" treated of matters that continued to preoccupy Spenser's attention throughout his life—the issue between sense and reason, action and contemplation, the corruption of a golden past into the leaden present, the instability of mortal affairs. Probably he had already penned some of the bitter expostulations against the inconstancy of fortune afterwards incorporated in the *Complaints*; certainly he had already begun to write *The Faerie Queene*, an epic of the warfare between flesh and spirit, a romance of old-time glory and of fantasies remote from material experience. But the concluding note sounded in his poetry is not one of despair; and it is more than likely that his mind ran back to the friendly remonstrance of his old friend, as in the "envoy" to *The Faerie Queene* he delivered his final answer to the plea that nature is "most of all delightid with vanitye" and that art "conformith herselfe to the like mutabilitye".

Whatever may have been his personal inclination, his appointment as Grey's secretary was emphatically a call to the life active; and the dedicatory sonnet to *Virgils Gnat*, written probably soon after his departure, is the complaint of a loyal servant who has been allowed to suffer for his very fidelity. But there were compensations in a new office which enabled him to live in financial security as the confidant of a man commanding his highest admiration and amid surround-ings that were destined to exercise a most favourable influ-ence upon all his subsequent writings. On August 12, 1580, he landed with his chief in Dublin. From that day onwards, except for two or three brief intervals, Ireland was his home for the rest of his life.

CHAPTER II

Life and Works

II

DURING the first few years after his arrival in Ireland Spenser was much occupied with the business and responsibilities of his new post. His chief, Lord Grey, had reluctantly accepted an office involving difficulties which neither his predecessor, Sir Henry Sidney, nor a private knight-errant like Walter, Earl of Essex, had been able to meet. A hard-headed soldier and an uncompromising Protestant, Grey firmly believed the only possible weapon for attacking the Irish problem to be the sword. Within a few days of his arrival he had embarked upon the policy of whole-sale suppression afterwards adopted by Strafford and Cromwell; and the result was an unsuccessful engagement against the rebel forces of James Eustace, Viscount Baltinglas, at Glenmalure in the Wicklow mountains. After this inauspicious beginning he had barely time to return to Dublin for the ceremony of his installation when it was reported that a band of foreigners, mostly Spaniards and Italians, supported by the Papal blessing, were fortifying the port of Smerwick, on the west coast of Kerry, as a naval base against England. Grey promptly marched upon Smerwick, secured the surrender of the fort after a three days siege and put practically the whole garrison to death. The details of his subsequent expeditions to Wexford, Munster and other parts of the country make one long story of carnage and destruction; but fortunately they do not concern us, though doubtless his secretary accompanied him. Suffice it to say that for two years, in an honest endeavour to restore order, he maintained a reign of terror, regardless of life or property and finally having to his credit " 1485 chief men and gentlemen slain, not accounting those of meaner sort, nor yet executions by law and killing of churls, which were innumerable".[1] But his royal mistress looked for something more than dead bodies and waste lands; and his enemies, trading upon the unpopularity of his measures, secured his recall in August, 1582.

It could hardly be expected that Spenser, always impressionable to his immediate environment, should judge Grey impartially, much less that he should offer a practicable solution to a problem which baffled professing statesmen for three centuries after his death. Like more than one politician of our own time he regarded the insurgent Irish not as a people struggling for their rights but simply as a "murder gang", and, according to a letter of Oliver Cromwell, dated March 27, 1657, "by his writings touching the reduction of the Irish to civility brought upon him the odium of that nation". His admiration for Lord Grey and for his policy finds full expression in *A View of the present state of Ireland* and in the fifth book of *The Faerie Queene*, where the Lord Deputy figures as Artegall, the champion of justice, who by a grim stroke of irony bears an Irish name. The *View* was completed after Grey's death, which occurred in 1593, and though conditionally registered in April, 1598, it was not published until 1633, a proof of the long disfavour attaching to its contents. Contrary to the general belief, Spenser asserts that his chief was by nature no man of blood but "most gentell, affable, loving, and temperate; but that the necessitye of that present state of thinges enforced him to that violence, and allmost chaunged his very naturall disposition". Under the control of this "most wise pilot" Ireland was steered into such smooth waters as to ride in peace "even by the space of twelve or thirtene yeares", and in that state she would have remained had not his enemies poisoned the mind of the Queen against him and so frustrated "that hope of good which was even at the doore". With the assurance of an eye-witness, "my selfe being as neere them as any", Spenser defends the massacre of the garrison at Smerwick on grounds similar to those alleged by Cromwell in justification of his conduct at Wexford; and the evil report spread by Grey's traducers inspires a rhetorical outburst recalling the tribute to Leicester in *The Ruines of Time*:

And now that he is dead, his immortall fame surviveth, and flourisheth in the mouthes of all people, that even those that did backbite him, are choaked with theyr owne venome, and breake theyre galles to heare his soe honorable report.[2]

The grievance is treated at greater length in the legend of Artegall, commissioned to deliver lady Irena from her foes but recalled to the court of Gloriana, whither he is pursued by the foul hags Envy and Detraction.

In the character of the native Irish the servant of the oppressor could find much to command his sympathy; and the pitiful conditions following on recent wars in Munster inspired the most moving passage that he ever penned:

Out of every corner of the woodes and glinnes they came creeping foorthe upon theyr handes, for theyr legges could not beare them; they looked like anatomyes of death, they spake like ghostes crying out of theyr graves; they did eate of the dead carrions, happy were they yf they could finde them, yea, and one another soone after, insoemuch as the very carcasses they spared not to scrape out of theyr graves; and yf they founde a plotte of watercresses or sham-rokes, there they flocked as to a feast for the time, yet not able long to continue therewithall; that in shorte space there were none allmost left, and a most populous and plentifull countrey suddaynly made voyde of man or beast.[3]

The picture is as graphic as the last record of the *Peterborough Chronicle*; but like all Spenser's longer works the *View* is a plea for the good old times, in this case for Grey's policy of repression and terrorism. The only effective remedy against lawlessness is military occupation and conquest by sword and famine; the milder measures of Sir John Perrot "could not be sounde nor holsome for that realme, being so contrarye to the former".

Personal considerations probably affected Spenser's judgment of Sir John Perrot, from whom he appears to have gained little or nothing. But in the meantime his post as secretary had proved a stepping-stone towards permanent office and honourable status in the ruling class. On March 22, 1580–1, he obtained the Clerkship for Faculties in the Irish Court of Chancery, which may have been no more than a sinecure entailing the registering of licences and dispensations granted under ecclesiastical authority. On July 15 he obtained the lease of the manor and abbey of Enniscorthy, county Wexford, which was conveyed temporarily to one Richard Synot on December 9. Early in 1581–2 he secured the six years' lease of a house in Dublin, and in August of the same year was granted New Abbey, Kildare, by letters patent. In May, 1583, he was appointed Commissioner for Musters in the county of Kildare, his duty being to assess the men and armour of all ranks according to the requirements of the law; and from October, 1587, till March, 1588, he acted as deputy clerk to the council of Munster in place of Lodowick Bryskett. Prior to this he was probably residing either at New Abbey or at Dublin, whence he addressed a sonnet to Gabriel Harvey on July 18, 1586. As Sir Philip Sidney died on October 17, *Astrophel* may have been written some time in the following year, when Bryskett's *Mourning Muse of Thestylis* was entered on the register; but in this case it is not easy to account for the withholding of the elegy from publication in 1591 or for the apology offered to the Countess of Pembroke at the opening of *The Ruines of Time*. Meanwhile negotiations were already afoot for the plantation of Munster by Undertakers, ostensibly with the object of increasing the prosperity of native tenants; and an article passed on June 27, 1586, assigned to Spenser 3028 acres. Thus he secured his final home, the castle, manor and lands of Kilcolman, about three miles from Doneraille, county Cork. His resignation of the clerkship of Chancery, on June 22, 1588, enabled him to reside at Kilcolman; and although the grant for his estate was not ratified until

October 26, 1591, he had settled there by 1589, when he was visited by Sir Walter Raleigh, who had himself secured about 40,000 acres as the result of the plantation.

Though Kilcolman could never have "commanded a view of above half the breadth of Ireland", as one historian asserted,[4] in the time of Spenser its surroundings were fair enough. It stood in the midst of a vast plain, bounded on the north by wooded uplands, and on the west and south by the River Awbeg, "Mulla mine, whose waves I whilom taught to weep", the daughter of "Old Mole" or the Ballyhoura range. Through the estate flowed Bregog, the lover of Mulla, in defiance of Father Mole, who intended to marry his daughter with Allo, or Blackwater, of which Awbeg is a tributary. But the wily Bregog found his own way to his desires:

> First into many parts his streame he shar'd,
> That, whilest the one was watcht, the other might
> Passe unespide to meete her by the way;
> And then, besides, those little streames so broken
> He under ground so closely did convay,
> That of their passage doth appeare no token,
> Till they into the Mullaes water slide.[5]

Such is the burden of Colin's ditty to "The Shepherd of the Ocean", and we may conclude that within the short time which elapsed between Spenser's settlement at Kilcolman and Raleigh's visit he had found ample material for poetry within the bounds of his own estate, amid scenery to which he often refers and invariably with pleasure and affection. The judgment of Mutability takes place on Arlo hill (Aherlow), "the highest head of my old father Mole", full of fair forests, once the seat of Diana but abandoned by the goddess to become the haunt of wolves and thieves. Nor was Spenser's knowledge of Irish topography by any means confined to the Kilcolman district. The guests at the marriage of Thames and Medway (*Faerie Queene*, IV, xi) include many of the principal Irish rivers—sandy Slane and stony Aubrian, swift Awniduff and Liffar deep (the Ulster Blackwater and the Foyle), pleasant Boyne and fruitful Ban, baleful Oure and sad Trowes (Avonbeg and Drowes), "spacious Shenan spreading like a sea". After such tributes we are not surprised to read in the *View* of Ireland as "a most commodious soil", "a goodly countrey", and of the northern province as "a most beautifull and sweet countrey as any is under heaven, seamed throughout with many goodly rivers, replenished with all sortes of fish, most aboundantly sprinckled with many sweet Ilandes and goodly lakes, like litle Inland Seas, that will carry even ships upon theyr waters, adorned with goodly woodes fitt for building of howses and shippes, soe comodiously, as that yf some princes in the world had them, they would soone hope to be lordes of all the seas, and ere long of all the world; also full of good portes and havens opening upon England and Scotland, as inviting us to come to them, to see what excellent comodityes that countrey can affoord, besides the soyle it self most fertile, fitt to yeeld all kind of fruite that shal be comitted therunto. And lastly, the heavens most milde and temperat, though somewhat more moyst then the part toward the West".[6]

The first half of the *View* is devoted to a survey of Irish laws, customs and religion, the second to the scheme of campaign requisite for the quelling of disorder. Some of the plans and statistics in the latter part were probably supplied by Grey; but for the bulk of his material Spenser is plainly drawing upon the first-hand knowledge of a government secretary and commissioner of musters, supplemented by the erudition of a topographer: "not certaynly affirming any thing, but by conferring of times, languages, monumentes, and such like, I doe hunte out a probabilitye of thinges, which I leave to your judgement to beleve or refuse". His "ripping up of ancient history" which extends to "Caesar, Strabo, Tacitus, Ptolomie, Plinie, Pompeius Mela, and Berosus, ... Vincentius, Aeneas Sylvius, Luddus, Buckhanan" shows proficiency in a branch of learning barely touched upon in his other writings; and the wealth of illustration cited in support of his views concerning the Scythian, Gallic and British elements in the Irish people gives us reason to regret that he never completed his projected treatise on the antiquities of Ireland. His notes on etymology, though by no means reliable, afford further proof of his interest in the country of his adoption. "Coygnye" and "Liverye" are presumably English, "for the Irishmen can make noe derivation nor analogye of them". "Kin-cogish" is "mingled of the English and Irish togither". The hills called "Folke-motes" must be distinguished from another kind called "Danerathes" because of their different origin. Criticising the vulgar error concerning the barbaric origin of the Irish people Irenæus points out that "the Saxons of England are sayd to have theyr letters, and learning, and learned men, from the Irish". Reverting to charges already laid against the Protestant clergy in *Mother Hubberds Tale* he cannot but contrast their indolence with the zeal of Catholic priests:

For they spare not to come out of Spayne, from Rome, and from Rhemes, by long toyle and daungerous travell hither, where they knowe perrill of death awayteth them, and noe rewarde nor richess is to be founde, onely to drawe the people to the Church of Rome; wheras some of our idell Ministers, having a waye for credit and estimation thereby opened unto them, and having the livinges of the countrey offered them, without paynes, and without perrill, will neither for the same, nor for any love of God...be drawen foorth from theyr warme nests and theyr sweete loves side to looke out into Godes harvest. [7]

Despite all prejudice, his romantic instinct responded inevitably to the spell of this wild land, the visible embodiment of the ancient world, harbouring a race of born warriors and haunted by ghosts of a half-vanished past. He admits that the Irish bards are "farr from instructing young men in morall discipline", summarising the contents of an Irish poem which was evidently more akin to the *Mabinogion* or the sagas than to *Amadis* or *Le Morte Darthur*; nevertheless he has "caused diverse of them to be translated", and finds that "they savoured of sweete witt and good invention, but skilled not of the goodly ornamentes of Poetrye; yet were they sprinckled with some prety flowers of theyr owne naturall devise, which gave good grace and comliness unto them, the which it is greate pittye to see soe abused, to the gracing of wickedness and vice, which would with good usage serve to beautifye and adorne vertue". The close study of native armour, costume and military tactic displayed in the *View* is all that might be expected from the author of *The Faerie Queene*; for here, at his very gate, were the manners and trappings of antiquity. In the quilted "jacke" of the Irish horseman he could recognise the "shecklaton" of Chaucer's Sir Thopas when he went to fight against the giant; "and there likewise by all that description ye may see the very fashion and manner of the Irish horseman most lively set foorth, his long hose, his shooes of costly corde-wayne, his hacqueton, and his habberjon, with all the rest thereto belonging". The deep smock sleeve hanging to the ground worn by Irish women recalled the fact "that Knightes in auncient times used to weare theyr mistress or loves sleeve, upon theyr armes, as appeareth by that which is written of Sir Launcelott, that he wore the sleeve of the Fayre Mayde of Asteloth in a turney, whereat Queene Guenever was much displeased".[8] So it is not surprising to encounter in *The Faerie Queene* touches of local colour as unmistakably Irish as names like Ferraugh, Brianor and Briana. The fight between Cambel and Triamond ebbs and flows like the Shannon tide, Scudamour and Blandamour come to grips like "two billowes in the Irish sowndes". The common hall in the House of Pride, with its minstrels, bards and chroni-clers is drawn from that of an Irish chieftain. The fugitive Florimell seeks refuge in a cottage like the Irish peasant's hovel,

> built of stickes and reedes
> In homely wize, and wald with sods around.

The foes of Alma, advancing from the rocks like gnats at evening over the Bog of Allen, constitute a typical band of native marauders:

> Vile caitive wretches, ragged, rude, deformd,
> All threatning death, all in straunge manner armd;
> Some with unweldy clubs, some with long speares,
> Some rusty knifes, some staves in fier warmd;
> Sterne was their looke; like wild amazed steares,
> Staring with hollow eies, and stiffe upstanding heares. [9]

But this rough exterior cannot obscure the vision of a regenerate Ireland, as bright and as baseless as Carlyle's picture of the same people left to the mercy of Cromwellian autocracy. Social, economic and agricultural conditions inspire the belief that, restored to order through the agency of English "captains", Gloriana's champions, this troubled land and its inhabitants might become a very Lycurgan commonwealth, enjoying "such sweetness and happy contentment, that they will afterwardes hardly be hayled away from it, or drawen to theyr woonted lewde life in theeverye and rogerye". [10] Both as retrospect and prospect the *View* is prose counterpart to *The Faerie Queene*.

Though in the course of time Spenser became more reconciled to his lot he could never regard his status in Ireland as anything but one of honourable exile, "in savadge soyle, far from Parnasso mount". "The Shepherd of the Ocean", hearing Colin's lay, casts

> great dislyking to my lucklesse lot,
> That banisht had my selfe, like wight forlore, [11]

and if, as seems probable, the dedication to *Virgils Gnat* was penned soon after August, 1580, the circumstances add poignancy to the gnat's complaint of his confinement "in a waste wilderness". Several kindred spirits were suffering the same fate. One of Grey's secretaries, who held office under a succession of Irish deputies, was Geoffrey Fenton, the translator of Bandello's novels and of Guicciardini's *Storia d' Italia*. Another prominent civil servant stationed in

Ireland was that stalwart Puritan, Barnabe Googe. It is more than likely that Spenser was acquainted with these and other such worthies.

But the most interesting record of his literary circle is supplied by Lodowick Bryskett, a private acquaintance as well as a professional associate. The son of a naturalised Italian, Antonio Bruschetto, Bryskett had been the chosen companion of Sir Philip Sidney during the latter's travels through Italy, and his two elegies upon Sidney were printed, along with *Astrophel* and *Colin Clouts Come Home Againe*, in 1595. He had accompanied Sir Henry Sidney to Ireland in 1575 as clerk to the Privy Council, and after the arrival of Spenser, five years later, the two officials appear to have become fairly intimate. Some time before Grey's recall in 1582 Bryskett had dedicated to him *A Discourse of Civill Life: containing the Ethike part of Morall Philosophie*, which was not published, however, until 1606. In the introduction to this work Bryskett describes a party held at his cottage near Dublin, and consisting of "Dr *Long*, Primate of Ardmagh; *Sir Robert Dillon*, Knight; M. *Dormer* the Queenes Sollicitor; Capt. *Christopher Carleil*; Capt. *Thomas Norreis*; Capt. *Warham St. Leger*; Capt. *Nicholas Dawtrey*; and M. *Edmond Spenser*, late your lordship's secretary; and *Th. Smith*, apothecary". The conversation turns on moral philosophy as treated by recent Italian writers; and Bryskett, confessing his own inability to deal satisfactorily with the subject, points out that there is "a gentleman in this company, whom I have had often a purpose to intreate, that as his leisure might serve him, he would vouchsafe to spend some time with me to instruct me in some hard points which I cannot of myselfe understand; knowing him to be not onely perfect in the Greek tongue, but also very well read in Philosophie, both morall and naturall". The said gentleman, Edmund Spenser, is thereupon requested to gratify the company "in declaring unto us the great benefites which men obtaine by the knowledge of Morall Philosophie, and in making us know what the same is, what be the parts thereof, whereby vertues are to be distinguished from vices; and finally that he will be pleased to run over in such order as he shall thinke good, such and so many principles and rules thereof, as shall serve not only for my better instruction, but also for the contentment and satisfaction of you al". But Spenser refuses the request on the ground that he has "already undertaken a work tending to the same effect, which is in *heroical verse*, under the title of a *Faerie Queene* to represent all the moral vertues, assigning to every vertue a Knight to be the patron and defender of the same: in whose actions and feates of arms and chivalry the operations of that vertue, whereof he is the protector, are to be expressed, and the vices and unruly appetites that oppose themselves against the same, to be beaten down and overcome. Which work, as I have already well entred into, if God shall please to spare me life that I may finish it according to my mind, your wish (M. *Bryskett*) will be in some sort accomplished, though perhaps not so effectually as you could desire". Spenser then proceeds to suggest that, instead, Bryskett should show his guests his own translation from the three dialogues of G. B. Giraldi on Civil Life; and "With this answer of M. *Spensers* it seemed that all the company were wel satisfied, for after some few speeches whereby they had shewed an extreme longing after his worke of the *Faerie Queene*, whereof some parcels had been by some of them seene, they all began to presse me to produce my translation mentioned by M. *Spenser* that it might be perused among them".

The historical value of this record is somewhat discounted by the contemporary taste for Platonic dialogue as a literary artifice and also by the fact that much of it, like the discourse to which it forms a preamble, closely follows Giraldi. On the other hand, the particulars added by Bryskett, including Spenser's speech, are too circumstantial to be summarily dismissed as fictitious. Bryskett had recently retired from most of his public duties in order to obtain more leisure for study, and his substitution of this particular group of individuals for the three characters in the original strengthens the probability of such meetings having taken place under the conditions he describes. Spenser's obvious debt to Giraldi's *Dialogues* in planning his ethical scheme would seem further to corroborate Bryskett's statement and therefore to suggest that *The Faerie Queene*, like many another literary product of the Renaissance, was in the nature of a group achievement and owed something to the throwing about of brains within the author's circle. Lastly we may conclude that, even at this early date, it was "already well entred into" and recognised by those who had read "small parcels" of it as the work of a philosophical poet whose name could suitably replace that of "Torquato" in Giraldi's *Dialogues*. But the task of a civil servant in Ireland was no light one; and Spenser was probably prevented from giving the final touches even to the first instalment of his poem until he had left the noises of a political post in Dublin for the comparative seclusion of a country seat at Kilcolman.

He may have known Sir Walter Raleigh before he left England, at the time when they were both enjoying the patronage of Leicester. In any case they must have met soon after Spenser's arrival in Ireland, for during the year 1580 Raleigh was commanding an English company in Munster and took part in the siege of Smerwick. Raleigh remained in Ireland until December, 1581, distinguishing himself throughout that time by carrying out Grey's policy of suppression. His absence from Ireland for the next eight years did not prevent him from taking a keen interest in the possibilities of that unhappy country as a source of wealth, and in 1586 he obtained a vast tract of land in Munster upon which he conferred at least one benefit by introducing the cultivation of potatoes. But the development of an estate in a half-civilised island could not for long monopolise the attention of so versatile an adventurer, who had graver business elsewhere. So like many of the Undertakers Raleigh remained an absentee landlord, and it was not until 1589 that a disagreement with the Earl of Essex drove him to seek refuge in Munster.

By this time the lease of Spenser's house in Dublin had expired and he had already settled in Munster, probably at Kilcolman. Here, as he relates in *Colin Clouts Come Home Againe*, he was visited by Raleigh, "the Shepherd of the Ocean", whose heroic achievements must assuredly have commanded his admiration and with whom he could find a common interest in poetry:

> He pip'd, I sung; and, when he sung, I piped;
> By chaunge of turnes, each making other mery;
> Neither envying other, nor envied,
> So piped we, untill we both were weary.

The upshot was a proposal that Spenser should accompany Raleigh back to London and try his fortunes on a soil more favourable than the barren wastes of Ireland:

> The which to leave, thenceforth he counseld mee,
> Unmeet for man, in whom was ought regardfull,
> And wend with him, his Cynthia to see;
> Whose grace was great, and bounty most rewardfull.[12]

The invitation was even more acceptable than the similar counsel tendered by Hobbinol eleven years previously, for both his literary projects and his private affairs rendered a visit to England imperative. The first instalment of *The Faerie Queene* was now ripe for publication and a stanza from Book II had already been quoted by Abraham Fraunce in his *Arcadian Rhetorike* (1588). Moreover, an Irish neighbour, Lord Roche, was preparing to lodge a suit against "Edmund Spenser, Clerk to the Council in Munster", the record of which is dated October 12, 1589. So there was every reason to welcome this opportunity of returning to London under the wing of such a patron.

They arrived, probably, in October, 1589,[13] and the three completed books of *The Faerie Queene* were registered under the date December 1. On January 23, 1589–90, Spenser addressed to Raleigh a "Letter of the Authors, expounding his whole intention"; and shortly afterwards the three books were published, prefaced by a dedication to the Queen and followed by the letter to Raleigh, seven poems of commendation and seventeen sonnets addressed by the author to the most conspicuous members of the court. Advertisement could hardly have gone to further extremities. Raleigh, extolling the New Poet as the supplanter of Petrarch and Homer, can no longer prize the verses of any "which speak our English tongue". Harvey, forgetting his former chagrin at the triumph of Hobgoblin over Apollo, rejoices that Colin's muse has lifted his notes "from Shepheardes unto Kinges" and commends the work to the grace of Elizabeth. One admirer bids the nymphs and syrens of Thames be silent at the song of this "Bryttane Orpheus". Another pronounces his workmanship to be beyond the praise of human pen. The band of worthies to whom Colin pays his addresses includes Raleigh "the sommers Nightingale", Lord Grey "the pillor of my life", Essex who may look for "more famous memory of thine Heroicke parts", Sir Francis Walsingham, the Mæcenas of the age, who by extending his patronage may win yet "bigger tunes", Lord Buckhurst, author of the Induction to *A Mirror for Magistrates*, whose "golden verse" merits immortal, fame, Lord Burleigh, who shoulders the "burdein of this kingdomes governement", the Countess of Pembroke, "goodly image" of her brother, and finally "all the gratious and beautifull Ladies in the Court".

So the romance of Hobgoblin, the philosophic poem discussed at Bryskett's cottage, was finally given out to the world as an English epic, the first of its kind, offered to a sovereign at the zenith of her power and to a people that had but recently learnt the full meaning of patriotism. Challenging comparison with Homer and Virgil the author admits within his "whole intention" a political allegory figuring contemporary events and living celebrities. "In that Faery

Edmund Spenser

Queene I meane glory in my generall intention, but in my particular I conceive the most excellent and glorious person of our soveraine the Queene, and her kingdom in Faery land." Without this explanatory note it would certainly not be easy for the reading public to detect anything beyond a vague correspondence between the material of the poem and its political purport. For the three books contained three distinct allegories—religious, ethical and romantic. Gloriana, the one character of whose identity there could be no question, did not appear, while most of the historical personages and incidents belonged to an earlier generation. Such detachment was only to be expected from a poet living in exile for a space of nine years, out of touch with affairs in the metropolis and leaning rather to fantasy than to fact. But in the light of his statement his general politic intention was unmistakable, independent of specific allusions. Under this dark conceit the whole array of virtues and vices appeared as a symbolic vision of the future now dawning upon a nation represented as the champion of civilisation against barbarism. Imagination had quickened the labour of years in the rich mine of philosophy, history and romance to a comprehensive epic of Humanism appealing alike to poet, patriot and moralist. Master "Immerito" now claimed attention as the laureate of a new Golden Age.

Far-reaching changes had overtaken English life and letters since Spenser's departure from London ten years before. The Muses no longer needed to bewail the abandonment of their shrines, for the Renaissance foreshadowed in *The Shepheardes Calender* was now at its prime. In *Colin Clouts Come Home Againe* honourable mention is made of no less than ten living poets, summarily appraised in epigrams that imply first-hand acquaintance with their works. The death of Sidney in 1586 and of Leicester in 1588 had finally severed the last threads of connection between Spenser and his first patrons, but other possibilities remained. If we may believe *Colin Clouts Come Home Againe*, through the good offices of

Raleigh he gained an audience with the Queen, a slight return for the unique tribute which he had paid to English imperialism; and he now prepared to consolidate his position by seeking favour from many new quarters. *Daphnaida*, an elegy on the death of Douglas Howard, wife of Arthur Gorges, was published early in 1591 with a dedication to Helena, Marquess of Northampton, her kinswoman by marriage. The subject of this very palpable imitation from Chaucer's *Book of the Duchess* had died, at the age of eighteen, on August 13, 1590; and it is more than likely that Spenser penned his tribute in the interests of "Alcyon" as opposed to the latter's father-in-law, who had attempted to thwart the marriage from the outset and whose brother twelve years later vented his wrath upon Ambrosia, pledge "of the late love the which betwixt us past" by raising doubts as to her legitimacy.[14]   Other pieces, some drafted at a much earlier date, were now prepared for the press with the object of gaining patronage. *The Ruines of Time*, an elegy on various members of the Dudley family, was inscribed to the Countess of Pembroke. The three Althorpe cousins, "Phyllis, Charillis & sweet Amaryllis", came in for their share of tribute, *Mother Hubberds Tale* falling to Lady Compton, *The Teares of the Muses* to Lady Strange, *Muiopotmos*, perhaps also the *Visions*, to Lady Carey, "pride and primrose of the rest".[15]

The publication of *The Faerie Queene* placed its author forthwith in the front rank of English poets and doubtless brought him to the notice of the whole reading public. But any hope that he may have cherished as to material advancement or permanent recognition at home was doomed to frustration. Had either circumstance or inclination allowed him to throw in his lot with that of the professing literary class, instead of still hovering on the fringe of the aristocracy, he would have found a genial concourse of kindred spirits ready to welcome him as one of their leaders. As it was, he stood in the unenviable position of the celebrity applauded by all circles but failing to establish himself in any of them. The picture of courtly and literary society presented in *Colin Clouts Come Home Againe* is that of an outsider, conscious of his detachment from the life that he portrays. Returning to England under the ægis of Raleigh Spenser might well have entertained great expectations. But he was in no sense an official dependant of Raleigh, whose preoccupation with his own affairs was more than sufficient to override a passing interest in the obscure owner of Kilcolman. The public recognition tendered him in return for *The Faerie Queene* was confined to a substantial pension of £50, which, according to tradition, Burleigh attempted to reduce.[16] All that was left for him was to return to honourable seclusion, breathing out his defiance at an ungrateful world.

The defiance found forceful expression in his *Complaints*, registered under the date December 29, 1590, and published in the following year soon after his "departure over sea", as we learn from the printer's address to the reader. Of the nine pieces included in this volume, only *The Ruines of Time* and *Muiopotmos* would appear to have been entirely of recent composition.[17] The former reads as a fresh bid for favour from the Dudley family through the good offices of the Countess of Pembroke to whom it is dedicated. In the latter the fable of the spider and the butterfly veils a dark conceit, the interpretation of which can only be conjectured. It may refer to the relations between Raleigh and Essex or between Spenser and Lady Carey; but whatever its purport *Muiopotmos* is unmistakably a work of its author's maturity, displaying to the full his easy mastery over his instrument and all the finer elements of his craft.[18]

The fact that each of the remaining poems in the volume represents earlier work lends some support to the statements of Ponsonbie, the printer, concerning his own responsibility in compiling it. *The Teares of the Muses*, a crude and pedestrian effort, presents a view of contemporary poetry more in keeping with "October" or with Sidney's *Apologie* than with *Colin Clouts Come Home Againe*.[19] The *Visions* are probably connected with the "Dreames", alluded to by both Spenser and Harvey in their correspondence of 1579–80. *Virgils Gnat* was "long since dedicated" to Leicester, *Mother Hubberds Tale* "long sithens composed in the raw conceipt of my youth". Even supposing that Spenser's present despondency prompted him to publish the dedicatory sonnet to the former—an address to a dead patron on an injury sustained ten years before—in the latter he could hardly have passed the now obsolete allusion to Leicester's marriage; and it is reasonable, therefore, to suppose that, as the result of his hasty departure, the work of final revision fell to the printer, Ponsonbie. On the other hand, Ponsonbie's equivocal statements, like the cautious annotations of E.K., can be accepted only with reserve. Had he been collecting "a fewe parcels" of his author's work in such haphazard fashion as he implies it is highly improbable that they should all have turned upon the common motive of "the worlds vanitie", which is in complete accordance with the melancholic fatalism that pervades the moralising passages of *The Faerie Queene*. Moreover, the inscription of various numbers to Spenser's new patrons, together with the registration of the volume some time before his departure, all go to prove that he himself fully intended publication and had collected the material with this specific object.

So the old Philippic, hitherto withheld, was adapted to suit the occasion and offered to the world. *Mother Hubberds Tale*, originally directed against Burleigh as the rival of Leicester, now did service as a personal manifesto on the part of the disgruntled poet, whose sense of injury finds poignant utterance in the lines upon the "poor suitor's state". And as if this were not enough the same charges, levelled at the same politician, were repeated in *The Ruines of Time*. The result was what might have been expected;

> *Spenser* therefore thy *Ruines* were called in,

wrote John Weever, the epigrammatist, with reference either

to *The Ruines of Time*, originally entitled *The Worlds Ruines*, or, as is more likely, to the whole volume which opens with this piece. The fact that in 1596 the *Complaints* were copied out by hand[20] implies that printed copies were difficult to obtain and had therefore been suppressed; and when in 1611 for the first time they were reprinted, along with Spenser's other collected works, it was still necessary to exclude *Mother Hubberds Tale* and to generalise the personal allusions in *The Ruines of Time*, doubtless out of deference to Burleigh's son, Robert Cecil. For a second time Spenser had proved his own worst enemy and his friends could only lament his precipitancy. Harvey, writing in 1592, acknowledged that "Mother Hubbard, in heat of choller, forgetting the pure sanguine of her sweete Feary Queene, wilfully over-shot her malcontented selfe",[21] to which Thomas Nashe promptly retorted by railing on him for a busybody whose long tongue would do his friend no good but only "rekindle against him the sparkes of displeasure that were quenched".[22] But the sparks had already wrought damage beyond repair; and no reader could possibly have been deluded by the offender's subsequent appeal to Raleigh for protection "against the malice of evill mouthes, which are alwaies wide open to carpe at and misconstrue my simple meaning" or by the ingenuous avowal of innocence at the close of *The Faerie Queene*, Book VI:

> Ne may this homely verse, of many meanest,
> Hope to escape his venemous despite,
> More than my former writs, all were they cleanest
> From blamefull blot, and free from all that wite
> With which some wicked tongues did it backebite,
> And bring into a mightie Peres displeasure,
> That never so deserved to endite.[23]

There was nothing for it but once and for all to abandon hope of the preferment which now for a second time had proved unattainable. *Colin Clouts Come Home Againe*, first drafted for Raleigh's benefit "from my house of Kilcolman, the 27 of December, 1591", though not published until 1595, breathes a new spirit of genial submission sharply contrasted with the despondency that overshadows all the pieces preceding it. Disillusioned by love, fortune and his fellow-men, the idealist who had demanded too much of life was at length resolved to accept life's proferred gifts, to seize the substance without vainly pursuing the shadow. Like Calidore at the homestead of Meliboe, Colin has gladly forsaken the intrigue and false luxury of Court for the "life so free and fortunate" not of preachers masquerading in pastoral weeds but of care-free shepherds piping as if they never would grow old. Untied by argument or ulterior object, for once he rejoices in pure irresponsible self-expression, "agreeing with the truth in circumstance and matter", humouring his fancy with favourite devices—the singing match, light burlesque, courtly eulogy and a hymn in honour of love, centred upon the person of his first mistress, Rosalind.

But Rosalind's star was already on the wane and her obduracy was no longer to prevent Colin, now past the fire of youth, from following the natural way of men. The courtship which inspired the greater part of *Amoretti* and which led to the occasion of *Epithalamion* appears to have begun towards the close of 1592. Its object was Elizabeth Boyle, daughter of Stephen Boyle of Bradden, near Towcester, Northampton. This lady had accompanied her brother, Alexander, on his migration to the Irish estate of their more famous kinsman, Richard Boyle; and prior to her marriage she appears to have been residing near the Bay of Youghal, "the sea that neighbours to her neare", possibly at Kilcoran.[24] Some of the *Amoretti* doubtless belong to an earlier date and may have been addressed to Rosalind or other ladies. But as published they represent a tribute to a single personality and an earlier draft of number 1, inscribed "To his mistress" by Spenser himself, was inserted in a copy of *The Faerie Queene* apparently presented to his bride.[25]

Edmund Spenser

The *Amoretti* cycle purports to tell the story of the suit, embellished by copious borrowing from Petrarchists and the Pléiade.[26] The dawn of a new year awakens love to greet the lusty spring, heralded by the cuckoo's note. The holy season of Lent incites the devout lover to service for his "Sweet Saynt", on whom his thoughts attend "lyke sacred priests that never thinke amisse". Summer reminds him that "ever sweet with soure is tempred still", and as the year wears on his lodestar is clouded and his ship wanders from her course. To his friend Bryskett he acknowledges the injury done to his "most sacred Empresse" through neglect to complete his unfinished epic; but he is "tost with troublous fit" by a mistress cruel and obstinate as panther or tiger, hard as marble, "no woman but a sencelesse stone". The second year brings a welcome change, as he descries the happy shore and enjoys the rest that follows toil. The lady accepts his favours and allows him to kiss her lips. She who had feared to lose her liberty now finds that she has gained more than she has lost and submits to her pursuer as spoil in the hands of the hunter. United in the joy of Easter they engage in the idle games of lovers. She weaves a device of herself as the bee ensnared by the spider. He writes her name upon the strand, the name

> The which three times thrise happy hath me made,
> With guifts of body, fortune, and of mind.[27]

His verses will immortalise her fame; for after completing one half of his *Faerie Queene* now he will sport his muse in praising his lady and so proceed to the second half, "as a steed refreshed after toil". The cycle closes with something of an anti-climax, perhaps occasioned by the displacement of some numbers or by the incorporation of earlier material. A venomous tongue has kindled strife between lover and mistress. But the difference, if it ever existed, was short-lived; for on the feast of "Barnaby the bright", June 11, 1594, the marriage took place, probably either at Cork or at

Youghal; and the consummation of the *Amoretti* romance
was celebrated by *Epithalamion*.

Upon this supreme masterpiece of its kind Spenser has
lavished all the resources of his matchless art. The courtly
maker of "April" and "November", who had long since
given proof of his skill in the invention of intricate strophic
patterns, is now the passionate lover in the first fine rapture
of satisfaction. Through a chain of "ditties", or miniature
odes, linked by the echoing refrain, the theme unfolds itself
as a complete word pageant of the country wedding, with not
a detail irrelevant or misplaced. For the first time in the
history of English poetry familiar conventions spring to life
as inevitable poetic expression, the spontaneous overflow of
powerful feelings:

> Tell me, ye merchants daughters, did ye see
> So fayre a creature in your towne before;
> So sweet, so lovely, and so mild as she,
> Adornd with beautyes grace and vertues store?
> Her goodly eyes lyke Saphyres shining bright,
> Her forehead yvory white,
> Her cheekes lyke apples which the sun hath rudded,
> Her lips lyke cherryes charming men to byte,
> Her breast lyke to a bowle of creame uncrudded,
> Her paps lyke lyllies budded,
> Her snowie neck lyke to a marble towre;
> And all her body like a pallace fayre,
> Ascending up, with many a stately stayre,
> To honors seat and chastities sweet bowre.[28]

But the cleanly wantonness is under control. Christian
marriage has sanctified these "sweet snatches of delight",
the satisfaction of normal human desire and the prelude to a
fuller life. *Epithalamion* is not only the crown of Spenser's
artistic achievement but the natural corollary to his epic of
perfect manhood.

But love and poetry were not to keep their way uninter-
rupted. In 1593 and 1594 Maurice, Lord Roche, whose
estate lay to the east of Spenser's, presented to the Lord

Chancellor two petitions against "one Edmund Spenser, gentleman", and a third against Joan Ny Callaghan, said to be supported and maintained by Edmund Spenser, "a heavy adversary unto your suppliant". This was not the first time in which Spenser was involved in litigation against Lord Roche, who had lodged a petition, on October 12, 1589, against five of his neighbours, including the poet, on the ground that they had misused his servants and property. Spenser and his supporters retorted by accusing their adversary of similar offences, also of speaking ill against Her Majesty's government, but the charges appear to have been unsubstantiated and for a time the matter was dropped. A guerilla warfare, however, was probably maintained, and four years later Lord Roche complained that Edmund Spenser had encroached upon three ploughlands, converting them to his own use. Spenser did not appear to defend his case, and in consequence the petitioner was successful in obtaining possession on February 12. It is not difficult to read between the lines concerning this affair, which may have occasioned the last four sonnets and which certainly prompted an attack upon Roche in the *View*. An Irish nobleman, who had remained loyal to the Queen during the Desmond rebellion, had no reason to love a foreign settler who had been concerned in the judicial robbery of Irish lands and whose estimate of the character and civilisation of his adopted country may be gathered from the *View*. It has been suggested that poverty rather than rapacity may have prompted Spenser's action; but though the "honour and large richesse" of *Amoretti*, LXXIV, may be a figure of speech there is no reason to assume that at this time he was suffering from want or living below the position of a country gentleman, for by the time of his death he had succeeded in acquiring, besides Kilcolman, several properties in different parts of the country.

The documents relating to the case with Lord Roche strengthen the supposition that by 1594 Spenser had resigned his clerkship in the Council of Munster, and this freedom from official duties would allow him more leisure for literary work. He had now completed another three books of *The Faerie Queene*, as we learn from sonnet LXXX, and was preparing other works for publication. *Colin Clouts Come Home Againe* was brought up to date by recent additions, including the references to Daniel's "tragick plaints"— *Cleopatra*, published in 1594,—and to the death of "Amyntas", or Ferdinando, Earl of Derby, which occurred in April of the same year. *Astrophel*, written probably several years before, was now completed by a dedication to the Countess of Essex, formerly Sidney's wife; and the two poems were published together by Ponsonbie in 1595. *Amoretti* and *Epithalamion*, likewise published together, appeared during the same year, having been registered under the date November 19, 1594. In the printed text the *Amoretti* were introduced by a letter from Ponsonbie to Sir Robert Needham, who had recently crossed from Ireland, probably bearing Spenser's manuscript with him, though ignorant of its contents.

Spenser himself must have followed soon after, for on January 20, 1595–6, the second part of *The Faerie Queene*, which he would certainly have seen through the press, was entered on the register. If the courtly tributes of *Colin Clouts Come Home Againe* meant a fresh bid for favour, any chance of this must have been considerably diminished by a fresh outburst against "Courtiers Schoolery". Nor were the new books of *The Faerie Queene* calculated to advance their author's status, notwithstanding his continued homage to the Queen. The complex political allegory of Book v centred upon Lord Grey, who had been dead three years and whose unpopular Irish policy had long been a thing of the past. Raleigh's scandalous love affair with Elizabeth Throgmorton and the Queen's consequent displeasure at her favourite, alluded to in the story of Timias, Amoret and Belphœbe, were events that, having occurred four years before, had now lost their interest. In Calidore discerning readers could recognise some traits of Essex; but the knight of Courtesy had at least as much in common with Sidney, the "brave courtier" of *Mother Hubberds Tale*, and the ambiguity was not cleared by the story of Pastorella, or the daughter of Walsingham ("Meliboe"), Sidney's widow, who afterwards married Essex. Moreover, certain references to the Queen's enemies were too outspoken to escape censure. In November, 1596, Robert Bowes, the English ambassador in Scotland, wrote to Burleigh on behalf of King James, protesting against the public affront offered against the memory of Queen Mary in *The Faerie Queene* and demanding the prosecution of its author, despite the privilege under which his book had been published.[29] The protest appears to have been ineffectual and probably did no more than advertise the poem; but it may well have served to maintain Spenser's reputation for dangerous patriotism.

His chances of preferment were now even more remote than in 1590, when at least he had Raleigh to befriend him, and at the opening of *Prothalamion*, written towards the end of the year 1596, he reflects bitterly upon his

> sullein care,
> Through discontent of my long fruitlesse stay
> In Princes Court, and expectation vayne
> Of idle hopes, which still doe flie away,
> Like empty shaddowes.[30]

The "spousall verse" introduced by this inauspicious prelude commemorates the double marriage of Elizabeth and Katherine, daughters of the Earl of Worcester, to Henry Gilford and William Peters, an event which took place on November 8. Like *Epithalamion*, *Prothalamion* is an English canzone, composed of complex stanzas, bound by a symmetrical rhyme system with continuous refrain. But the lyrical note is wanting and the prevailing tone more subdued. The self-abandoned lover of *Epithalamion* is back in his habitual rôle of polite poet, devising pretty fancies and developing his theme with the detachment of the objective artist. A society wedding in town calls for grace and urbanity rather than the display of boisterous animal spirit; so the event is figured under a stately allegory of two swans, "softly swimming downe along the Lee". *Prothalamion* is the proud and glowing eulogy of a Londoner to his native city, Cleopolis, the fair and venerable home of civility.

The allegory affords Spenser occasion for courting a new patron, Robert Devereux, Earl of Essex, the "noble peer" who lodges by the river-side in Leicester House, once the poet's home, and who appears, accordingly, as *deus ex machina* at the close. Largess might well be expected of such a protector, fresh from his triumph at Cadiz,

> Whose dreadfull name late through all Spaine did thunder,
> And Hercules two pillors standing neere
> Did make to quake and feare,[31]

and whose enlightenment recalled the spirit of that other "faire branch of Honor, flower of Chevalrie", Sir Philip Sidney. Six years before, in a sonnet prefixed to *The Faerie Queene*, this "Magnificke Lord" had been promised "more famous memory Of thine Heroicke parts" in one of the later books; and another tribute, even more pointed, was to follow. During his stay in London Spenser was probably completing his *View of the present state of Ireland*, which internal evidence proves to have been written in England some time during the deputyship of Sir William Russell (1594–7). Apprehensive of the impending catastrophe and despite warnings from Eudoxus, Irenæus openly attacks the present Irish policy and the incompetence of officials, concluding that in the interests of all parties supreme authority should be delegated to a Lord Lieutenant, "of some of the greatest personages in England (such an one I could name, upon whom the eye of all England is fixed and our last hopes now rest)".[32] But his outspoken criticisms were too dangerous to be allowed to reach the public ear. The *View* was not registered for publication until 1598 and then only on condition that the publisher "gett further aucthoritie before yt be prynted". Thirty-five years were to elapse before it appeared in print. But as it was undoubtedly circulated in 1596, the date of some half-dozen extant manuscripts, it probably came to the notice of Essex, who might well have been gratified by his protégé's flattering suggestion, destined to be carried out three years later with all too tragic consequences.

On September 1, 1596, writing from Greenwich, Spenser inscribed to Margaret, Countess of Cumberland, and "Marie" (Anne), Countess of Warwick, his four *Hymnes*, the first two composed "in the greener time of youth", and the other now offered "by way of retractation". The latter statement is clearly a blind, intended to satisfy the scruples of two Puritanical patronesses; if youth sucked poison from the two earlier *Hymnes* what was to be said of *Amoretti, Epithalamion*, or many episqdes in *The Faerie Queene*? The fervid neo-Platonism which illumines the earlier *Hymnes* had penetrated too deeply into Spenser's being to be thus easily "retracted"; on the other hand the narrow dogmatism of *An Hymne of Heavenly Love* is a fatal curb to inspiration and frequently collapses into flat prosaic verbiage. The *Hymne of Heavenly Beautie* is more successful and the closing stanzas represent Spenser at his best; but the attempt to reconcile Platonism with Christianity involves considerable confusion of thought and recapitulation of authorities. Each of the two later hymns suffers from the inevitable disadvantage attending work written to order rather than at the urge of genius; and it was probably the realisation of this fact that persuaded Spenser to include the two earlier pieces, from a poet's standpoint the "retractation" of the others.

Before leaving England Spenser was again involved in litigation, on this occasion as plaintiff. Elizabeth Spenser's mother, Joan Boyle, married to a second husband Ferdinando Freckleton, had lent £100 of the Boyle children's legacy from their father to Edmund Lucey of Kingston, Warwickshire, the trustees being Thomas Emyly and John

Mathewe. The suit of Edmund Spenser, his wife and her brothers, George and Alexander, against Emyly and Mathewe for payment of the said £100 was entered in the Court of Chancery on November 20, 1596; and it is therefore highly probable that the plaintiffs protracted their stay in England until it was concluded in the early part of the following year.[33]

It may have been after his return to Ireland, in 1597, that Spenser wrote the cantos of Mutability, drawing much of his local colour from the surroundings of Kilcolman and Arlo Hill. By this time he had at least two children, bearing the suggestive names Sylvanus, heir to the wooded Kilcolman, and Peregrine, "an exile". In September, 1598, a few weeks after the death of his old foe, Burleigh, he was recommended for the office of High Sheriff of Cork as one well known "for his good and commendable parts being a man endowed with good knowledge in learning, and not unskillful or without experience in the service of the warrs". Almost simultaneously with this new honour fell the catastrophe, when the Earl of Tyrone, after a victory over the English near Armagh, succeeded in conveying a force to Munster and arousing the province to insurrection. Short shrift was to be expected for the unfortunate owner of Kilcolman, formerly the family seat of Desmond. The castle was plundered and burnt, its occupants barely escaping; and according to a report preserved by Ben Jonson and adopted by Landor in his "Conversation between Spenser and Essex" a new-born child perished in the flames. Practically destitute, Spenser made for Cork whence, in December, he embarked for London, bearing despatches with details of the rebellion from Sir Thomas Norreys, President of Munster, to the Secretary of State. Sir James Ware, a trustworthy authority, states that already he had "finished the later part of that excellent poem of his *Faery Queene*, which was soone after unfortunately lost by the disorder and abuse of his servant, whom he had sent before him into England";[34] but this report is unconfirmed.

He may have been responsible for "A brief note" to the Queen respecting the recent rebellion and reiterating the arguments for military conquest propounded in the *View*.[35] But he was not destined to see any amelioration of the conditions which had occasioned the calamity. His sufferings and anxieties during the last few months must have told upon his health; and on January 13, 1599, three weeks after his arrival in England, he died at Westminster.

He left three children, two sons, Sylvanus and Peregrine, and a daughter, Catherine. Within less than two years of his death his wife, Elizabeth, was married to Roger Seckerstone, and on March 3, 1612, in the study of Sir Richard Boyle, she took as her third husband Captain Robert Tynte, to whom she bore seven children. She died in 1622.

According to Camden and other authorities Spenser died in poverty, which might naturally have resulted from the plundering of his possessions at Kilcolman. "Poorly, poor man he liv'd; poorly, poor man he died", says Phineas Fletcher, while the author of *The Returne from Parnassus* is even more explicit:

> And yet for all this, unregarding soile
> Unlac't the line of his desired life,
> Denying mayntenance for his deare reliefe.
> Carelesse (ere) to prevent his exequy,
> Scarce deigning to shut up his dying eye.

Ben Jonson states that he died for lack of bread, having "refused 20 pieces sent to him by my Lord of Essex, and said, He was sorrie he had no time to spend them".[36] "The famous Spenser", says Henry Peacham, "did never get any preferment in his life, save towards his latter end he became a Clerk of the Council in Ireland, and dying in England he dyed but poore. When he lay sicke, the noble and patterne of true honor, Robert Earle of Essex, sent him twenty pound either to relieve or bury him".[37] These statements are neither so incredible nor so contradictory as might at first appear. Spenser's friends in London would hardly have allowed him

Life and Works

to starve, while his pension should have kept him from absolute want. On the other hand he probably left Kilcolman with nothing but his personal necessities, and his death almost certainly resulted from the privations he had suffered between the time of his escape from Ireland and his arrival in England. In this case the reply to Essex would be perfectly understandable—he knew that he had reached his end and therefore had no time for spending the money. To judge from his own accounts, poverty would seem to have dogged him through life, as is plainly hinted by his eulogists; and though, as we have seen, his implications on this matter can only be accepted with some reserve, literary fame has never been a guarantee of prosperity and until his later years he had probably no independent means. It would have been no more than the irony of fate if the poet who had been educated through the charity of an acquaintance was brought to his end through want.

He was buried in Westminster Abbey, by his own request (as is said) near to his master Chaucer:

> Nigh Venerable Chaucer, lost,
> Had not kinde Brigham reared him Cost,
> Found next the doore Church-outed neere,
> And yet a Knight, Arch-Lauriat heere.[38]

His obsequies, the expenses of which were borne by Essex, were celebrated with the honour befitting England's laureate, his brother poets following the bier and dropping pens and elegies into his grave. Tradition says that the Queen ordered a monument to be erected over his remains but that the order was not fulfilled. In 1620, at a cost of £40, Anne Clifford, Countess of Dorset, caused the erection of the present monument,[39] worthily inscribed to the memory of "Edmond Spencer, the Prince of Poets in his tyme, whose Divine Spirrit needs noe other witnesse then the works which he left behinde him".

CHAPTER III

Humanism

LITTLE is known of Spenser the man apart from his writings. The extant portraits are less reliable than those of Shakespeare or Chaucer, and the one note that has come down concerning his outward appearance only tells us that "he was a little man, wore short haire, little band and little cuffs".[1] Though his poetry is profoundly affected by the impress of his personality, it lacks the intimate self-revelation that continually strikes the reader of Dante or Petrarch, Milton or Donne. His plastic genius was moulded by environment and by the spirit of an age more interested in objective achievement and character portrayal than in self-analysis or the growth of a poet's mind. Spenser the individual is largely eclipsed by Spenser the representative apostle of that English Renaissance which revealed itself, under different aspects, in geographical discovery, religious reformation and the revival of learning. Sidney's "Areopagus" and the party at Bryskett's cottage were as symptomatic of their times as the meetings of the first Petrarchans in the Alberti garden or of the neo-Platonists at Cosimo's Florentine Academy. The "new poetry" inspired by such formative influences claims notice not simply as a detached monument of individual genius but as a group achievement, a dome to the temple of Humanism.

A sensitive and assimilative mind, trained in orthodox schools, qualified Spenser to assume the rôle of correct poet and conscious interpreter of his age. His conformity with the creed and usage of the ruling majority was no less pronounced than that of Pope or Tennyson. The studious craftsman of the juvenilia, surpassing all his predecessors in skilful imitation of prescribed patterns, foreshadows the fashioner of a gentleman and author of the national epic. His writings present a figurative panorama of Elizabethan

Humanism

England in which the personality of the maker identifies itself with the spirit of his age. To the question "What is Humanism?" the whole answer is contained in the *Republic*, the *Nicomachean Ethics*, *Utopia* and *The Faerie Queene*. For though Spenser's intellectual endowment does not compare with the universal culture of an Alberti or a Leonardo, no English writer is so much preoccupied with the humanistic ideal, the man of men, scholar and artist, excelling in virtue private and politic. His minor pieces are as side chapels of the Gothic cathedral dedicated to human prerogative, capacity and achievement; and the main portal bears the inscription: "Homo sum; humani nihil a me alienum puto". Colin is the peerless poet singing to a royal paragon of excellence and to a perfect mistress, whose praises "cannot be expressed by any art". The shortcomings of his baser co-mates draw tears from the Muses who bewail such prostitution of their sacred gift, the divinely appointed means of raising man above the level of the beast. The task of the New Poet was to transform commonplace into a thing of enduring beauty. Assured of his success he would admit of no doubt as to its permanence, proffering his bride "an endlesse moniment", boldly inscribing his masterpiece to his sovereign, "To live with the Eternitie of her Fame".

The writings of Spenser represent the meeting between old tradition and new experiment; and his Humanism, though largely derivative, was not circumscribed by the dictates of any one school. His classical scholarship was probably sufficient to deserve Lodge's tribute, "Spencer, best read in ancient poetry",[2] for his writings show acquaintance, direct or indirect, with all the principal ancient poets and moralists. But he is equally indebted to mediæval authors and to contemporaries, while his invention plays so freely upon his material that particular sources are often impossible to identify. His Platonism was derived mainly, if not wholly, through Italian channels, and two specific allusions to the "father of philosophy" in *The Faerie Queene*[3] involve misstatements of fact that match such inaccuracies as the designation of the Muses as daughters of Apollo. His scheme of virtues "as Aristotle hath devised" is not strictly Aristotelian but compounded "according to Aristotle *and the rest*". His interest in hexameters was short-lived and never advanced beyond the stage of benevolent neutrality. He shows none of Petrarch's sense of fellowship with antiquity or of Milton's veneration for the "divine volumes" of Plato and the ancient poets. Perhaps his old schoolmaster first taught him discrimination, reminding him that "it is no proufe, bycause *Plato* praiseth it, bycause *Aristotle* alloweth it, bycause *Cicero* commendes it, bycause *Quintilian* is acquainted with it, or any other else,...that therfore it is for us to use".4 Be this as it may, the New Poet parades his preference for native homespun as against foreign importation, acknowledging Chaucer alone as his master.

This catholicity of taste is equally evident in the form and substance of his poetry; for "imitation", the humanist's watchword, entailed new emphasis upon the mutual relation subsisting between the two components of a work of art. "They be not wise, therefore", writes Roger Ascham, "that say, what care I for a mans wordes and utterance if his matter and reasons be good?"; while the barbarous writing of "Stoickes, Anabaptistes, and Friers, with Epicures, Libertines and Monkes" provides fit drapery for their fond and pernicious opinions, the "wisest in judgement of matters" have ever proved "purest in uttering their myndes".5 As the sculptor modelled his life studies upon an ideal human figure, so the poet looked to models universally accepted, the ancient patterns of drama, epic, eclogue and lyric. The correlation of art with life bore directly upon technique; the counterpart to propriety in conduct was "decorum", "the good grace of everything in his kind", the due adapting of manner to matter. Here at least Spenser conformed with authority in consistently selecting his medium with the judgment of a true artist. With justice, therefore, Master

E.K. could praise his "dewe observing of Decorum everye where, in personages, in seasons, in matter, in speach; and generally, in al seemely simplycitie of handeling his matter, and framing his words".

But at this point the editor was necessarily on his defensive; for the language of the New Poet brought to a head the issue between decorum and classic purism that followed any attempt to stabilise the vernacular. For the purists "imitation" of the ancients was the first and last principle in literary composition. Sir Thomas Wilson, condemning archaism along with other affectations of speech, Ascham supplying "English matter in the English tongue for Englishmen" were both content to write Latinised prose. E.K.'s allusion to "those auncient solemne wordes" of Livy and Sallust was palpable special pleading on behalf of a writer who admitted not only archaism and dialectal speech but neologisms and linguistic vagaries of every description. The "pastoral rudeness" suitable to bucolic poetry did not require the coinage of a new tongue, nor was it easy for a sixteenth-century reader to appreciate the decorum of a "seemely simplicitie" exaggerated far beyond the accepted limits of seemliness. The New Poet, in short, fairly fluttered the dovecotes of the intelligentsia by admitting licences in flat defiance of all that had been said upon the subject since Wilson had launched his famous attack upon inkhorn terms. For even decorum must needs submit to the ruling of the tribunal which had prescribed it, the authority of the ancients, wherein "we finde alwayes wisdome and eloquence, good matter and good utterance, never or seldom a sonder"; and Sidney doubtless voiced a general opinion in bluntly stating the real cause of offence: "That same framing of his stile to an old rustick language I dare not alowe, sith neyther *Theocritus* in Greeke, *Virgill* in Latine, nor *Sanazar* in Italian did affect it".

The problem which Spenser solved for himself in so drastic a fashion had already been faced by the "new poets" of other lands. The task of Politian had been an easier one, owing to the proximity between Latin and the Italian vernacular. In France the matter had been duly debated and settled by the Pléiade school, more particularly by Ronsard and Du Bellay, whose *Deffence et Illustration de la Langue françoise* contains the liveliest and most comprehensive treatment of the imitation theory as interpreted by a staunch upholder of the native tradition. Spenser followed the lead of Du Bellay in refusing to be hoodwinked by the dictates of any clique, reactionary or progressive; popular and academic strains merge easily in the new poetry which he inaugurated. For a time the precious wits of Cambridge evidently regarded him as fair game; and long after he had come into his own Thomas Nashe was girding at Gabriel Harvey, "this mudborn bubble, this bile on the browe of the Universitie, this bladder of pride new blowne",[6] for daring to parade his intimacy with the arch-poet whom he had vainly sought to misdirect. But Spenser was never a complete convert to the hexameter school. Even while discussing the subject he displays equal interest in alternative possibilities, and the entire absence of hexameters from his published works tells its own tale. The most significant feature in his contribution to the debate is his insistence upon the poet's prerogative in the matter of diction: "For, why a Gods name, may not we, as else the Greekes, have the kingdome of oure owne language, and measure our Accentes by the sounde, reserving the Quantitie to the Verse"?

The chaotic condition of English poetry compelled even an instinctive conformist to cleave a way for himself, regardless of Philistine opposition from either camp. The courtly maker looked for something better than the barbarism of metre-ballad-mongers. On the other hand, the successors of Wyatt and Surrey, "first reformers of our English metre and style", had merely followed the path of least resistance by a blind process of imitation. Hampered by the instability of language and verse they plodded laboriously, in constant danger of pitfalls which no restrictive purism could avert.

Humanism

The new instrument fashioned by Spenser in defiance of all authority save that of a poet's taste and judgment rendered possible the expression of a new Humanism in English poetry. The publication of *The Shepheardes Calender*, dividing an age of pedestrian effort from one of inspired achievement, gave passage to forces altogether beyond the author's control. As an historical event it was comparable with the appearance of *Tamburlaine*, *Tom Jones* or *Lyrical Ballads*.

For the outward formality of Spenser's first efforts reflects a new self-consciousness, the humanist's exultation in his art which had already inspired Petrarchans and the Pléiade and which now for the first time found full expression in English poetry. Decorum requires the perfect adjustment of form and matter in imitation of the ideal. So the poet, true to his calling as seer and inspired leader of men, will turn with disdain from the barbarous dissonance of those who would defame his sacred art and will spare no pains in the process of scaling Parnassus. Sufficient evidence is available to show that upon this basic principle Spenser's lost "English Poet" agreed in substance with Sidney's *Apology for Poetry*. The thought of poetry's immortal heritage transforms the turgid declamation of *The Ruines of Time* into winged words:

> For deeds doe die, how ever noblie donne,
> And thoughts of men do as themselves decay;
> But wise wordes, taught in numbers for to runne,
> Recorded by the Muses, live for ay;
> Ne may with storming showers be washt away,
> Ne bitter-breathing windes with harmefull blast,
> Nor age nor envie, shal them ever wast.[7]

Polyhymnia, bewailing the abandonment of her shrines, recapitulates the familiar text of Minturno:

> Whilom in ages past none might professe
> But Princes and High Priests that secret skill;
> The sacred lawes therein they wont expresse,
> And with deepe Oracles their verses fill:
> Then was shee held in soveraigne dignitie,
> And made the noursling of Nobilitie.[8]

Piers can only echo the reproach of Sidney, that poetry "from almost the highest estimation of learning, is falne to be the laughing stocke of children". Princes are content to die in oblivion, boasting only of arms and ancestry, "underkeeping" the "learned imps". Poetry, their pledge of immortality, is profaned through wanton rhymes, scurrility and ignorance. "Romish Tityrus", befriended by Mæcenas, left his "oaten reede" to sing of wars and shake the heavens with his song. But now Mæcenas is "yclad in claye", virtue stoops for age and poetry is forced to feign nothing better than men's ignorance and folly.[9]

In "October" the New Poet announces himself as the imitator of Virgil, aspiring later to abandon "the base and viler clowne" for bloody Mars and doubted knights. Behind this unmistakable advertisement lies the whole humanistic conception of poetry. For the imitator strove after a higher seat than that of poet's poet, supreme craftsman in words and numbers. Fine execution is but the symbol of high seriousness in purpose; the graceful show of ornament gilds the hidden meaning, an imitation of life. Ben Jonson would have Spenser read for this matter, Milton found him "a better teacher than Scotus or Aquinas".[10] The feigned teaching that drew their admiration, the natural corollary to the new poetry, is the art of right living, the new philosophy of Humanism.

In substance, therefore, as in form, the poetry of Spenser is circumscribed by the tastes and beliefs of his age. His criticism of life is founded upon a preconceived theory of human nature, affording little evidence of insight into individual character. Reversing the course of the dramatic poet, such as Shakespeare or Browning, he draws concrete examples from the abstract type; and this preoccupation with types, ranged according to a pre-determined scheme, allows little scope for the delineation of personality. Such evidence of penetration into the mainsprings of conduct as his writings afford is confined to passing notes or comments and never extends to the full-length portrait. He sees men through the spectacle of books or through a vista of intellectual concept. His knowledge of women is as slight as would be expected of an active public servant who spent the greater part of his life probably as a celibate in a half-civilised outpost. His descriptions and imagery are spectacular rather than psychological, though in this respect some advance can be traced throughout his later works; and even when he descends to the plane of realism, as in the picaresque *Mother Hubberds Tale*, the characterisation is two-dimensional. He draws men not as they are but as they ought or ought not to be. Whether the theme be love or warfare, eulogy or elegy, it presupposes the absolute type, the perfect lover, warrior, courtier, as measure to the scale of values.

In common with other moralists of the Renaissance, as opposed to those of the Middle Ages, Spenser grounds his rule of living upon ethics rather than theology. Gloriana's laureate is the champion of Protestantism, compelled by virtue of his office to vindicate the sanctity of the individual state and the sovereign right of private judgment in spiritual affairs against the claims of proud and ambitious pastors. But he bears no love for the iconoclast, typified in Kirkrapine and the Blatant Beast, nor is his religious dogma in any sense sectarian. The Calvinism of the House of Holiness is little more distinctive than the Catholic mysticism of *An Hymne of Heavenly Beautie*. Extensive borrowings from the Bible throughout Spenser's extant works lend support to the statement of Ponsonbie, his publisher, who attributes to him translations from *Ecclesiastes*, *Canticum Canticorum* and seven Psalms, besides two devotional pieces entitled "The Howers of the Lord" and "The Sacrifice of a Sinner". But the general trend of his thought has more in common with the gnomic books of the Old Testament than with anything in the New; and the fact that only one of his extant poems, *An Hymne of Heavenly Love*, treats of dogmatic theology confirms an assertion in *A View of the present state of Ireland*: "For religion litle have I to saye, my selfe being (as I sayd) not professed therin". His Christianity is overlaid with the paganism of the Renaissance, with concepts of a widely diffused mythopœic genius which, a century before, had prompted the Greek Platonist Gemistos Plethon to invent for himself a fantastic hierarchy of deities, part Christian, part Platonic. "Great Pan", the god of shepherds, feeds his blessed flock "upon mount Olivet". Pilate suffers torment along with Tantalus and other "damned wights" upon the banks of Cocytus. The few references to religion in *The Faerie Queene* are vague and inconclusive. Christian theology contributes nothing to the allegory apart from the legend of Holiness. In one episode, imitated from Tasso, an angel appears as divine agent, otherwise the supernatural machinery is either mythical or romantic. The naturalism of the "Mutability" cantos owes nothing to orthodox Christianity, and the "Mass" at the Temple of Isis is as pagan as the rites that conclude *The Broken Heart*.

Spenser's interpretation of current philosophical notions will be treated at greater length in another chapter. Here it will be sufficient to notice his conformity, on general principles, with the commonplaces of Renaissance ethic loosely compounded from Plato, Aristotle, Plutarch and the Latin moralists. Virtue, "the life according to nature" as the Utopians had defined it, is to be pursued on its own account, irrespective of an afterworld to redress the balance of the present. It is the unique prerogative of man which renders him lord of creation by enthroning reason as the master of animal instinct and appetite. It enables its possessor to spiritualise his faculties, to avoid excess and to act with moderation.

So rigid and abstract a code of morals, the creed of the Stoic reinforced by the dead weight of English Puritanism, would seem ill-adapted to poetic presentation were it not tempered by the humanist's sense of beauty and joy of living. "Our sage and serious Spenser" savours of Tasso rather than of Ariosto, the gravity of his argument allowing little scope for ribaldry or mirth. But if less voluptuous he is quite as sensuous as Ariosto and equally responsive to the appeal of physical beauty. The law of conduct deduced from the victory of reason over passion at Alma's castle and in Acrasia's bower is one of moderation rather than repression and the half-draped enchantress has no place amid the hundred naked maidens dancing to Colin's melody. *The Faerie Queene*, its allegory apart, is "vain and amatorious" as *Arcadia*. All the principal personages, save Guyon, are ardent lovers with normal sex instincts. The moral drawn from their amorous adventures differs fundamentally from that of Petrarch's *Secretum*, of *Paradise Regained* or of *Samson Agonistes*. After the first two books "Thou shalt not" gives place to "Thou shalt", "Be bold, be bold, be not too bold". The chastity of Britomart is not renunciation but the dedication of pure love untainted by wantonness.

Less passionate, but more romantic than either Petrarch or Milton, Spenser habitually plays or philanders with sense impression; the one poem in which he follows through an emotion is *Epithalamion*. His objective, surface view of life as the image of eternity, unblemished by original sin, renders possible the sublimation of fleshly desire into that of the spirit; the will to live becomes the means of self-fulfilment:

> Poure out the wine without restraint or stay,
> Poure not by cups, but by the belly full,
> Poure out to all that wull,
> And sprinkle all the postes and wals with wine,
> That they may sweat, and drunken be withall.
> Crowne ye God Bacchus with a coronall,
> And Hymen also crowne with wreathes of vine;
> And let the Graces daunce unto the rest,
> For they can doo it best.[11]

The voice of Stoic conscience is drowned by the Pindaric strain, for the occasion allows such abandonment on "this one day" to the life of sensations rather than thoughts. Acrasia would be as misplaced at the wedding feast as at the court of Gloriana; but mirth and revelry are the fit accompaniments to a consummation that conforms with natural and social law. The humanist, in restraining the Puritan, has sacrificed none of his principles.

Ideal humanity, the concrete imitation drawn from accepted ethical theories, becomes the hero of *The Faerie Queene* which, from this aspect, belongs to the same order of literature as *The Boke of the Governour*, *The Courtier*, and *Euphues*. As Plato delays the confirmation of his case for justice by Divine revelation until it has been fully proven through inductive reason, so Spenser confines his allegory to the earthly warfare, admitting only occasional reference to the after-life. The faerie knight is first and last the complete gentleman, owning fealty to his sovereign, his fellows and himself, skilled not merely in battle but in horsemanship, falconry, swimming and the chase. His moral virtue is tempered by the social graces of courtesy, friendliness and urbanity. By uniting the scattered threads of allegory in the person of Prince Arthur, the symbol of Magnificence, "which vertue is the perfection of all the rest and conteineth in it them all", Spenser evidently sought to preserve the semblance of epic design. But to plan an epic upon a pre-determined ethical scheme, substituting an abstraction for a personality, is to start from the wrong end. The result is not "an heroic poem, properly so called", but a hybrid of epic, romance and allegory, all character with the minimum of characterisation. Arthur figures in the capacity of *deus ex machina*, striking the finishing blow when the battle is well-nigh ended and aiding his inferiors in their advance towards that perfection which he has attained. But perfection is too unfamiliar a quality to attract except from a distance; and the superman equipped with magic resources clean contrary to the law of arms arouses less interest than his weaker brethren, men of like passions to our own. It is through their adventures that the allegory unfolds itself as a tale of chivalric conflict and of the pilgrimage from weakness to strength.

The analogy between the perfect man and the perfect commonwealth, dating back to Plato's *Republic*, suggests the logical extension of Humanism from ethics to politics. "The citizens beinge gathered into one societye doe make as it were one man, whiche with diversitie of wytte and memorie doth excell, with many eyes seeth, with many handes worketh, and with almost infinite feete endeavoureth himselfe in his affayres."[12] In stressing the distinction between private and politic virtue Spenser follows the authority of Aristotle, Giraldi and Tasso, the last of whom "formed both parts in two persons, namely that part which they in Philosophy call Ethice, or vertues of a private man, coloured in his Rinaldo: the other named Politice in his Godfredo". But the nature of heroic poetry will not allow the maintenance of such a distinction to any appreciable extent. Tasso's "allegory" is nothing but an ingenious piece of special pleading, designed to meet the hostile criticism of a clerical hierarchy. Any attempt to press the alleged cleavage between his two principal characters, who differ in circumstance rather than temperament, would have undermined the structure of his epic; and Spenser was in much the same position. His letter to Raleigh leaves no doubt as to the politic intention underlying his allegory. "In that Faery Queene I meane glory in my generall intention, but in my particular I conceive the most excellent and glorious person of our soveraine the Queene, and her kingdome in Faery land." "Life active" is inseparable from a poem such as *The Faerie Queene*, even when, as in Books I and II, the ethical motive predominates and is enforced by such figures as the House of Holiness the Hill of Contemplation, the Castle of Alma and the Bower of Bliss. The story of Britomart is avowedly offered in deference

to the Queen, as a tribute to woman's achievement outside
the domestic sphere:

> But by record of antique times I finde
> That wemen wont in warres to beare most sway,
> And to all great exploites themselves inclind,
> Of which they still the girlond bore away;
> Till envious Men, fearing their rules decay,
> Gan coyne streight lawes to curb their liberty:
> Yet sith they warlike armes have laide away,
> They have exceld in artes and pollicy,
> That now we foolish men that praise gin eke t'envy.[13]

From this point private virtue recedes into the background.
Britomart at the outset of her career is perfected in that
holiness and temperance which the Red Cross Knight and
Guyon have gained through conflict. The subjects of
Books IV, V, and VI—friendship, justice and courtesy—
extend still further beyond the bounds prescribed in the
prefatory letter; and had Spenser completed the second part
of the poem it is difficult to see how he could have effected
any substantial change in the character of the later legends,
ostensibly representing "virtue politic".

Political theory in England during the sixteenth century,
though crude and incomplete, is clearly influenced by the
humanistic notion of the state as a work of art imitated from
ancient patterns. But while the moralist or pedagogue could
freely disseminate doctrines gleaned from foreign authorities,
the politician had necessarily to show greater respect for
national conditions and prejudices. Time and again throughout the Middle Ages the English people had given proof of
their aversion from anything that savoured of tyranny or of
foreign encroachment; and it was to an English philosopher,
William of Occam, that Pope Clement VI attributed the
invention of the subversive doctrines upon Church and
State propounded by Marsilio of Padua in his *Defensor Pacis.*
Both the Yorkists and the Tudors were willing, at need, to
take a leaf from the book of Italian despots; but they did not

dare to say so, and when an English nobleman—John Tiptoft, Earl of Worcester (*c*. 1427–70)—was suspected of such
Italianate proclivities he lost his head, to the satisfaction of a
furious mob who would have none of the "Paduan law" in
England. English political writers of the sixteenth century
point with pride to their "very and true commonweal",
compounded of monarchy and oligarchy, as a happy medium
between tyranny and anarchy; and such is the constitution,
though hinted only in vague outline, of Spenser's romantic
Faeryland.

Gloriana is too obscure a figure to stand as sole representative of her original, the reigning monarch, whose several
attributes, accordingly, fall to others—truth to Una, virginity
to Belphœbe, benevolent justice to Mercilla, commanding
sword and sceptre yet willing to show mercy to her fallen
foe.[14] The task of "elvish knights" is to safeguard the security
of the commonwealth by quelling the various forces of disorder. On the one hand is the petty princeling, "tyrannising
and oppressing all", on the other the Anabaptist leveller,
winning "fooles, women and boys" by sophistry which
recalls the specious reasoning of the fox in *Mother Hubberds
Tale*:

> For now a few have all, and all have nought,
> Yet all be brethren ylike dearly bought:
> There is no right in this partition,
> Ne was·it so by institution
> Ordained first, ne by the law of Nature,
> But that she gave like blessing to each creture,
> As well of worldly livelode as of life,
> That there might be no difference nor strife,
> Nor ought cald mine or thine.[15]

The spread of this mischievous doctrine is associated with
the two besetting social evils of the day, vagrancy and un-
employment; its logical outcome, in the eyes of an average
sixteenth-century politician, is mob law or "democracy",
condemned on all sides as "a horrible monster of many

heads without reason". For even the socialist republics of Lycurgus, Plato and More maintain a speciality of rule that distinguishes the governing from the governed classes; and when Shakespeare can abandon his habitual attitude of impartiality to express his contempt for the fool multitude we can hardly expect more tolerance from the conservative Spenser. Artegall meets the demagogue upon his own ground with a favourite retort of monarchist to leveller:

> What though the sea with waves continuall
> Doe eate the earth, it is no more at all;
> Ne is the earth the lesse, or loseth ought,
> For whatsoever from one place doth fall
> Is with the tide unto another brought:
> For there is nothing lost, that may be found if sought.[16]

Any one of Gloriana's knights, with the possible exception of Calidore who has a weakness for the lowly, would have shown Artegall's distaste for the "rascall crew" at close quarters; for all are "heroes" of the ancient stamp, half human, half divine, even when their upbringing and demeanour belie their origin.

The *Faerie Queene* and the *View* contain a substantial body of evidence indicative of Spenser's interest in "generall poyntes of governement, and the great archepollycyes of all ould and newe common welthes".[17] A letter addressed to him by Harvey deals at some length with the political writers in vogue at Cambridge; nor is it difficult to trace analogues to his political ideas in the writings of Machiavelli, Luther, Calvin and Jean Bodin, the last of whom, according to Harvey, was an author to be found in every scholar's library. A quotation from the *Discourses on Titus Livius* in *A View of the present state of Ireland* would lead us to believe that he had formed a juster estimate of the great Florentine patriot than the majority of contemporary writers, for whom "Macheval" meant "Make-evil", the fictitious monster of "policy" invented by Innocent Gentillet. But the commonplaces of Renaissance politics would have provided him with his conception of the State as an harmonious work of art, the security of which must be maintained, if necessary, by violence and at the sacrifice of personal interest. Arthur, Guyon, Britomart and Artegall are all alike distinguished by their virtue or persistency in the pursuit of their object; and the political theories underlying the fifth legend are developed at much greater length in *A View of the present state of Ireland.*

To the sixteenth-century militarist, vindicating the sanctity of government as by law established, the notion that might is right was as axiomatic as to the Athenians invading Melos. King Henry VIII had assumed the title of King in Ireland, but nothing more: "For all other absolute power of principalitye he had in himself before derived from many former Kinges, his famous progenitors and woorthy conquerours of that land . . . . It was in the power of the conquerour to take upon himself what title he will over the dominions conquered. For all is the conquerours, as Tully to Brutus sayth". A panegyric upon the "most wise and valiaunt handling" of Lord Grey introduces a brief discourse on justice, the peculiar virtue attributed to him in *The Faerie Queene.* Although "true justice punnisheth nothing but the evill act or wicked woord", the mere premeditation of a crime against the Prince is a capital offence, since the commonwealth would suffer more by the loss of their Prince than by the execution of the malefactors. "Soe that *jus politicum,* though it be not of it self just, yet by application, or rather necessitye, it is made just; and this only respect maketh all lawes just." So where the security of the State is involved the end justifies the means, and in Ireland the only means is the sword. "For all these evills must first be cutt away with a strong hand, before any good can be planted." On the same assumption, although laws should generally be accommodated to the manners of subjects, it was bad policy to apply the laws of William the Conqueror to Ireland without safeguarding their due observance: "Soe as it is in vayne to speake of planting of lawes, and plotting of pollicyes, till they are altogither subdued".[18]

Seeing that Spenser had nothing to gain from the publication of the *View*, which was not written until ten years after the death of Grey, his treatise must be read not as the special pleading of a sycophant but as a reasoned statement of opinion, supported by first-hand acquaintance with Irish conditions and by such knowledge of law as would be expected of a civil servant in his particular position. The delusion that it was possible to impose upon disunited tribal communities humanistic notions of loyalty to an undivided state was shared by the great majority of ministers in Ireland throughout the sixteenth and seventeenth centuries. The defence of politic expediency by the champion of Platonic justice is not more anomalous than the persecution of heretics by the author of *Utopia*; in each case such inconsistency is the inevitable outcome of contemporary thought and conditions. Of the twenty years comprising Spenser's literary career nearly half were spent in the toils of active service and the remainder in the aftermath of a great war. His politics, therefore, are those of the man who in his time plays many parts and whose sense of values is necessarily affected by changing conditions. The jingoism of the militarist cannot avert the disillusion which allows a serious interpretation to Ariosto's banter:

> So oft as I with state of present time
> The image of the antique world compare,
> When as mans age was in his freshest prime,
> And the first blossome of faire vertue bare;
> Such oddes I find twixt those, and these which are,
> As that, through long continuance of his course,
> Me seemes the world is runne quite out of square
> From the first point of his appointed sourse;
> And being once amisse growes daily wourse and wourse.[19]

So the politician, foiled of his hopes, perforce submits to the poet, finding refuge in a romantic world of his own

Humanism

choice, like Calidore among the flocks of Meliboe. But his vision has been pre-determined by the operations of waking consciousness; its fabric, though unstable, is not utterly baseless but grounded in the life around him. The spectacle of a triumphant nation reaping daily more and more of the civility afforded by arts and learning confirms the humanist's faith in the vitality of the past. For all its fantastic foundation *The Faerie Queene* is no elegy upon faded glory but the eulogy of a patriot addressing a united people, the nearest approach to a national epic in the cycle of English poetry. Viewed in the aura of Elizabethan achievement the insubstantial pageant of Faeryland became a solid reality within the reach of every man true to himself and to his country:

> Of faery lond yet if he more inquyre,
> By certein signes, here sett in sondrie place,
> He may it fynd; ne let him then admyre,
> But yield his sence to bee too blunt and bace,
> That no'te without an hound fine footing trace,
> And thou, O fayrest Princesse under sky!
> In this fayre mirrhour maist behold thy face,
> And thine owne realmes in lond of Faery,
> And in this antique ymage thy great auncestry.[20]

The vision of Camden's "Britannia", of Drayton's "Polyolbion" enjoying a new age of chivalry and illumined by a galaxy of Arthurian Knights—here is fine matter for heroic poetry. The world is yet unreformed, monsters of vice are rampant, virtue has still to fight desperately for the restoration of "antique use". But Gloriana reigns, Arthur has come out of Faerie, heroes stand ready to serve the cause of the right. The author of the *View* and of *Mother Hubberds Tale* was shrewd enough to see through the characters whom he selected as living originals for his images of virtue. He must have recognised in Elizabeth a woman of small mind and inordinate vanity, in Leicester an unscrupulous intriguer, in Grey a thick-skinned soldier, in Raleigh a capricious adventurer. But with all due allowance for the flattery of a courtly

75

maker the fact remains that somehow he believed in the Elizabethan régime as transformed by his poetic view of the world. The apostrophe of Prince Arthur on learning of his "famous auncestryes" breathes a spirit of true patriotism devoid of sentimentality:

> At last, quite ravisht with delight to heare
> The royall Ofspring of his native land,
> Cryde out; "Deare countrey! O! how dearely deare
> Ought thy remembraunce and perpetuall band
> Be to thy foster Childe, that from thy hand
> Did commun breath and nouriture receave.
> How brutish is it not to understand
> How much to her we owe, that all us gave;
> That gave unto us all what ever good we have".[21]

Humanism quickens and orders Spenser's Romanticism by providing a tangible object to his fugitive fancies. His faery realm is founded not simply upon beautiful ineffectual dreams but upon the firm basis of past and present civilisation. A century earlier Marsilio Ficino had argued that it is good for man to change, since he alone of all creation possesses free-will and therefore has a history; and though Spenser has but little conception of progress, in the modern sense, his cantos of Mutability, embodying the advanced ideas of Giordano Bruno, look forward to the scientific cosmic Humanism of the later Renaissance. In such an age of expansion and discovery the Titaness could find ample evidence to support her claim. But Spenser was too conservative, too Platonic to allow it. The *Sturm und Drang* which kindled in others the spirit of violence and rebellion drove him rather to take refuge in accepted belief and realities. So his map of man figures not the restlessness of the intellectual adventurer but Platonic aspiration towards absolute good, the life of virtue ordered by law and the rule of reason over sensuality. The closing stanzas to *The Faerie Queene*, like the envoy to *Troilus and Criseyde*, strike a note of anti-climax to the brave story that has gone before; but Spenser's last word on the subject ever uppermost in his mind is contained in Nature's retort to Mutability. Loving the principle of beauty in all things he is dismayed at the prospect of its evanescence. From one aspect Mutability—the ever-changing countenance of the visible world—is so fair to behold that even Jove himself stands enraptured before her. But from another she is the personification of turbulence and misrule. So her boasted empire is but a delusion, the changing accident outlived by immortal substance; and her beauty is as the shadow to the cave men, the fitful reflection of the eternal idea.

CHAPTER IV

Romance

H UMANISM and Romanticism imply two distinct modes of consciousness and expression. The humanist imparts significant form to objects perceived with detachment; the romantic, identifying self with object, represents concepts of the associative imagination. To the humanists of the Renaissance classical antiquity stood for a composite civilisation, an intelligible whole; but the Middle Ages were barbarous, intangible, meaningless, an opinion that appeared to be fully confirmed by the most typical of mediæval literary monuments. For chivalric romance, from its origin, reflected the artificiality of the society which had created it and to which it was addressed. The replacement of primitive *comitatus* by Douzeperes and Round Table, of the *Volsungasaga* and the *Chanson de Roland* by the *Nibelungenlied* and *The Four Sons of Amon* meant the dilution of ancient epos to suit the taste of a feudal community; and the universal popularity of romantic tales among all classes quickly opened the way to every sort of commonplace absurdity and extravagance. The minstrel scored his success not by apt presentation of the age and body of the time but by skill in the invention and refurbishing of monsters and marvels utterly remote from human experience. The incredible fictions, the unnatural setting and disorderly conduct of romance in its dotage contravened every principle of classic decorum.

With good reason, therefore, Thomas Nashe could follow the lead of Montaigne in fulminating against "worne out impressions of the feyned no where acts of Arthur of the rounde table, Arthur of litle Brittaine, Sir Tristram, Hewon of Burdeaux, the Squire of low degree, the foure sons of Amon".[1] Others, like Vives, Roger Ascham and Francis

Meres, based their objection chiefly upon moral grounds. But none the less these "worn out absurdities" continued to divert a large public and to supply material for heroic poetry throughout the Renaissance era. A typical specimen is *Amadis of Gaul*, originally a Portuguese product of the fourteenth century, which enjoyed an immense vogue up to the time of Sir Philip Sidney and, together with two other works, survived the conflagration of Don Quixote's library. With *Amadis* as chief exemplar of its kind, it is not surprising that Italian poets of the new school, with the logical and critical instinct of their race, showed scant reverence for their romance originals. Luigi Pulci (1432–84) amused the wits of Medicean Florence with the burlesque fable and low comedy of his *Morgante Maggiore*. At Ferrara romance fared better, as a thing of beauty which, though faded, was worthy of retention. Count Matteo Maria Boiardo (1434–94) founded the plot of his *Orlando Innamorato* upon the rival suits of Orlando and Rinaldo for Angelica, a typically romantic situation of conflict between love and honour. Lodovico Ariosto (1474–1533), whose *Orlando Furioso* nominally completed the unfinished *Orlando Innamorato*, shifted the interest to the fortunes of Ruggiero and Bradamante, traditional ancestors of his patron, Cardinal Ippolito d'Este. Both Boiardo and Ariosto fully appreciate the bravery and fine sentiment of their theme; but the romantic illusion serves them only as fair game for the exercise of poetic fantasy. They refuse to believe in it, to quit solid earth in pursuit of shadows. Boiardo's hero is in love, and this is sufficient to make him slightly ridiculous. To Ariosto, for all his moralising and mock gravity, the main argument is irresistibly comic, a wild-goose chase after an impossibly elusive heroine, admitting endless wonders and wizardry by way of diversion. Romance, so sceptically treated, is three parts on the way towards mock heroic. The alternative, in Italy, was romantic epic, first attempted by Trissino in his tedious *Italia Liberata* (1547–8) and finally brought to perfection by Tasso, whose *Gerusalemme Liberata*

(1581) provided a pattern for all subsequent work of the same kind.

But in England the *chanson de geste* was a native heritage, transmitted by direct line from the Anglo-Norman writers of the twelfth century. Arthur, Lancelot, Bevis, Guy, and a score of others still held their own, and had even gained ground since the invention of printing. The first Christian worthy was a British prince, still venerated as the national hero and therefore ranking in a class apart from foreign rivals like Orlando or Godfrey, whose chief claim to recognition lay in their legendary repute as champions of the true religion. Elizabeth and her court could draw the analogy between their princely pleasures and the tourneys of the Round Table; but the real strength of Arthurian romance lay in the familiarity which for generations had endeared it to the masses.

Among all Spenser's originals the place of honour must be assigned to Malory's *Morte Darthur*, that "booke of Chevalrie" which, despite the objections of pedant and Puritan, preserved the most complete record not merely of the hero himself but, as Caxton reminds his readers, of all the finer elements of antique usage:

And I accordyng to my copye have doon sette it in enprynte, to the entente that noble men may see and lerne the noble actes of chyvalrye, the ientyl and vertuous dedes that somme knyghtes used in tho dayes, by whyche they came to honour, and how they that were vycious were punysshed and ofte put to shame and rebuke; humbly bysechyng al noble lordes and ladyes wyth al other estates of what estate or degree they been of, that shal see and rede in this sayd book and werke, that they take the good and honest actes in their remembraunce, and to folowe the same. Wherin they shalle fynde many Ioyous and playsaunt hystoryes, and noble and renomed actes of humanyte, gentylnesse and chyvalryes. For herein may be seen noble chyvalrye, Curtosye, Humanyte, frendlynesse, hardynesse, love, frendshyp, Cowardyse, Murdre, hate, vertue and synne. Doo after the good and leve the evyl, and it shal brynge you to good fame and renommee.

The proximity between these reflections and the ethic of

The Faerie Queene is so close as to suggest that Spenser planned his allegory with Caxton's preface in mind, admitting within his scheme the virtue of Courtesy, which he could not have found in Plato or Aristotle. True, in the unmoral world of old romance, of lawless love self-justified in scorn of consequence, the issue between right and wrong with due assignment of reward or punishment is hardly so plain and direct as Caxton would infer. But his defence of "noble chyvalrye" carries more weight than Ascham's attack upon its "bold Bawdry", and won a better following. In the history of Arthur, Spenser, like Sidney, could find nothing to displease a soldier, but rather the very mirror of nobility, the pure heroic mettle without fear or reproach, unsullied by custom and unshattered by abuse. The sinewy strength of authentic romance, rarely recaptured by the Italian poets, springs spontaneously from the naïve, pregnant English of Malory:

And soo the knyght arose up hastely and putte his helme upon his hede, and gat a grete spere in his hand, and without ony moo wordes he hurled unto sir Tristram, and smote hym clene from his sadel to the erthe, and hurte hym on the lyfte syde that sir Tristram lay in grete perylle. Thenne he wallopped ferther, and fette his cours, and came hurlynge upon sir Palomydes.

And thenne he tooke hym a scarlet cote so that shold be in stede of his sherte, tyll he had fulfylled the quest of the Sancgreal; and the good man fond hym in soo merveillous a lyfe, and soo stable, that he merveilled and felte that he was never corrupte in flesshely lustes.[2]

Spenser, in comparison, is diffuse and artificial; but at points of dramatic climax he is often nearer to Malory than to Ariosto:

So stoutly he withstood their strong assay;
Till that at last, when he advantage spyde,
His poynant speare he thrust with puissant sway
At proud Cymochles, whiles his shield was wyde,
That through his thigh the mortall steele did gryde:
He, swarving with the force, within his flesh
Did breake the launce, and let the head abyde.
Out of the wound the red blood flowed fresh,
That underneath his feet soone made a purple plesh.[3]

The similarity extends from diction to tone, suggesting kinship of mind, a common attitude towards a common theme.

This community of spirit is more significant than any specific borrowings; for so freely does Spenser adapt his material that it is impossible to determine precisely the extent of his debt to any one original. As the invincible knight-errant, Prince Arthur resembles his namesake in *Arthur of Little Britain*; and the conception of a "faery knight" was authorised through his traditional association with the ladies of the lake, his departure to Avalon and the popular report, preserved by Malory, that he was yet alive and would one day return. But his career prior to his accession is briefly dismissed by most of the earlier romancers. Spenser follows Malory in stating that the hero, after being taken from his parents in infancy, was entrusted to the care of a guardian ("Ector" in Malory, "Timon" in Spenser), and to the tutelage of Merlin, who endows him with supernatural power; but the suitor of Gloriana is substantially a new invention. Merlin is the child of a nun, seduced by a spirit, as stated by Geoffrey of Monmouth. He meets his end, as in Malory, through the guile of a false lady of the lake, but is "buried under beare" and inhabits the underground cave of enchantment before and not after he has met his doom. Spenser again follows Malory in his account of Tristram's ancestry and early career, but makes nothing of the more important part of the story. The familiar motive of knight and dame bound upon the same quest, parted through misunderstanding or treachery and finally reunited, occurs in the tales of Gareth and of Geraint, though it might equally well have been suggested by the episode of Olympia and Bireno in Ariosto. The "wylde man" who beneath a churlish exterior hides a noble heart is a commonplace of Renaissance fiction, anticipated, however, by Malory's Balen in his retort to the disdainful damsel:

Worthynes and good tatches and good dedes are not only in arrayment, but manhood and worship is hyd within mans persone and many a worshipful knyghte is not known unto all people, and therfore worship and hardynesse is not in arayment.[4]

The castle of Radigund resembles the castle of maidens assailed by Galahad and both maintain a similar "wicked custom". The episode of Crudor and Briana probably derives from Malory's story of King Ryence, who, after working himself a mantle from the beards of Arthur's knights, demanded that of the King himself for its completion. The Blatant Beast is Malory's "Questing Beast", "that hadde in shap a hede lyke a serpentes hede, and a body lyke a lybard, buttocks lyke a lyon, and foted lyke an herte, and in his body there was such a noyse as hit had ben the noyse of thyrtty coupel of houndes questyng, and such a noyse that beest made where somever he wente".[5] Finally, Malory supplies such names as Placidas, Pelleas, Pellenore, Percivall, Joyous Gard, all redolent of romantic suggestion.

Besides *Le Morte Darthur* the common stock of romance, with which Spenser was well acquainted, provided him with abundant material. Most of the chronicle canto (II, x) and of Merlin's prophecy concerning Britomart's offspring (III, ii) comes from Geoffrey of Monmouth and the sixteenth-century historians, including Holinshed who "muche furthered and advantaged " Spenser in his "Epithalamion Thamesis". The scheme of knights-errant owing allegiance to one sovereign and setting out upon successive quests of deliverance is common to many of the cycles and may have been partly suggested by *The Seven Champions of Christendom*, which undoubtedly supplied hints for Book I. The situation of the Red Cross Knight resembles that of Libeaus Desconus, the original of Gareth, while the adaptation of this motive to an allegory of the Christian's pilgrimage to salvation had already been attempted by Stephen Hawes in his *Pastime of Pleasure*. Cambell and Canacee come from *The Squire's Tale*, completed through the invention of a lover for Canacee and the introduction of a favourite romantic *motif*, the sealing of eternal friendship between two mortal foes meeting in combat. *The Parliament of Fowls,* possibly also its original, the *De Planctu Naturæ* of Alain de l'Isle, gave suggestions for the trial of Mutability and the pageant of seasons in Book VII. Huon of Bordeaux is mentioned once in connection with Guyon, though nothing is made of his relations with Oberon and the fairy train. The belt of Chastity which serves to distinguish the true from the false Florimell has several analogues. In *The Boy and the Mantle* a mantle fulfils the same function at Arthur's court; in the fable of *The Wright's Chaste Wife* the lady's fidelity is vindicated by means of a magic girdle; and at the conclusion of *Gawain and the Green Knight* the hero's peers agree to wear green belts in token of his victory over temptation.

But for particular details Spenser stands far more deeply indebted to Ariosto and Tasso than to any single mediæval author. The episodes, images and phrases which he has adapted from the former are so numerous as to suggest that *Orlando Furioso* was open at his side while he was penning his work; and though his debt to *Gerusalemme Liberata* is mainly confined within certain episodes, particularly that of Armida, the influence of Tasso's glowing and coloured descriptions was sufficient to enable Fairfax, when translating Tasso, often to do little more than reproduce Spenser. But though Spenser derived from Tasso the idea of an allegorical romance his ethic differs fundamentally from Tasso's militant Catholicism, while from Ariosto, in spirit, he is worlds apart. Purporting to be a serious poem of love nd chivalry presented through a succession of diverting scenes, the *Orlando Furioso* is dominated by the imp of mischief and mockery. Throughout one-third of it the nominal hero, driven desperate at the news of his lady's infidelity, cuts the ludicrous figure of a maniac rending his clothes, uprooting trees, stealing horses, slaying their owners and performing such impossible feats as swimming the Straits of Gibraltar. Ruggiero, the principal character, in the fourth book is abruptly separated from the heroine by a flying hippogryph and transported to Alcina's enchanted island. Astolfo, having neither razor nor scissors to cut the lock of hair that confers immortality upon Orrilo, holding the severed head of the magician by the nose, shears the lock with his sword. And through all this comedy sparkles the irony of the poet's grave reflections and assurance. How fortunate were the old-time cavaliers who could find in deserts, caves and forests ladies of such beauty as cannot now be seen in palaces! The wonderful tales which Turpin related of Ruggiero he knew to be true, but you must believe as you list. Achilles, Æneas and the rest owe their renown not to their own merits but to the generosity of their descendants, to the villas and palaces presented to poets who, as everyone knows, are the greatest of liars.

Such levity, the very life and soul of the *Orlando Furioso*, is incompatible with the aim and temperament of Spenser, who will often adapt Ariosto's mocking sallies to his own serious purpose. The reconciliation between Guyon and Britomart at the opening of Book III calls forth a eulogy of ancient chivalry freely translated from a stanza in the first canto of *Orlando Furioso*. But the difference in situation is characteristic. Whereas Guyon abandons the fight solely at the instigation of Prince Arthur and Palmer, Rinaldo and Ferraù compose their differences for the very good reason that the lady for whom they are fighting has vanished. The praise of woman and of her heroic achievements, which serves to introduce the legend of Britomart, derives from the bantering preamble to the account of Orontea and her domain, in which ten men are allowed to every hundred women. Ariosto's admonition to the squeamish reader of the Host's very merry tale (*Orlando Furioso*, xxviii), which is on a par with Chaucer's similar apology for his churls, inspires the introduction to the tragic history of Malbecco and Hellenore.

But despite fundamental difference in temper Spenser's debt to the *Orlando Furioso* is profound and far-reaching.

Artegall and Britomart are modelled on Ruggiero and Brada-mante, and both pairs of lovers are encouraged to pursue their adventures by prophecies of their ultimate union and glorious progeny, in the one case the D'Este family, in the other the Tudor dynasty. Guyon's temporary submission to the charms of Phædria recalls Ruggiero's sojourn at the island of Alcina, the original of the Bower of Bliss. Alcina, like Acrasia, treats her victims with Circean hospitality and, when unmasked, proves hideous and deformed as Duessa. Astolfo, like Fradubio, transformed into a tree discovers himself at the wounding of the bark, though here Spenser adds a dramatic touch by allowing the enchantress Duessa to be present and to overhear the recounting of her victim's wrongs. Radigund and her realm are suggested by Orontea and her Amazons. Braggadochio, the one purely comic figure in *The Faerie Queene*, is much nearer the norm of Ariosto than of Spenser, and all the main details respecting him—the horse-stealing that leads to his advancement, his boastfulness, cowardice and final "uncasing"—are paralleled in *Orlando Furioso*. The adventures of the Squire of Dames in the performance of his vow form a milder version of the host's tale of Giocondo. Trompart is another Pinabello. Most of Spenser's supernatural machinery comes from the same source. Arthur's shield and horn, Artegall's sword, Chrysaor, and Britomart's magic lance have the same virtues as the shield of Atlante, the horn presented by Logistilla to Astolfo and the lance of Bradamante. "Brigadore" is an anglicised version of "Briglia d' oro", the name of Orlando's horse.[6]

The parallel extends to language and imagery. Guyon attacks two knights simultaneously, like a ship rolled by two contrary waves. Satyrane restrains the monster pursuing Florimell as a husbandman dams a sudden flood. Talus defends Artegall against an unruly mob like hawk descending upon a "flush of Ducks". Irena, learning of her deliverance, revives like a withered rose at the first drops of rain. Mal-

becco, watching the satyrs around Hellenore and finding
himself cuckolded in his own demesne,

> out of the bush
> Upon his handes and feete he crept full light,
> And like a Gote emongst the Gotes did rush;
> That, through the helpe of his faire hornes on hight,
> And misty dampe of misconceyving night,
> And eke through likenesse of his gotish beard,
> He did the better counterfeite aright.[7]

For all these and many like figures Ariosto gave the suggestion; and though comparison affords good evidence of his
brevity beside Spenser's diffuseness the adaptation is often
little more than free translation. If any one work may be
described as the original of *The Faerie Queene* it is the *Orlando
Furioso*, Spenser's first model, as we learn from his correspondence with Harvey, duly honoured along with the ancient
epics in his prefatory letter and transparently imitated in each
of the six legends.

While Ariosto had fully exploited the possibilities of
chivalric romance as theme for narrative poetry Tasso re-
fined upon the work of his uninspired predecessor, Trissino,
in imparting to his romantic material the solidity of an
heroic poem fashioned after conventional design. The
Gerusalemme Liberata is a regularly constructed epic, consisting of one continuous action to which all digressions are
directly related; and the religious object which inspired it
impels a high seriousness of tone more akin to that of *The
Faerie Queene* than of *Orlando Furioso*. But Tasso's fidelity to
classic authority forbade the intrusion of much romantic
commonplace freely admitted by Ariosto and Spenser. There
is a world of difference between the apparition of angels or
devils as ministers of grace or disaster to a crusader and, on
the other hand, the astonishing array of dragons, orcs,
monsters and phantoms which people Ariosto's kingdom of
nonsense; between an epic strictly observing the traditional
laws of design and a romance of Faerie in which time and

space count for nothing. Reverencing the heroic spirit and fine sentiment of romance, Tasso had no use for its irresponsibility, for the pursuit of the quaint or fantastic on its account. His burden is not

> Le donne, i cavalier, l' arme, gli amori,
> Le cortesie, l' audici imprese,

"of Knights and Ladies gentle deeds", "of Faerie Knights, and fayrest Tanaquill", but

> l' armi pietose, e 'l Capitano,
> Che 'l gran Sepolcro liberò di Cristo.

The first concern of his heroes is neither amorous adventure nor the pursuit of virtue, but a crusade on behalf of true religion.

Temperamentally Spenser had not a little in common with Tasso, whose epic is specifically cited in the legend of Friendship.[8] Both were idealists with a profound sense of spiritual values, thwarted outwardly by circumstance and inwardly by a restlessness of disposition which, in the case of Tasso, bordered on insanity. Whilst Ariosto could supply Spenser with copious fine material his poem is totally lacking in the gravity essential to an allegory of virtue, and this defect Tasso made good. His heroes are no carpet cavaliers seizing the present moment to gratify their passing fancies but, like Spenser's, stout champions united in their devotion to a common object. His women likewise—Erminia, Clorinda, the warrior maid, won to the truth through love, even the enchantress Armida—are more closely related to Una, Britomart or Belphœbe than to any of Ariosto's volatile damsels. Without slavishly following either of his Italian masters Spenser could learn from them both. *The Faerie Queene* combines the exuberance and irresponsibility of Ariosto's romantic medley with the austere solemnity of Tasso's sacred epic. In Spenser we miss the intimacy of Ariosto, who is continually obtruding himself, nudging his readers and chuckling at his characters. On the other hand his Muse

works with less effort than that of Tasso, who sacrifices
something of his freedom as a poet to his admiration for
his models, particularly for the elegance and dignity of Virgil.

The first impression created by such diversity of motive and
matter is one of Gothic inconsequence rather than of classic
coherence. Pigna's note on *Orlando Furioso*—"D' errante
persone è tutta la poema"—is still more applicable to *The
Faerie Queene*, in which every character possesses the ubiquity
of Artegall,

> ne wonneth in one certeine stead,
> But restlesse walketh all the world arownd.[9]

Whereas Ariosto relates every digression and side-show to
the main design, leaving nothing unexplained, Spenser has
considered neither beginning, middle nor end of his fable,
apart from the allegory to which it is related. Guyon, or the
Red Cross Knight—there is some ambiguity as to which—
turns up unexpectedly with Britomart. Calidore drops out
of the picture throughout half the legend that bears his name.
Most surprising of all, Arthur offers no response to Scudamour's tale of woe concerning the loss of Amoret when he
himself, at that very moment, has the unfortunate lady under
his protection and almost within earshot. Spenser has, in
fact, clean forgotten Amoret, who forthwith disappears from
the field, unrestored to her lover.[10] The stock apparatus of
romantic fiction and drama adds further complexity and im-
probability. The appearance of a phantom Florimell occasions
much of the adventure and intrigue in Book IV. Mistaken
identity and disguising play a prominent part in the legends of
Britomart and Artegall, especially in the stories of Dolon and
of Samient. The pastoral interlude in Book VI, clearly influenced by *Arcadia*, perhaps also by Sidney's originals,
Montemayor, Longus and Heliodorus, embodies all the
traditonal *motifs* of its kind—the foundling heroine, the
birthmark disclosing her identity, the warrior turned shepherd, his clownish rival, the rescue of the heroine from the
wild beast. In moments of crisis everyone behaves in orthodox

romantic fashion. Hearing that Artegall has been worsted by a "tyrannesse", without waiting for explanations Britomart rushes to her chamber, nursing her delusion till restored balance of mind impels her to return to Talus and learn the truth. Timias, scorned by Belphœbe for infidelity, betrays his remorse by carving her name on every tree and ultimately recovers grace through the good offices of a dove which bears his jewel to its donor, the disaffected lady.

Even the principal figures of *The Faerie Queene*, though ostensibly distinguished as allegorical types, are for the most part conditioned by their romantic setting. The hero does not make the legend but evolves within it. St George is neither holier than Guyon nor less courteous than Calidore. The difference lies in presentation rather than in character, arising from the division of the fable into six distinct types of romance.

The Red Cross Knight pays the common penalty of "blameless fool" in having no mind of his own. His crudity and inexperience are stressed from the outset, when he appears as "a tall clownish younge man", seated upon the floor, "unfitte through his rusticity for a better place". With Truth herself as guide and despite her warnings, at the first provocation he accepts the advances of a suspicious-looking stranger and deserts her. Duped by Duessa, whom he continues to accompany after she has lured him into the disreputable House of Pride, he falls an easy victim to Orgoglio and would have succumbed to Despair, but for the timely aid of his mistress. Finally, after a special course of discipline at the House of Holiness, he succeeds in quelling the dragon only after three days' conflict and with the aid of magic balm. In so pale and ethereal a "Saint George of mery England, the signe of victoree" the sturdy dragon slayer of *The Golden Legend* and *The Seven Champions* is scarcely recognisable; for the interest aroused by his story depends upon neither personality nor adventure but upon the adaptation of both to an allegory of the Christian pilgrimage.

The Odyssey of Guyon, Spenser's nearest approach to

travel romance after the order of the *Argonautica*, allows for much firmer character delineation. The adventurer pursuing the quest for Acrasia's bower is of pure heroic mould, no neophyte but thoroughly versed in the ways of chivalry and the pitfalls of knight-errantry. Playing the active and un-selfish part, as rescuer of the distressed, he appears to better advantage than the Red Cross Knight, who is fully occupied in extricating himself from difficulties occasioned through ignorance and indiscretion. Guyon's impulsiveness, evinced throughout his earlier adventures before he has fully acquired the virtue of Temperance, appears as the natural outcome of heroic virtue; and his temporary submission to the charms of Phædria is more in keeping with the part than his subsequent treatment of Acrasia. That the trial at the cave of churlish Mammon, unlike the counsels of Despair, should prove utterly unavailing is only to be expected. For Guyon possesses strength of will together with instinctive gentleness and nobility, a gracious combination befitting the type of chivalric virtue in active life.

The character of Artegall, on the other hand, suffers through the entire subordination of romance to allegory. His supernatural origin, his relations with Britomart and the prophecies respecting their royal descendants endow him with heroic attributes second only to those of Prince Arthur himself. But the nature of his exploits and the unseemly ministrations of his henchman Talus tend to convert him into an inhuman symbol of justice, unseasoned by mercy. His story is one long record of terrorism. The drowning of Pollente and Munera may have been a public necessity; but we might have been spared the barbarous mutilation of the victims and the exposure of their remains. Arguments with demagogues and interference in property disputes better become the legislator than the knight at arms, especially as Artegall's methods of executing justice have more in common with the Elizabethan criminal code than with the goodly usage of chivalry. The fable cannot be classed under any traditional type, but falls into a series of mechanical episodes manufactured to point the moral and culminating in the artless reduplication of the last two cantos. In Book v the politician completely overrides the romancer; Arthur, Lord Grey, has eclipsed the memory of Arthur and the Table Round.

At the opposite pole to Artegall is Calidore, the "very perfit, gentle knight" of Courtesy, a purely chivalric virtue, standing second on the list prefixed by Caxton to *Le Morte Darthur*. The opening to Book vi spells an entire change of *motif* and atmosphere, transporting us from grim reality to the idyllic fantasy of *Arcadia* and the Greek romances. Calidore, Tristram and the wild man belong to the Saturnine age of natural living and primitive refinement. The knight of Courtesy is a man of peace, subduing violence by arbitration and reform. His easy settlement of differences in the episodes of Crudor and Briana, of Aladine and Priscilla offer a welcome contrast to the rough justice of Artegall; and having early abandoned the heroic life for the bucolic he leaves the field with the minimum of bloodshed, claiming only Maleffort and Pastorella's abductors as victims of his sword.

The legend of Courtesy evolves from that of Justice. But the way for Calidore has already been prepared by the scenes and actors of Books iii and iv, in the course of which faery society has undergone considerable transformation. The knight of Holiness wooing his mistress Truth, Prince Arthur serving a phantom Gloriana, Guyon the celibate captor of Acrasia are far removed from the traditional romantic lover. But the story of Britomart, with its attendant episodes, allows for the tempering of heroic virtue by heroic sentiment. The pure flame of passion that held Lancelot and Guenevere, Tristram and Iseult—elemental, self-sufficient, subversive— is inadmissible within the ideal commonwealth of *The Faerie Queene*. But passion spiritualised urges its possessor towards the highest good. Britomart is no unsexed Radigund but the ornament of "true feminitee", hiding beneath the armour of a valkyrie the "amiable grace" of woman, a rose secured from the spoiler by thorns and briars. She enters as the child princess of romance, sleepless for love of a knight unknown, confiding in her nurse, saying her prayers "with great devotion and with little zele". Everything about her betrays the natural touch—her confusion on being taxed by Guyon as to the reason for her disguise, her perversity when slandering Artegall in order to learn the truth about him, the womanly arts whereby she would stay his departure:

> And by the way she sundry purpose found
> Of this or that, the time for to delay,
> And of the perils whereto he was bound,
> The feare whereof seem'd much her to affray;
> But all she did was but to weare out day.
> Full oftentimes she leave of him did take;
> And eft againe deviz'd some what to say,
> Which she forgot, whereby excuse to make;
> So loth she was his companie for to forsake;[11]

finally the pitiful scene of her desolation:

> One day when as she long had sought for ease
> In every place, and every place thought best,
> Yet found no place that could her liking please,
> She to a window came that opened West,
> Towards which coast her love his way addrest:
> There looking forth, shee in her heart did find
> Many vaine fancies working her unrest;
> And sent her winged thoughts, more swift than wind,
> To beare unto her love the message of her mind.[12]

The entry of Britomart brings the love *motif* into the foreground, where it is represented under every aspect—as physical and spiritual desire, at once a disease and a remedy, as friendship, domestic affection, idyllic sentiment. The Christian champion has yielded priority to the romantic lover, whose trials and adventures tend to obscure the basic moral issue. The "loose life" and "ungentle trade" at Malecasta's castle prefigures a new and welcome secularity. As the noise of war diminishes to the milder note of joust and tourney interest becomes more evenly distributed among minor actors and episodes included "rather as accidents than intendments" and less remote from common experience. Abstract figures of good and evil give place to familiar types of chivalric legend—to "Cupid's man" Scudamour, to Braggadochio the comic mountebank, to Paridell, Blandamour and the Squire of Dames, whose worldly wisdom and urbanity make ample amends for their easy virtue. A train of fair ladies follows the warrior heroine—Belphœbe, vital and majestic as Diana, Florimell, forlorn type of fugitive beauty, Amoret, chosen of Venus, the very embodiment of afflicted innocence and fidelity, Pastorella, another "Flora, peering in April's front". Two-dimension figures, confined within their romantic setting, they are timeless.

The faery world which Spenser has fashioned from the raw material of myth and folk tale, legend and chronicle is no less peculiar to himself than is his diction. The unseen Gloriana has little in common with the mistress of Launfal, still less with a fairy Mab no longer than an agate stone, commanding an airy palace with walls of spiders' legs, windows of cats' eyes and roofing of bats' skin. Hers is no golden age when

> All was this land fulfild of fairye:
> The elf queene with her joly compaignye
> Daunced ful ofte in many a grene mede.[13]

Guyon was knighted by Huon of Bordeaux "when with King Oberon he came to Faeryland". But Oberon has left none of his faery crew, none of the pucks and hobgoblins exorcised in *Epithalamion*; nor is this surprising since Oberon is actually no faery monarch but King Henry VIII. For the defenders of Gloriana life is a grim business and any approach to the wonder and delight of traditional faerie stands suspect. Guyon may not submit to the charms of Acrasia nor Scudamour tarry within the Temple of Venus. Spenser's faery lore is a lore within itself.

The diversity of his material covers a single poetic concept. *The Faerie Queene*, for all its inconsequence, preserves unity

of place, unbroken from the entry of the Red Cross Knight
to the capture of the Blatant Beast. "The reader never knows
where he is, but still he knows, from the consciousness within
him, that all is as natural and proper, as if the country where
the action is laid were distinctly pointed out, and marked
down in a map."[14] The romantic device is not artificially
contrived by the compounding of this and that original but
evolves as a whole, "out of space", from creative imagination. The fable, apart from the allegory, has neither beginning,
middle nor end. Scenes change, figures enter and vanish
without prologue, epilogue or relevance to their context.
But the complete spectacle conveys the kaleidoscopic effect
of a dream, where disconnected objects and incidents merge
easily without abrupt transition. "All is marvellous and
extraordinary; yet not *unnatural* in one sense, as it agrees to
the conceptions that are readily entertained of these magical
and wonder-working Natures."[15] Nothing is unexpected.
Sansloy, Braggadochio, Scudamour and the rest, entering
suddenly out of the void, seem to have been there all the
time. Against the charges of incoherence and discursiveness
the poet—a Pygmalion, beguiled by his own handiwork,—
proffers an unanswerable defence:

> The waies, through which my weary steps I guyde
> In this delightfull land of Faery,
> Are so exceeding spacious and wyde,
> And sprinckled with such sweet variety
> Of all that pleasant is to eare or eye,
> That I, nigh ravisht with rare thoughts delight,
> My tedious travell doe forget thereby;
> And, when I gin to feele decay of might,
> It strength to me supplies, and chears my dulled spright.[16]

For this land of Faerie is but a concrete symbol of the
poet's dream, the ideal realm of fantasy expressed under
different attributes through epic, pastoral and allegory but
common to them all. Without conscious effort the faerie way
of writing, with its quaint diction, haunting music and

95

phantom imagery, effects spontaneously "that willing suspension of disbelief, which constitutes poetic faith":

> A shepeheards boye, (no better doe him call,)
> When Winters wastful spight was almost spent,
> All in a sunneshine day, as did befall,
> Led forth his flock, that had bene long ypent:
> So faynt they woxe, and feeble in the folde,
> That now unnethes their feete could them uphold.

> A gentle Knight was pricking on the plaine,
> Ycladd in mightie armes and silver shielde,
> Wherein old dints of deepe woundes did remaine,
> The cruell markes of many a bloody fielde.[17]

Here is no palpable artifice for the gradual inducing of atmosphere. The spell works at a stroke, plunging us into the middle of things.

Though we may not always follow our bearings the objects that we encounter are sharply outlined and easily recognisable. The one exception is the House of Busirane, deliberately set in the conventional romantic atmosphere of wonder and terror; for here the nature of the tale, embodying the Child Roland-Comus *motif* of rescue from an enchanter, calls for the full paraphernalia of horror—prolonged suspense, mysterious inscriptions, midnight thunder, ritual drama—half masque, half Black Mass,—the sealing of the spell with the blood of the victim. But as a rule Spenser prefers open daylight and quick-changing spectacle to gloomy interiors and lengthy concentration upon the eeriness of the unseen. His giants, witches and monsters, though of incredible strength and dimension, are supernormal rather than supernatural, creatures of the same universe as their opponents. Though treacherous and malicious they lie within reach of attack and fight in the open. Their few supernatural allies are too familiar to cause any cold shudders; "snowy Florimell" too closely resembles a common harlot, Archimago a "Vice", or Lord of Misrule, often more comic than sinister. Magic armour, healing waters, love wizardry are

freely adopted as narrative machinery; but the mumbo-jumbo
of sorcery is only fair game for laughter:

> But th'aged Nourse, her calling to her bowre,
> Had gathered Rew, and Savine, and the flowre
> Of Camphora, and Calamint, and Dill;
> All which she in an earthen Pot did poure,
> And to the brim with Coltwood did it fill,
> And many drops of milk and blood through it did spill.
>
> Then, taking thrise three heares from off her head,
> Them trebly breaded in a threefold lace,
> And round about the Pots mouth bound the thread;
> And, after having whispered a space
> Certein sad words with hollow voice and bace,
> She to the virgin sayd, thrise sayd she itt;
> "Come, daughter, come; come, spit upon my face;
> Spitt thrise upon me, thrise upon me spitt;
> Th'uneven nomber for this business is most fitt".[18]

Heroic argument calls for the semblance of actuality, for
vigour and energy in presentation. Far more typical than the
Busirane episode at the close of Book III is Book v, canto ii, in
which fifty-four stanzas suffice to describe the combat with
the Pagan, the drowning of Munera and the overthrow of the
giant with his adherents. Time and again dramatic touches
vivid as those of Chaucer or Ariosto serve to connect the
land of Faerie with common experience. The woeful history
of Florimell, despite her fugitive appearances, is a most effective study in pathos developed through complex intrigue to
a highly theatrical dénouement. Another striking instance
of such contact between fantasy and fact is the scene after the
slaying of the dragon:

> Some feard, and fledd; some feard, and well it faynd;
> One, that would wiser seeme then all the rest,
> Warnd him not touch, for yet perhaps remaynd
> Some lingring life within his hollow brest,
> Or in his wombe might lurke some hidden nest
> Of many Dragonettes, his fruitfull seede:

Edmund Spenser

Another saide, that in his eyes did rest
Yet sparckling fyre, and badd thereof take heed;
Another said, he saw him move his eyes indeed.

One mother, whenas her foolehardy chyld
Did come too neare, and with his talants play,
Halfe dead through feare, her litle babe revyld,
And to her gossibs gan in counsell say;
"How can I tell, but that his talants may
Yet scratch my sonne, or rend his tender hand?"
So diversly them selves in vaine they fray;
Whiles some more bold to measure him nigh stand,
To prove how many acres he did spred of land.[19]

In Spenser romantic sentimentality is tempered and controlled by the objective alertness of the humanist who would repair the ruins and rekindle the dying embers, not content to stand entranced before their half-spent radiance. The fairyland of his poetic consciousness is no ruin peopled by misty wraiths and shadows, like the erections of his early "Gothic" admirers, but a well-defined structure, peopled by the figures of living originals or lively conventions, vividly imaged and portrayed. Its history, as he naïvely reminds his reader, is hardly more astounding than the logs of voyagers to "Indian Peru", "Amazon huge river", "fruitfullest Virginia" or other unknown lands,—authorities in which the incredulous could have found authentic record of Fancy's painted plumes,

> Like as the sunburnt Indians do aray
> Their tawney bodies in their proudest plight,

of Maleger turning at bay,

> As wonts the Tartar by the Caspian lake,
> Whenas the Russian him in flight does chace,

or of the features, dress and gestures of "salvage men".[20]
The defence, offered but half seriously, bears upon his poetry as a whole. His ideal concept is an image of the actual, he extols

the past as a pattern for the present, breathing new life into a dying tradition. The numerical correspondence between the twelve knights of the Round Table, the twelve virtues of Aristotle and the twelve books of the heroic poem is the outward symbol of an inward union between the old world and the new. The last of those "lofty fables and romances which recount in solemn cantos the deeds of knighthood" becomes the epic of Humanism.

CHAPTER V

Allegory

To many readers Spenser's allegory has proved a veritable Serbonian bog not easily to be escaped or left to take care of itself, as Hazlitt advised. Even in his own age the orthodox view of poetry as "delightful teaching" could not prevent Joseph Hall from tilting at his "misty moral types" or Henry Reynolds, in his *Mythomystes* (1632), from sympathising with those who wished "that he had therein beene a little freer of his fiction, and not so close rivetted to his Morall". For Spenser's allegory does unquestionably cramp and stiffen his romantic invention. Confronted with so plain an issue between abstract right and wrong we are prevented from judging each character according to his deserts as we can judge those of Malory. The commendable grief of Abessa and Corceca at the death of Kirkrapine, the fraternal affection of Sansjoy, Sansloy and Sansfoy is counted to them for unrighteousness. But we must applaud the harshness of Artegall and bear with the vacillation of the Red Cross Knight in the face of the resourceful Archimago, whose energy and perseverance fully substantiate Bishop Latimer's tribute to the devil as "the most diligentest bishop and prelate in all England". The religion of Faeryland is rooted in totemism and taboo.

But the allegory has to be faced. Its threads are so closely interwoven with those of the narrative that the one pulls awkwardly against the other, often compelling the poet to cut short the action and assume the rôle of expositor:

> Tho, wrapping up her wrethed sterne arownd,
> Lept fierce upon his shield, and her huge traine
> All suddenly about his body wound,
> That hand or foot to stir he strove in vaine.
> God helpe the man so wrapt in Errours endlesse traine!

Allegory

In stead thereof he kist her wearie feet,
And lickt her lilly hands with fawning tong,
As he her wronged innocence did weet.
O, how can beautie maister the most strong,
And simple truth subdue avenging wrong.[1]

But fiction and signification are not always thus mutually dependent. The tales of Cambel and Triamond, of Calidore and Pastorella, Timias and Belphœbe are for the most part pure romance, devoid of moral purport, while the physiological symbolism of Alma's house soon develops into a realistic study of an Elizabethan interior. At the opposite extreme are automata of allegory like the witnesses against Duessa—"People's Cry", "Law of Nations", "Commons' Suit"—which have no value apart from their names. Here the zeal of the partisan has outrun his better judgment, landing him in the position of the mediæval allegorist at uninspired moments; the whole episode of Duessa's trial smacks rather of the fourteenth century than of the sixteenth, at many points recalling the trial of Lady Meed in *Piers Plowman*.

The toll of grievances against the Hydra-headed monster allegory is indeed heavy; but in employing it Spenser was no more retrograde than the majority of his contemporaries. The revival of learning tended to encourage the mode of thought which, during the Middle Ages, found expression through the parable, the beast fable and the erotic vision. Upon certain detached instances of authentic allegory in ancient poetry, notably in Virgil and Ovid, Petrarch and his successors had erected an elaborate superstructure of allegorical interpretation, which rendered possible the reconciliation of Paganism with Christianity and which survived until the age of Voltaire. Tasso's representation of Godfrey as reason, Jerusalem as civil happiness, the army as mankind and so forth was far outpaced by similar special pleading on behalf of *Orlando Furioso*, which Sir John Harington could find "full of Christen exhortation, doctrine, and example", worthy to stand beside the masterpieces of the ancients, who "wrapped, as it were, in their writings divers and sundry meanings, which they call the senses or mysteries thereof".[2] Chapman followed the French commentator, Spondanus, in representing Homer's description of Achilles' shield as a symbol of the round world, the four elements and the signs of the Zodiac. To satisfy discerning critics a sixteenth-century poet must needs edify as well as please; and when his moral was not self-evident the extraction of a dark conceit, no matter how far-fetched, was calculated to win favour.

Practice followed precept. Fable and allegory retained all their appeal for the author and his public. The romance of Reynard the Fox gave Spenser the hint for a masterly satire in the form of "Prosopopoia or the Counterfait in Personation", still a favourite literary device. Thenot's tale of the Oak and the Briar, though ascribed to "Tityrus", savours rather of Æsop than Chaucer, as E.K. points out, and the same may be said of other similar fables in the *Calender*. The marginal notes to the Geneva Bible supplied appropriate beast symbolism for *The Ruines of Time*. The personified abstraction remained a familiar figure in poetry, and had recently been used with signal success by Sackville whose "loftie numbers and heroicke stile" left marked influence upon the *Complaints* and upon such episodes as that of Despair.

Other arts, besides literature, had much to offer the allegorist, who readily availed himself of their resources. A line in "November"—"All musick sleepes, where death doth leade the daunce"—presumably refers to the popular theme of the *Danse Macabre*, versified in English by Lydgate and frequently represented in mural paintings. Of far greater moment is the extensive influence of allegorical drama, which had been kept alive through interlude, pageant and masque and in which Spenser himself may have taken part at school or college. The Red Cross Knight at the House of Holiness loses such individuality as he possesses to become "Humanum Genus" of the morality and to pass through similar experiences. Other characters, such as Una and the Palmer, play the traditional rôle of Expositor. The visions at the close of *The Ruines of Time* pass like "tragic pageants" and "Pageants" was the title of a lost work mentioned by E.K., very probably a first draft of episodes afterwards incorporated in *The Faerie Queene*. The episode of Malengin and the "Epithalamion Thamesis", a year before their publication, supplied material for two masques, of Amity and Proteus, by Davison and Campion, which were performed in the winter of 1594–5.[3] The account of the Masque of Cupid is the minute record of an eye-witness, complete with stage directions. First enters Ease, bearing a branch of laurel and clad "in costly garments, fit for tragic stage". Signalling for silence he proceeds to indicate the argument in dumb show. Then follows the anti-masque of wanton bards and minstrels, and finally the masque proper with its regular procession of symbolic figures appropriately arrayed. Elsewhere the "manner of a masque", though not specifically mentioned, is plainly implied. Whereas Langland, depicting the seven deadly sins as penitents, is chiefly concerned with their lives and characters, Spenser, like Dunbar, in his *Dance of the Seven Deadly Sins*, visualises the House of Pride as the scene of a morality, concentrating attention upon the outward appearance of each passing figure. Gluttony, clad in vine leaves and crowned with an ivy garland, holds a "bouzing can" from which he sups so oft that he can barely sit upright upon the filthy swine that carries him. Lechery rides upon a goat, Avarice upon a camel, Envy upon a wolf, each coupled with its symbolical associate after the manner of the old Bestiaries. Another theatrical piece is the pageant of months and seasons attending the suit of Mutability before the bar of Nature, who herself supplies appropriate emblems for her auditors. The months ride upon the Zodiacal beasts, Spring is "all dight in leaves of flowers", Summer "in a silken cassock, coloured greene", Autumn "all in yellow", Winter "all in a frize".

Edmund Spenser

To Spenser allegory is a natural mode of poetic expression. His creative faculty instinctively transforms abstract thought to concrete image. He sees nature alive with the creations of traditional lore or of his own fugitive fancy. His genius thrives on pretty tales made or recollected for the occasion. The rivers encircling his home at Kilcolman call up the myth of Mulla and Bregog, the union of Thames and Medway suggests an "Epithalamion Thamesis", ruined Verulam becomes "A woman sitting, sorrowfullie wailing". Converging with this mythopœic genius, in which he resembles Ovid and which inspires some of his finest inventions—the Garden of Adonis, the Temple of Venus, the trial of Mutability—is the contemporary taste for allegory, distinct from myth in bearing an ulterior significance but no less serviceable for a poet seeking to mask ethic under the guise of romance. Each eclogue in the *Calender* reflects some aspect of human character or temperament, intensified by the accompanying woodcut and the concluding emblem. Pictures "singularly set forth" and perhaps identical with the emblematic woodcuts in *A Theatre for Worldlings* were to have accompanied the "Dreames". Symbolism illumines allegory throughout the *Visions, Prothalamion* and *The Faerie Queene*, where it serves to distinguish the principal figures as a badge of office. Arthur's magic shield becomes the shield of truth, dazzling the eyes of beholders. Una's veil hides her from the stare of the impious. The three theological virtues at the House of Holiness are distinguished by appropriate attributes and gestures. Fidelia, clad in white, bears the sacramental cup of wine and water containing the serpent of health; Speranza, in blue, leaning upon a silver anchor prays with her eyes raised steadfastly to heaven; Charissa, in yellow, crowned with "tyre of gold" and accompanied by a pair of turtle-doves, tends her prolific offspring. As the blood of Amavia upon the hands of her babe seals Guyon's pledge of vengeance, so Mirabella's bag and bottle serve as a perpetual reminder of her penance. Other symbols, like the belt of Chastity or the scales of the demagogue, have the effect of converting a sermon into an object lesson.

But symbolism is an insidious device, which may tempt the symbolist either to invent a system bearing no direct relation with its object or, on the other hand, to labour analogy beyond all reasonable limits. The former was the course adopted by Blake; the latter was a besetting fault of the mediæval allegorist and the occasion of several lapses in Spenser. The public exhibition of Charissa's maternity errs on the side of extravagance. Até goes many stages better than Dante's soothsayers, doomed to walk backwards, by simultaneously walking backwards and forwards, hearing and speaking double, marring with one hand what she makes with the other. Iron Talus and Lady Munera with her golden hands and silver feet, the dragon with a tail of three furlongs and a roar like that of a hundred lions are better suited to the child's story-book than to poetic allegory. But they are mere commonplaces beside the Blatant Beast with its mouth as wide as a peck, containing teeth of rusty iron and a thousand tongues of men, dogs, cats, bears, tigers and serpents. Allowing for a touch of misplaced humour, even as allegory this fails, and for good reason. While the dragon is easily recognisable as an uncanny wight long established in popular belief, the Blatant Beast is no beast but merely a formula for detraction, wherein the abstract idea has completely undermined the concrete representation.

Conditions of Elizabethan authorship favoured the use of allegory. The *chanson obscur*, with its *double entendre*, has ever proved a serviceable ruse for the poet seeking to gratify a circle of initiates without exposing himself to unnecessary risks. For all E.K.'s florid advertising *The Shepheardes Calender*, in common with the rest of Spenser's minor poems, was addressed not to the masses but to the few, and even *The Faerie Queene* was in substance a courtly panegyric rather than a popular best seller. Spenser had ample precedent for figuring contemporaries and current gossip under the guise of beast fable or pastoral, and there was nothing to prevent heroic romance from being put to the same use. To his first readers the signification of these innuendoes was doubtless sufficiently obvious; but though they have since provided a happy hunting-ground for commentators, many of them are too equivocal to admit of final solution. The element of snobbery underlying all such ingenuity necessarily discounts its value, which is historical rather than literary. The knowledge that Artegall is Lord Grey, the fox Burleigh, or the spider Lady Carey adds little to our appreciation of *The Faerie Queene* as romance, *Mother Hubberds Tale* as satire, or *Muiopotmos* as a mock heroic. Nor do we welcome the cold blast of disillusion which reduces episodes like that of Timias and Belphœbe or Calidore and Pastorella to the intrigues of court adventurers. The political interests of *The Faerie Queene* imposed their own restrictions. As Gloriana never appeared it was necessary to compliment the Queen in the person of other characters—Una, Britomart, Belphœbe and Mercilla, each a distinct individual. Similarly Duessa the harlot and Radigund the shrew may both figure the same original, Mary Queen of Scots. Plausible identifications have been found for every one of the characters throughout the complex historical allegory of Book I, which summarises the course of the Protestant Reformation in England; but not one reader in a hundred concerns himself with this aspect of the legend. Generally, the more palpable the allusion the more laboured the episode, as shown all too plainly throughout Book v, particularly in the stories of Irena and of Belgè with her seventeen sons. The political allegory, only surface deep, may indeed be treated as Hazlitt recommends and left to take care of itself.

But it is otherwise with the philosophical allegory, which represents the fullest expression not merely of one poet's ethic but of the whole humanistic idea concerning poetry and its function. If poetry is to be regarded as means to an end, a delectable way of righteousness, the poet will best fulfil his priestly function by investing his creations with moral significance. Here, at least, schoolman and humanist could agree. In the *Convivio* Dante divides the possible interpretations of any work or passage into four—the literal, the allegorical, "truth hidden under a fair fiction", the moral, which every teacher may apply to himself and to his pupils for their benefit, and the anagogical, or spiritual, transcending the literal sense and signifying "the sublime things of eternal glory". The account of the entry to Purgatory (*Purgatorio*, IX) admirably illustrates this union of fourfold sense within a single concept, which follows inevitably from Dante's scholastic thought and mystic consciousness. To Spenser, living in an age of intellectual upheaval and propounding ethic rather than theology, such fusion of sense was impossible. Nevertheless the four modes of interpretation can be applied at various points of *The Faerie Queene*. The purely mythical and romantic fabric strikes the imagination directly and independent of any ulterior meaning. But permeating this "fair fiction" is the "continuous allegory or dark conceit", the representation of moral truths which, if not immediately obvious, stand out unmistakably in full-length studies of human life and character. The third or "moral" interpretation may be applied to the analysis of conduct which occupies so much attention throughout the first three books. Finally an isolated instance of "anagogical" or "supersensual" interpretation is provided in the account of the House of Holiness and the vision of New Jerusalem, which together compose the one purely religious episode throughout *The Faerie Queene*.

That Spenser himself regarded the allegory as the very stuff and substance of his poem may be inferred from his frequent references to a hidden meaning, which are quite as emphatic as Dante's appeal to the initiated reader:

> O voi ch' avete li 'ntelleti sani,
> Mirate la dottrina che s' asconde
> Sotto il velame de li versi strani.4

Plato and the Platonists suggested the infinite possibilities of myth and allegory as theme for poetry and by 1582, as we learn from Bryskett's *Discourse*, *The Faerie Queene* had already been planned as a philosophical epic. The prefatory letter, describing "the author's whole intention", tells the same tale. In the first twelve books "the twelve private morall vertues, as Aristotle hath devised" are to be represented in the person of Arthur and of other heroes. If these are well received the poet may be persuaded to undertake another twelve books, framing the political virtues in a similar romance of Arthur after he became king. Though this method may be unpleasing to some readers, it is suited to "the use of these dayes, seeing all things accounted by their showes, and nothing esteemed of, that is not delightfull and pleasing to commune sence". For the romantic allegorist enforces doctrine by "ensample", which is ever more profitable and gracious than rule. Free to select and arrange his material with the object of pleasing his readers, he differs from the historiographer who "discourseth of affayres orderly as they were donne". So the peerless poet fulfils the function of both philosopher and historian without the restrictions of either, as Sidney argues throughout the early part of the *Apology*, and emphasis upon the didactic value of poetry, "thus clowdily enwrapped in Allegoricall devises" follows as a matter of course.[5]

Seeing that Spenser compounded his scheme from Aristotle *and the rest*, any attempt to draw a close analogy between *The Faerie Queene* and the *Ethics*, except in certain detached passages, must necessarily prove abortive. The ten virtues enumerated in the *Ethics* are Courage (ἀνδρεία), Temperance (σωφροσύνη), Liberality (ἐλευθεριότης), Magnificence (μεγαλοπρέπεια), Magnanimity (μεγαλοψυχία), a nameless quality, probably Love of Honour (φιλοτιμία), Gentleness (πραότης), Truthfulness (ἀλήθεια), Urbanity (εὐτραπελία), and Friendliness (φιλία), to which are added Modesty (αἰδώς), and Righteous Indignation (νέμεσις), the last two "mean states" to be treated as emotions rather than virtues. In the *Republic* Plato enumerates the four Cardinal Virtues as Courage, Temperance, Wisdom (σοφία), and Justice (δικαιοσύνη), to which, in the *Protagoras*, he adds Holiness (ὁσιότης). Spenser's fragmentary scheme of Magnificence, Holiness, Temperance, Chastity, Friendship, Justice and Courtesy partakes of both Plato and Aristotle, with additions from independent sources. "Holiness", as portrayed in the first legend, is a purely Christian virtue; "Justice", in Book v, is more Machiavellian than classical. "Magnificence", "the perfection of all the rest", is an inaccurate rendering of Aristotle's μεγαλοψυχία or magnanimity, the attribute of the man who deems himself worthy of great things and who must therefore shine in all virtues. Any author aspiring to fashion a gentleman is inevitably laid under heavy obligation to the succinct, lucid sketches of Aristotle, the fountain head to the whole literature of Theophrastian character portrayal both in poetry and prose. But apart from this general influence the only two books in which Spenser follows his nominal authority at all closely are the second and the fourth.

His debt to neo-Platonic sources was far more effective. The scheme of personified abstractions reacting upon each other is comparable with Plato's dramatic presentation of differing types of mind brought into relation or conflict and ultimately compelled to submit to the verdict of a superior intelligence. The whole conception of Faeryland, the vision of a perfect world swayed by images of virtue that exist only in heaven, beyond the bounds of time and space, is the philosophy of ideas in romantic dress. The analogy between private and politic virtues culminating in the idea of justice recalls the *Republic*. The entire moral basis of the first two books rests on the life of discipline and self-mastery set forth in the *Republic* and the *Phædrus*. The allegory of the third, fourth and fifth books turns on neo-Platonic notions of love, treated more theoretically in the first two *Hymnes*, much of which ultimately derive from the *Symposium*. It may be safely asserted that, without Plato and the Platonists, *The Faerie Queene* would never have reached its present form, and further that, in respect of his allegory, whenever Spenser descends from the world of ideas to that of fact, as a rule his inspiration begins to flag.

But in order to appreciate the full extent of his debt to authorities in formulating this ethical scheme we must look well beyond Plato and Aristotle, to Cicero and the Latin Stoics, to moralists of the Middle Ages as well as to those of the Renaissance. The seven virtues of Christian ethic are Faith, Hope, Charity, Prudence, Justice, Fortitude and Temperance. In *L'art de chevalerie selon Vegece*, translated by Caxton as *The Fayt of Arms and of Chevalrye* (1489), the twelve chivalric virtues are Noblesse, Foy, Feaultie, Honneur, Droicture, Prouesse, Amour, Courtoisie, Diligence, Nectete, Largesse, Sobresse; and this may have supplied Caxton with a hint for the list included in his *Morte Darthur* of which notice has already been taken. The Italian philosophers cited in Bryskett's *Discourse* owed something to their mediæval forbears as well as to the classics, and similarly Spenser, framing a poem on current ethics, draws his philosophical material not from any one original but from commonplaces familiar to every sixteenth-century moralist. His ethical allegory, like his romantic narrative, is a "gally-maufray" of ideas derived from many sources but harmonised in one poetic whole. In the light of ancient and modern philosophy the far-off things and battles long ago re-awaken to a new life, affording ample scope for the analysis of character and for dramatic situation occasioned by the interplay of mind against mind. On the surface *The Faerie Queene* has all the inconsequence of romance. But its epic vitality and any unity it possesses beyond that of place must be sought in the philosophical allegory, which binds the loose threads of narrative into at least some semblance of continuous argument.

Allegory

In allowing himself this freedom Spenser showed a true sense of his own powers and limitations. His poem is not a single spiritual autobiography but a discursive and fanciful presentation of ideal types treated objectively. He had none of the schoolman's logical instinct, the mystic's eagle vision which could inspire Dante to devise a complete cosmic scheme, where every soul has its proper place and every episode adds its own special contribution to the drama of the universe. His Faeryland is no pit of Hell or mount of Purgatory representing progressive stages of existence, but a world of one plane, spacious, wide and sprinkled with the sweet variety of a day-dream. The philosophic scheme, though partly pre-arranged, develops along with the rambling romantic narrative. Though the letter to Raleigh was written after three books were completed Spenser must already have realised that an heroic poem should take account of politic, along with private virtues; and in the later books he practically abandons the original plan by admitting the purely political justice of Book v as well as friendship and courtesy, which are social accomplishments rather than moral virtues. Rigid adherence to any one system was incompatible with his wayward fancy, and would have had the effect of hardening his poem into an allegory as wooden and conventional as *The Pastime of Pleasure* or a score of others after the same school.

At the very outset he departs from classical authority by introducing a legend of Holiness treating of Christian ethics after the manner of mediæval allegory. The legend is a spiritual biography, a tale of progress in private virtue from weakness and ignorance to strength and knowledge. The hero is a crusader not merely in appearance but in action, duly enrolled among the Seven Champions, girt in "the armour of a Christian man, specified by Saint Paul", fighting the enemies of religion—Error, Blind Devotion (Corceca), Superstition (Abessa) and Despair. His "solemn sadness" and disinclination to enjoy this world's goods distinguish him from the "Humanum Genus" of morality drama, whom in other respects he resembles. He is Graund Amoure spiritualised; not Everyman, but an exceptional type whose trials are those of the spirit rather than of the flesh and whose quest is not an education through the seven sciences but the soul's pilgrimage by the light of reason and with the help of grace. Through experience and victory over temptation his character evolves; but before he can destroy his last enemy and behold the Beatific Vision he must pass through an intermediate stage of purgation at the House of Holiness. Protestantism inevitably deprives the religious allegorist of much invaluable material, for the symbolic attributes and outward manifestations of the "inner light" cannot compare with those of the sacramental system. Nevertheless the Red Cross Knight's spiritual pilgrimage falls into the same stages and points the same moral as that of Dante. Both descend in order to ascend, gaining their initiation through a life of action in which they have laboured and not fainted.

The Christian mysticism of the first legend is enforced through neo-Platonism. Una is absolute Truth, the perfection of wisdom and beauty, the highest good and the object of spiritual love. Her face, even veiled, can tame the savage passions of lion and satyr, and when she reveals herself in her awful loveliness, like Beatrice in Paradise or the image of beauty as figured in the *Phædrus*, she inspires first terror and then reverence in her beholders. As law-bringer, quelling the forces of disorder, she plays a part similar to that of Truth in Bruno's *Spaccio della Bestia trionfante*, appointed by Jove to be deputy ruler of the universe. The Red Cross Knight, inspired by Una to heroic achievement, is the ideal lover of the *Symposium*:

> The noble hart that harbours vertuous thought,
> And is with childe of glorious great intent,
> Can never rest, untill it forth have brought
> Th'eternall brood of glorie excellent.[6]

His victory illustrates the Platonic principle of reason's mastery over passion. Unruly desires and outward semblances, figured in Archimago, Duessa and their allies, lure the soul from its mistress eternal Truth, and reason nearly succumbs to Despair, whose plea for suicide is finally met by the retort of Socrates to Cebes in the *Phædo*. The whole ideal of contemplative life as treated in this legend, especially in canto x, is deeply tinged with Platonism. But it is Platonism interpreted through Fidelia's "sacred Booke, with blood ywritt", as infallible to the Protestant as the visible Church to the Catholic; and the sacred book supplies some of the most effective symbolical machinery. Duessa and her seven-headed beast, the fight with the dragon and the vision of New Jerusalem come from the Apocalypse, recommended by Dante to Giotto as worthy material for his art and preferred by a Divine, in the hearing of Gabriel Harvey, "before al the veriest *Metaphysicall Visions*, and jollyest conceited *Dreames* or *Extasies*, that ever were devised by one or other".[7] If, as is probable, Spenser began the legend of Holiness while he was still moving in Puritan circles this would account for his exceptional dependence upon sacred texts, here employed with a freedom which Warton could only regard as "an impropriety amounting to an impiety".

Despite outward appearances the allegory of *The Faerie Queene* was clearly planned as a single structure, "builded some dozen stories high", though only half the stories were completed. Holiness, confirmed through discipline, forms the basis of Christian conduct. Its natural emanation is temperance, ranging between pure asceticism and the Hellenic idea of wholesome restraint. But the control of passion, Plato's neutral steed, is only a preliminary to its proper use, which is manifested in the exercise of love and friendship as a spur to noble action. The man who has gained such mastery over his faculties has reached the state of inward harmony compared by Plato with political justice. But before he can be regarded as a complete gentleman his virtue must be graced with courtesy whereby the world may know him for what he is.

With the opening of Book II the Christian note is practically lost. The safest guide to conduct which the Palmer can enjoin upon Guyon is the Aristotelian mean,

> Nether to melt in pleasures whott desyre,
> Nor frye in hartlesse griefe and dolefull tene,[8]

the principle personified in Elissa, Perissa and Medina. The first six cantos treat of intemperate fury, the remainder of intemperate desire. Amavia's "raging passion" at the tragic end of Mortdant, robbing reason of its "due regalitie", lures her to suicide and leaves the brand of blood upon her babe. The unbridled rage of Phaon, having driven him to violence, places him at the mercy of Furor and Occasion. The story of Pyrochles and Cymochles points the same moral. In his classification of anger Spenser follows Aristotle, who treats of the subject in his sections on courage and meekness, or "the mean state of anger". Irascibility, which ultimately destroys itself, and the spurious "courage of anger" ($\theta\upsilon\mu\acute{o}\varsigma$), prompted not by deliberation but by injury, which incites men to behave like beasts, are figured under the quaint imagery of the mediæval homilist:

> "Wrath, gealosie, griefe, love, do thus expell:
> Wrath is a fire; and gealosie a weede;
> Griefe is a flood; and love a monster fell;
> The fire of sparkes, the weede of little seede,
> The flood of drops, the Monster filth did breede:
> But sparks, seed, drops, and filth, do thus delay;
> The sparks soone quench, the springing seed outweed,
> The drops dry up, and filth wipe cleane away:
> So shall wrath, gealosy, griefe, love, die and decay."[9]

From this point myth and romance do service for allegory, the *Odyssey*, Ovid and Tasso corroborating Aristotle on the dangers of intemperate desire. Guyon's narrow escape from Phædria (Mirth) arms him for the more formidable trial at the Bower of Acrasia (Incontinence), which is modelled in

detail upon Tasso's Garden of Armida. Mammon, "mort-
gaging his life to covetize" and thereby perverting lawful
possessions into a moral canker, resembles both the illiberal
man and the intemperate glutton as depicted by Aristotle.
Finally Plato's notion of temperance as not merely best
policy in practical conduct but a virtue inherent in the soul
suggests the allegory of Alma and her castle, curiously compounded of Humanism and Scholasticism. The physiological details come from the *Timæus*, supplemented, perhaps,
by the *Somnium Scipionis*, the *Natura Deorum* and the *Sepmaine* of Du Bartas (First Week, Sixth Day). The *De Planctu
Naturæ* of Alain de l'Isle offers several striking analogues to
the account of the three turret chambers, which represent the
three functions of mind—imagination, judgment, memory,—
with their respective properties—fancy, philosophy, history,—classified as in *The Advancement of Learning*. But for
the main device it was unnecessary to depart from traditional
Christian allegory as developed from the Pauline figures of
fleshly lust warring against the soul and of the Christian's
equipment against the darts of the Devil. The comparison
between the organs of the body and the "keepers of the
house" is at least as old as the book of *Ecclesiastes*, which at
some time Spenser transversed, and it recurs in Grosseteste's
Chasteau d'Amour, Langland's Castle of Care, *The Castle of
Perseverance* and elsewhere. But the closest parallel to the
House of Alma is provided in the thirteenth-century English
homily of "Soul's Ward", which tells of a king defending
his castle with the aid of his daughters, the five wits, against
a foe who attacks it with the connivance of the five senses.

It is not surprising that the quaint device of Alma should
have appealed to the "metaphysical" taste of the seventeenth century. More than twenty years before Phineas
Fletcher saw fit to enlarge upon it in his *Purple Island* it had
apparently supplied the basis to *Roome for a Messe of Knaves*
(1610), "A narration of a strange but true battel fought in
the little Isle (or worlde) of Man". Sir Kenelm Digby, in

a letter to Sir Edward Esterling, commented at length upon the geometric symbolism of ii, ix, 22, which, in his opinion, would alone establish Spenser as "no whit inferior to the most famous men that have ever been in any age; as giving evident testimony herein that he was thoroughly versed in the mathematical sciences, in philosophy and in divinity". The circle, most perfect of figures, and the triangle, least perfect, represent soul and body. The baser feminine particles in nature are quickened by life-giving masculine emanations, the "imperfect, mortall" by the "immortall, perfect". The quadrate, symbolising the four elements and the four Platonic virtues, is proportioned as seven to nine, possibly in reference to the seven stars that preside over the new-born body and the nine orders of guardian angels. The excess of "fine conceit" that follows, extending from the

> wandring vine,
> Enchaced with a wanton yvie twine [10]

to the graceless ministrations of Concoction and his "kitchen clerk", Digestion, belongs to an age which numbered wit among the cardinal virtues of poetry. But the logical relation of the episode as a whole to the allegory of Temperance is made clear at the encounter with Shamefastness:

> "Why wonder yee,
> Fair Sir, at that which ye so much embrace?
> She is the fountaine of your modestee:
> You shamefast are, but Shamefastnes it selfe is shee." [11]

For here in Alma's house Guyon is confronted with the living embodiment of the natural parts that have swayed his conduct throughout the legend. His sojourn is as necessary as that of the Red Cross Knight at the House of Holiness.

The idea of Temperance presented in Book ii is much nearer Christian renunciation than Hellenic moderation. Whereas Aristotle cannot conceive of the man who delights in pleasure less than he ought, since such insensibility is contrary to human nature, Guyon, the Puritan celibate, em-

bracing the Pauline rule of life, has little inclination to in-
dulge the lusts of sense and appetite. But the introduction of
a new love motive at the opening of Book III tends to break
down this rigidity and greatly to enlarge the human interest
of the fable. In proceeding from Temperance to Chastity
Spenser may have been influenced by Plutarch, who distinguishes temperance (σωφροσύνη), a state of rest in which
reason has quelled sensuality, from continence (ἐγκράτεια),
"less than virtue", a state of flux and conflict in which reason
merely controls the senses without destroying their activity.
"For remorse, sorrow, displeasure, and indignation do not
as yet abandon and quit continence: whereas in the mind of
a temperate person all lieth plain and even on every side:
nothing there but quietness and integrity." Similarly, in-
temperance is distinguished from incontinence (ἀκρασία),
"less than vice".[12] Spenser's "chastity" certainly represents
a higher degree of perfection than Plutarch's "continence";
but the two qualities bear a somewhat similar relation to
"temperance". Britomart is an ardent lover, less Stoic, more
temperamental and passionate than Guyon. Her chastity is
not the negative "Holy Maidenhood" of the mediæval
ascetic but an active enthusiasm for the noble and beautiful,
inspiring its possessor to deeds of praise. As Guyon the
temperate quells the irascible Pyrochles and the sensual
Acrasia so Britomart the chaste is brought into conflict with
various types of ignoble love—the shallow Squire of Dames,
the wanton Hellenore, the lustful Paridell, to each of whom
love is a snare. Her romantic love for a fair unknown, of
whom she has seen no more than a shadow, is a spiritual
passion, an inward yearning for the fame which will render
her worthy of his regard:

> For love does alwaies bring forth bounteous deeds,
> And in each gentle hart desire of honor breeds.[13]

This is the ideal love of the *Phædrus* and the *Symposium* as
opposed to the selfish frigidity of Marinell, the ardent passion

that allows the lover no rest until he has attained the highest good:

> Ne suffereth it uncomely idlenesse
> In his free thought to build her sluggish nest,
> Ne suffereth it thought of ungentlenesse
> Ever to creepe into his noble brest;
> But to the highest and the worthiest
> Lifteth it up that els would lowly fall:
> It lettes not fall, it lettes it not to rest;
> It lettes not scarse this Prince to breath at all,
> But to his first poursuit him forward still doth call.[14]

The concupiscence of Malecasta and her minions, the bestiality of Argante, the sodomy of Oliphant are but a profanation of this pure affection, divine in origin and devoid of sensuality:

> Most sacred fyre that burnest mightily
> In living brests, ykindled first above
> Emongst th' eternall spheres and lamping sky,
> And thence pourd into men, which men call Love!
> Not that same, which doth base affections move
> In brutish mindes, and filthy lust inflame,
> But that swete fit that doth true beautie love,
> And choseth vertue for his dearest Dame,
> Whence spring all noble deedes and never dying fame.[15]

So the third legend turns upon the same motive as the *Hymnes*. The distinction between temperance and chastity is marked not only by Britomart's immunity from the temptations which beset Guyon but by changes in the whole character of the fable. Her assumption of masculine dress symbolises not the repression of sexual desire but its direction towards a laudable object. Though at the start she appears to possess the virtue attained by her predecessor there is still room for development and the third allegory embraces a far wider range of interest than the second. Possessed of the self-mastery which the Red Cross Knight and Guyon have acquired through successive temptation, Britomart is ready to approve in action the grace within her, the enthusiasm

that will ultimately render her worthy of her lover. The love
of Scudamour, "Cupid's man", for Amoret, the chosen of
Venus, though innocent, is too engrossing; powerless to
save her from the toils of the enchanter Busirane, he forfeits
his manhood by forswearing arms. The tragic history of
Florimell and her wrangling suitors illustrates the disastrous
consequence of submission to the outward semblance of
beauty. Against all such baser passions shines the "fresh,
flowring Maidenhead" of Belphœbe, which renders her a
"perfect complement" of her sex, and the chastity of Britomart, which enables her to achieve her task by rescuing
injured innocence from the fetters of brutal lust.

By the close of Book III the love motive has so completely
transformed the "Stoic censor's" rule of repression as to
call for apology:

> Such ones ill judge of love that cannot love,
> Ne in their frosen hearts feele kindly flame.
> Forthy they ought not thing unknowne reprove,
> Ne naturall affection faultlesse blame
> For fault of few that have abusd the same;
> For it of honor and all vertue is
> The roote, and brings forth glorious flowres of fame,
> That crowne true lovers with immortall blis,
> The meed of them that love, and do not live amisse.

> Which who so list looke backe to former ages,
> And call to count the things that then were donne,
> Shall find that all the workes of those wise sages,
> And brave exploits which great Heroes wonne,
> In love were either ended or begunne.[16]

This foreword links the allegory of Chastity with that of
Friendship, which follows it without interruption of the
narrative. Friendliness is represented by Aristotle as the
mean between peevishness and flattery, the quality of the
man who treats everyone according to his desert, neither
praising nor blaming indiscriminately. Though the Platonic
association of friendship with love persuaded Spenser to

attach to it more of an emotional value than is implied in the *Ethics*, the outlines of his allegory are plainly drawn from Aristotle. Até, Sclaunder, Corflambo and Druon, who "unto ladies love would lend no leisure", are all peevish and quarrelsome, "opposing everything and not caring an atom for the pain they cause", as Aristotle describes the man deficient in friendliness. Até works mischief through "false rumours and seditious strife", with the aid of Duessa, Sclaunder and Corflambo. Between them they succeed in provoking endless disputes between Blandamour, Paridell, Claribell and the competitors for the false Florimell, all vying with each other and incapable of reconciliation except through the aid of "God, or godlike man". Alliance between such as these can never be more than a friendship of policy:

> Ne certes can that friendship long endure,
> However gay and goodly be the style,
> That doth ill cause or evill end enure;
> For vertue is the band that bindeth harts most sure.[17]

All alike err through excess, but the excess is of love rather than of friendship in the sense employed by Aristotle. The typical specimen of Aristotelian complacency or excessive friendship, the man "who praises everything with view to pleasure and opposes nothing at all", is the Squire of Dames. On the other side stand the true friends Cambel and Triamond, Placidas and Amyas, bound by mutual love free of rancour, a brotherhood "combyned with vertues meet", which overrules all other ties of affection, whether to mistress or to kin.

The last three cantos of Book IV, partly inspired, perhaps, by the circumstances to which we owe *Amoretti* and *Epithalamion*, compose one great hymn to the praise of love as the source of all happiness and the object of all desire. The erotic allegory which predominates throughout the greater part of the poem reaches its climax in the vision at the Temple of Venus, the "Epithalamion Thamesis " and the nuptials of Marinell and Florimell; but the climax has been anticipated by a change in tone which steadily develops throughout the latter part of Book IV. The testy suitors, pacified through the timely intervention of Arthur, appear in more favourable light, as well-spoken gallants rather than mere types of lawless passion. At the request of *good* Sir Claribell, who, but twenty stanzas before, was *lewd* Sir Claribell, Scudamour regales the company with the story of his adventures at the court of Love, a secular allegory after the order of the *Romant de la Rose*, which comes as a welcome relief from the clash of arms and the saws of the moralist. His encounters with those old-time worthies Doubt, Delay, Danger, Concord, Love and Hatred are but a preliminary to the apocalypse that follows, the mighty concourse of lovers hymning the Queen of Beauty and the silent group encircling the object of his desire:

> Thus sate they all around in seemely rate:
> And in the midst of them a goodly mayd
> Even in the lap of Womanhood there sate,
> The which was all in lilly white arayd,
> With silver streames amongst the linnen stray'd;
> Like to the Morne, when first her shyning face
> Hath to the gloomy world itselfe bewray'd:
> That same was fayrest Amoret in place,
> Shyning with beauties light and heavenly vertues grace.[18]

So the magic of Spenser quickens and beautifies a moribund convention, worn and enfeebled by long use. For one moment the twelve virtues of Aristotle are forgotten and the court of Gloriana dissolves before the court of Venus.

The spell lasts throughout the two cantos following. Storm and stress give place to reconciliation and midsummer merriment. But the opening of a new book means a fresh start, an unwelcome awakening from a lover's day-dream to the sterner life of action. The prologue of Book V might stand at the beginning of a new poem, and the change of tone is so marked as to suggest that a considerable interval of time separated the composition of the two books. The allegory likewise, though related to the preceding scheme, is of a radically different order. The triumph of reason over wayward passion, already treated under the aspects of holiness, temperance, chastity and friendship, bears issue in justice, the inward harmony induced by self-control. So far Spenser can follow Plato, without doing violence to the plan proposed in the prefatory letter. But private justice has already been treated, though not at full length, incidentally in the adventures of Arthur, the Red Cross Knight, Guyon and Britomart. The growing encroachment of historical allegory throughout Book IV can be seen in such thinly disguised portraits as Paridell and Blandamour, Timias and Belphœbe. So when Artegall, hitherto a subsidiary figure, finally has the stage to himself, the Knight of Justice is three parts eclipsed by Lord Grey, while the delightful land of Faery is brought violently down to earth by means of such familiar landmarks and personages as the river Lee, Lady Irena, Bourbon, Floudelis and Geryoneo, "that whylome in Spaine so sore was dred".

The entry of Artegall is prepared at greater length and with more flourish than that of any other character. He is first mentioned by Guyon to Arthur just before they reach the House of Alma as one of the most famous of Gloriana's knights. His image inspires Britomart throughout her adventures and he appears in three out of the six completed books. Yet for all this, and partly because of it, the "salvage knight" of Britomart's young dreams is less convincing than any of his fellows. Whereas the latter are represented as human personalities distinguished by traits appropriate to the allegory, Artegall is either Lord Grey or simply abstract Justice personified. For exercise "in justice law" Astræa at first appointed him to arbitrate in disputes between the beasts of the forest; but this part of his career, which might have made a good story, is dismissed in a few stanzas, and we meet him already an accomplished justiciar, inspiring terror rather than affection:

> That even wilde beasts did feare his awfull sight,
> And men admyr'd his over-ruling might;
> Ne any liv'd on ground that durst withstand
> His dreadfull heast, much lesse him match in fight,
> Or bide the horror of his wreakfull hand,
> When so he list in wrath lift up his steely brand.[19]

The part he plays is by no means so impressive as the brave words promise. At his first encounter with Britomart, after a preliminary success at Satyrane's tournament, he is badly worsted. He prefers preaching to action, leaving the heavier responsibilities to Talus whom on more than one occasion he most ungallantly sends in advance,

> to invent
> Which way he enter might *without endangerment*,[20]

and who is generally called off in the name of mercy when the field has already become a shambles. The achievement of his task—the rescue of Irena—is protracted beyond endurance. Deprived, for the first time, of the help of Talus he succumbs to Radigund, and after being ignominiously rescued from a woman by a woman he goes his way,

> ne ever howre did cease
> Till he redeemed had that Lady thrall.[21]

Yet he finds time to engage with Arthur, to play the lesser part in an intrigue for entrapping the Soldan, to stand by whilst Talus tackles Guile and at Samient's request to tarry for an indefinite period at the court of Mercilla. His self-reproach is indeed well founded:

> "Too much am I to blame for that faire Maide,
> That have her drawne to all this troublous strife,
> Through promise to afford her timely aide,
> Which by default I have not yet defraide";[22]

and we cannot but recognise a certain poetic justice in the fate that condemns him, after his long-delayed battle with

Grantorto, to return to Gloriana with nothing but the insults of Envy and Detraction to reward him for his pains.

His supernatural endowments likewise ill become a champion of heroic virtue. It might have been supposed that Chrysaor, the traditional sword of justice which nothing can withstand, would have sufficed. But Chrysaor is almost negligible in comparison with the astounding "iron groom", Talus. The pseudo-Platonic *Minos* makes mention of one Talus, appointed by Minos to travel thrice a year throughout Crete, bearing the brazen tables of the law and on this account surnamed "the Brazen". Apollonius Rhodius comes nearer Spenser in speaking of the same Talus as "made of brass and invulnerable". The tower of Dunother, in *Huon of Bordeaux*, is guarded by two men of brass, each holding an iron flail. But neither authority nor the demands of allegory can palliate the offence of admitting this grotesque automaton, Thor with his hammer but without his humour, upon the shores of old romance. Talus is a very affront to the hero's dignity, a lapse on the part of Spenser that can only be attributed to waning power.

The legend of justice manifestly is not at unity with itself. It collapses into a series of unrelated episodes representing the operation of justice in various directions, as the supreme legislator, the foil to tyranny and anarchy, the infallible arbiter between truth and falsehood. The continuous theme of the first four books being exhausted, a fresh start was necessary, entailing certain radical changes in the nature of the allegory. The *Ethics* had already served its purpose, since the remaining Aristotelian virtues hitherto untouched, such as liberality or munificence, are not specially adapted to the heroic theme. The distinction between private and public virtue having already broken down, justice, a cardinal virtue according to Plato, claimed attention: and what better occasion than a legend of justice in defence of Lord Grey, who had suffered something approaching the fate of the just man in the *Republic*? But in this case justice meant wholesale repression, and the single foes hitherto encountered by the champions must give place to bands of rebels and brigands, to be utterly crushed before Irena could be rescued from Grantorto. At the same time Artegall must not compare unfavourably with his fellows, as a ruthless man of blood. So the work of carnage is delegated to Talus, personifying the execution of justice by force and deliberately represented as a machine of destruction, devoid of ruth or feeling, quelling the "rascall many" "with a few sowces of his iron flail". Artegall, on the other hand, embodying merely the abstract principle of justice, giving instructions to Talus and calling him off when he has done enough, plays the inglorious part of headquarters staff, the necessary consequence of his compromising position.

By the close of Book v the ethic of *The Faerie Queene* has moved several stages from both Plato and Aristotle; and the natural complement to the virtues already treated is Courtesy, represented not as an acquired accomplishment but as a quality inherent in the moral being,

> Which though it on a lowly stalke doe bowre,
> Yet brancheth forth in brave nobilitie,
> And spreds it selfe through all civilitie.[23]

"The gentle mind by gentle deeds is known", blood will tell and nothing bewrays the man, wild or civil, so well as his manners. Discourtesy, slander or malice, on the contrary, are not merely breaches of etiquette but offences against humanity itself. Mirabella, despising love, is by love the more tormented and compelled to do penance for her crime against nature; and when no outward salve can cure Timias and Serena of the wounds inflicted by the Blatant Beast they find the remedy within themselves. Aristotle's illustrations reinforce the commonplaces of Renaissance text-books. For Courtesy resembles friendliness, the subject of the fourth legend, in inclining its possessors

> to beare themselves aright
> To all of each degree as doth behove.[24]

But it approximates still more closely to "urbanity" (εὐτρα-πελία), the mean between ribaldry and rusticity, which Aristotle places second among the social virtues: hence the emphasis upon rural simplicity in the character of Tristram and the "wild wood man" as well as in the concluding pastoral episode.

By his own confession Calidore begins his quest where Artegall retires. Justice must be consolidated through the quelling of Envy and Detraction, and once again the allegory serves to maintain continuity and unity of action. The necessary counterpart to justice is pity, the absence of which infallibly marks the coward and the bully,

> For wheres no courage, theres no ruth nor mone.[25]

The new motive induces a new change of tone; and as relentless justice gives place to mercy and pity so the noise of war gradually modulates into the piping of Colin and Coridon. Admitting historical allusions when occasion serves, Spenser is no longer obsessed with them, as the defendant of a particular individual and his policy. Instead he reverts to the moral allegory, using it, however, more casually and, on the whole, less seriously than in the earlier books. The interests of Raleigh (Timias), as of Lord Grey, require an attack on his traducers; hence the introduction of that wooden trio,

> The first of them by name was cald Despetto,
> Exceeding all the rest in powre and hight;
> The second, not so strong but wise, Decetto;
> The third, nor strong nor wise, but spightfullest,
> Defetto.[26]

But no attempt is made to develop them, as in the case of Sansloy, Sansfoy and Sansjoy. The discourse of the Hermit with Timias and Serena, poisoned by the teeth of the Blatant Beast, marks a return to psychological allegory and to the moral of the first two legends:

Allegory

For in your selfe your onely helpe doth lie
To heale your selves, and must proceed alone
From your owne will to cure your maladie.
Who can him cure that will be cur'd of none?
If therefore health ye seeke, observe this one:
First learne your outward senses to refraine
From things that stirre up fraile affection;
Your eies, your eares, your tongue, your talk restraine
From that they most affect, and in due termes containe.[27]

But the episode is related to the hero, Calidore, only as an example of the evil wrought by the object of his pursuit. The story of Mirabella ends in being much ado about nothing, leaving the unhappy lady in precisely the same predicament in which she was placed at Prince Arthur's first intervention. The allegory of courtesy falls into detached sketches, interspersed with much that is purely romantic. Its position is rather analogous to that of Shakespeare's last romances as summed up by Mr Strachey: "It is difficult to resist the conclusion that he was getting bored himself. Bored with people, bored with real life, bored with drama, bored, in fact, with everything except poetry and poetical dreams".[28] Substitute for "people" and "drama" "allegory, historical and philosophical" and the statement will apply to Spenser. So it is not surprising to find his last hero, at the conclusion of his recorded adventures, lifted bodily from the toil and turmoil of Faeryland to disport himself on the swards of Arcadia; yet even here the first authority, Aristotle, gave some sanction for such an interlude in connecting urbanity with the necessity for rest, recreation and amusement.

Calidore leaves his task but half achieved by chaining the Blatant Beast so insecurely that the monster succeeds in regaining his liberty. And thus the allegory draws to a conclusion in which nothing is concluded. The gentleman has been fashioned, his virtues have been systematically examined and portrayed at full length. But this task, proposed in the preface and duly fulfilled, involves another, the quest into origins, an attempt to solve the eternal problem of evils yet unsubdued. If the plan of the allegory is Aristotelian the underlying thought is Platonic. Holiness, temperance, chastity and all the other virtues have an existence independent of the individuals possessing them, as eternal ideas and powers that make for righteousness. In the millennium, as in the antique world, they will reign supreme and unchanging as heaven itself. But how may they be enthroned in a world of universal instability? The question is left unanswered in *The Faerie Queene*, a kaleidoscopic medley of episodes each complete in itself, an allegory of truths and objects unrelated to one final cause. But a solution is attempted in the allegory of Mutability; and though inadequate, it is the poet's last word, left for what it is worth. Changing accident is but an outward and visible sign of eternal substance evolving towards a final perfection, wherein the images of vice and corruption shall dissolve in the eternal ideas of virtue and truth.

CHAPTER VI

Diction

THE announcement by E.K. of a New Poet, together
with Sidney's admission that "the *Shepheardes Calender*
hath much poetry in his Eglogues", established for
Spenser a claim to pre-eminence that has since passed un-
disputed. A century before Lamb invested him with the
title of "Poet's Poet" John Hughes had hailed him as the
father of more poets than any other English writer. Cowley
confessed that a copy of Spenser within his mother's parlour
"filled my head first with such chimes of verse, as have never
since left ringing there".[1] Incidental objections on the score
of diction, fable or allegory have in no wise affected the
general verdict, which even the incorrigible Thomas Rymer
could endorse with the acknowledgment that "he had a
large spirit, a sharp judgment and a *Genius* for *Heroic Poesie*,
perhaps above any that ever writ since *Virgil*".[2]   Many
features that captivated his first admirers offer but little direct
appeal to an age that has long outgrown the Elizabethan taste
for allegory and fine conceit. But his work remains as something infinitely more vital and precious than a treasured
antique. The passage of time can never impair the legacy
with which he has endowed three centuries of English
poetic tradition.

The New Poet assumed office with all the honest haughti-
ness of a self-conscious creator, of Marlowe, Milton or
Shelley. The formal apology of "Master Immerito" for
his rustic quill spells no lack of assurance or of faith in the
immortality shared by the poet with the object of his song.
Colin is the "shepheards joye", the paragon of his compeers,
silencing the very Muses with his "silver sound" and re-

awakening the woods of Kilcolman on his return; the peerless poet who can inscribe *Amoretti* and *Epithalamion* to his
lady as "an endlesse moniment", "vowd to eternity", and, to
his sovereign, *The Faerie Queene*, "to live with the eternitie
of her fame". Ἐνθουσιασμὸς, treated at large in his lost
"English Poet", the divine madness transcending sense and
reason, exalts the poet to a plane above the common reach.
"Ravished with a Poetical furie" even the clodpate Cuddie
can echo the sentiments of Mantuan's Candidus in winged
words which Ben Jonson committed to memory, perhaps for
the benefit of his sons at the Mermaid:

> The vaunted verse a vacant head demaundes,
> Ne wont with crabbed care the Muses dwell:
> Unwisely weaves, that takes two webbes in hand.
>
> Who ever casts to compasse weightye prise,
> And thinkes to throwe out thondring words of threate,
> Let powre in lavish cups and thriftie bitts of meate,
> For Bacchus fruite is frend to Phœbus wise;
> And, when with Wine the braine begins to sweate,
> The nombers flowe as fast as spring doth ryse.
>
> Thou kenst not, Percie, howe the ryme should rage,
> O! if my temples were distaind with wine
> And girt in girlonds of wild Yvie twine,
> How I could reare the Muse on stately stage,
> And teach her tread aloft in buskin fine,
> With queint Bellona in her equipage.[3]

But this trencher fury of a riming parasite, raised from the
vapours of wine, is no better than a travesty of the Platonic
frenzy that possesses Colin as he discourses of love:

> "Shepheard, it seems that some celestiall rage
> Of Love (quoth Cuddy) is breath'd into thy brest,
> That powreth forth these oracles so sage
> Of that high powre, wherewith thou art possest."[4]

The humanistic notion of the poet as seer and oracle of
"delightful teaching" allows neither "profuse strains of un-
premeditated art" nor "art for art's sake". The poet's pride

"is virtue to advance and vice deride" and the divine fury finds expression through conscious effort, "not table talk fashion or like men in a dream" but "peyzing each syllable of each word".[5] The burden of complaint that predominates throughout *The Teares of the Muses* descends with equal weight upon "scoffing scurrility" and "rymes at random".

The ancient definition of poetry as a mode of imitation has proved sufficiently elastic and equivocal to meet the demands of widely divergent schools of criticism; and the cult of ideal form throughout the Renaissance era encouraged the artist, in imitating nature, to attempt to refine upon her. "Arte and nature strived to joyne", "nature had for wantonesse ensude Art", "art playing second natures part", "art, striving to compayre with nature", "Art at nature did repyne"—such phrases all bear the same implication. The faculty enabling the artist thus to imitate, even to improve upon his model is "invention", which bears something of the same relation to "fury" as "fancy" to "imagination". "The first and most necessarie poynt", writes George Gascoigne, after Ronsard, "that ever I founde meete to be considered in making of a delectable poeme is this, to grounde it upon some fine invention. . . . What Theame soever you do take in hande, if you do handle it but *tanquam in oratione perpetua*, and never studie for some depth of devise in the Invention, and some figures also in the handlyng thereof, it will appeare to the skilfull Reader but a tale of a tubbe. . . . If I should undertake to wryte in prayse of a gentlewoman, I would neither praise hir christal eye, nor hir cherrie lippe, etc. For these things are *trita et obvia*. But I would either finde some supernaturall cause wherby my penne might walke in the superlative degree, or els I would undertake to aunswere for any imperfection that shee hath, and thereupon rayse the prayse of hir commendacion. Likewise, if I should disclose my pretence in love, I would eyther make a strange discourse of some intollerable passion, or finde occasion to pleade by the example of some historie, or discover my disquiet in shadowes *per Allegoriam*, or use the covertest meane that I could to avoyde the uncomely customes of common writers. Thus much I adventure to deliver unto you (my freend) upon the rule of Invention, which of all other rules is most to be marked, and hardest to be prescribed in certayne and infallible rules; . . . that beyng founde, pleasant woordes will follow well inough and fast inough."[6] The principle here enunciated by a literary mechanic, whose theories were better than his practice, needed little recommendation to a crew of courtly makers whose pens walked, as if by nature, "in the superlative degree". So Gabriel Harvey could praise the "lively hyperbolicall amplifications" of the fine conceited Grecians and Sidney depict himself as

Studying inventions fine, her wittes to entertaine,
Oft turning others leaves, to see if thence would flowe,
Some fresh and fruitfull showre, upon my Sunne-burnt braine.[7]

At its worst this aversion for the *trita et obvia* proves a snare to the poetaster, Aguecheek with his "Odours, pregnant and vouchsafed; I'll get 'em all three all ready"; but in the other scale must be set the incalculable resources of diction and imagery which later English poets have owed to the fertility of Elizabethan invention.

In content, style and temper the poetry of Spenser fully satisfied the demands of authority. But the coining of a new tongue was too bold an invention to escape censure. In a passage noted by E.K., Cicero allows the orator to elevate his speech by means of unusual and metaphorical words, adding, however, that such licence is generally more proper to poetry than to oratory. For the same reason one of the speakers in Castiglione's *Courtier* contends that ancient Tuscan words, though unsuited to conversation, give "a great grace and authoritie unto wrytings, and of them is compact a tongue more grave, and more ful of majestie, than of the new". The problem of standardising the vernacular by a judicious blending of native and foreign words, discussed by successive writers from the time of Dante to that of Voltaire, had come to a head in the middle of the sixteenth century. Du Bellay allowed a moderate admixture of native words, "not always too common". Sir John Cheke's censure of Sallust's archaisms comes ill from one who attempted a translation of the New Testament into Wardour Street English composed exclusively of Germanic words. Wilson's allegation that "the fine courtier will talke nothing but Chaucer" implies that the use of archaism was a favourite affectation of polite speech. E.K. had, therefore, substantial support for his defence of "such good and naturall English words, as have ben long time out of use, and almost cleane disherited". But the defence could hardly justify a hybrid of archaisms, provincialisms and neologisms selected at the caprice of one poet; and many a contemporary reader may well have been disposed to endorse the verdict of Ben Jonson in condemning this "gallymaufray" as "no language".

Logically the criticism is irrefutable. Spenser's artificial diction can be justified solely as an extreme poetic licence, an instrument of fantasy fashioned for a unique purpose. "Woordes", says Irenæus in the *View*, "are the Image of the mynd, soe as, they proceeding from the mynd, the mynd must needes be affected with the woordes." In the selection of a literary vocabulary, therefore, the guiding principle will be that of decorum. The stark directness of

> Pray you, undo this button,

or

> Cover her face; mine eyes dazzle; she died young

emanates from within, as the inevitable, spontaneous over-flow of powerful feeling. But the "seemely simplicitie" of the *Calender* is a stage artifice, whereby each personage appears appropriately garbed, a knight in the accoutrements of chivalry, a shepherd in English homespun. Low and rustic life supplies a basis to the argument not "because in that condition the essential passions of the heart find a better soil in which they can attain their maturity", but because it affords Colin an effective rôle for the exercise of his Muse. When the shepherd turns courtier, as in "April " and "November", his speech changes accordingly; we could hardly imagine the eulogist of Dido or Elisa adopting the idiom of Cuddie or Thenot and speaking of "my beaten hyde" or "thou brutish blocke".

To the poet language is both restrictive and refractory, imposing absolute laws upon the free play of invention. It is a hard taskmaster, and every poet must find himself chafing at times against this tyranny of an instrument not of his own making and therefore not entirely under his control. In striving to meet the difficulty he will adopt an attitude of more or less passive resistance, often achieving some of his greatest triumphs in the process. Aristotle allows the use of rare or even invented words that may serve to elevate style above the mean or commonplace, and the licence has been tacitly assumed by the great majority of poets. In this respect Shakespeare and Milton were both arch-rebels, the one a Prometheus, his own law-giver, the other rejecting native authority for the regiment of a foreign power. By affecting the obsolete, therefore, Spenser was not exceeding the privileges of his profession; but he chose an easier path than any of his predecessors in devising a language so purely decorative and so little bound by traditional usage or the exigencies of grammar. It has been well said of Shakespeare's diction that hardly any word looks old until we consider it. With Spenser's the position is exactly reversed. E.K. would have it that his author "hath laboured to restore, as to theyr rightfull heritage, such good and naturall English words, as have ben long time out of use, and almost cleane disherited", tentatively suggesting that they are admitted as "fittest for such rusticall rudenesse of shepheards. . . or els because such olde and obsolete wordes are most used of country folke". The real ground of his defence, however, is not the poet's object but the happy result, "so delightsome for the roundnesse, and so grave for the straungenesse". The sole criterion or authority governing the selection is tone and effect; the pedantic distinction drawn between *trewe* and *true* in "July", 163, is quite exceptional. A vocabulary so entirely unfettered, so open to the caprices of "casualtye and custome", offers to its possessor the line of least resistance. In the interest of rhyme or euphony *vile* may become *vilde, mislike misleeke, waves wawes, abandon aband.* Nothing short of the triumphant end could have justified such means pursued to such extremities.

But Jonson was barely judicious in summarily dismissing as "no language" this "gallymaufray" which, though hybrid, was not entirely unhistoric. Wilson's censure of inkhorn terms, which include Latinism, Italianisation, Gallicism and the Chaucerian speech specially attributed to the "fine courtier", goes to prove that many of the anomalies in Spenser, though doubtless outside the range of "King's English", were not far removed from the living speech of his day. Colloquialisms still heard in the dialects, Chaucerisms still freely admitted in conversation and writing, could not justly be described as "no language", and several of the words glossed by E.K. as presumably unfamiliar— e.g. *soote, queynt, virelaies, borrell*—occur in other contemporary writers. Though the purist might look askance upon these vagaries the average reader, then as now, probably accepted them at their face value as a natural cloak to the image of antiquity. A possible analogue to Spenser's venture is afforded in *Gawain and the Green Knight* and other works of the so-called west midland poets, who appear to have adopted a mixed dialect compounded specially for literary usage. Such a vocabulary differs fundamentally from Wardour Street English like that of William Morris in deriving from current as distinct from dead language and in possessing the authority of literary usage. Still farther is it removed from sham archaism like that of Chatterton, an artless fake made up of ill-assorted fragments, the spuriousness of which could hardly escape even the illiterate. Morris relies far more than Spenser upon "good and natural English words *that have been long disherited*", while the language of the Rowley poems is, indeed, "no language".

Spenser's interest in the history of language is attested not merely by the gloss to the *Calender* but also by notes upon Celtic words embodied in *A View of the present state of Ireland* and by playful guesses at etymology such as "baleful Oure" and "bounteous Trent" with his "thirty sorts of fish, and thirty sundry streames". His sensitive ear must have been continually on the alert for an unusual and effective word in earlier literature or provincial speech. The former supplied a rich store, represented in such specimens as *attemper, chevisaunce, peregall, sneb, swink, tottie*; moreover, Spenser's frequent tributes to Chaucer as "well of English undefiled" are somewhat misleading in view of his indebtedness to other older writers, including Lydgate, Caxton and Skelton. The prevailing dialect of the *Calender*, however, is not east midland but northern, a fact that accords with the supposed Lancastrian origin of Spenser's family and with E.K.'s allusion to Colin's descent from the northern parts. The clearest proofs of this are afforded by the appearance of northern grammatical forms such as the present participle in *-and* (*glitterand*) or the uninflected *thou was*, of words and phrases peculiar to the north—*busket, gate, hidder* and *shidder* —and of northern forms, as distinct from their southern cognates—*wae, kerke, gang, sike, war* (worse). But against these must be set midland and southern forms like *yeven, liggen*, as well as the southern prefix to the past participle (*y-clad*, etc.). Anomalies in vocabulary are less decisive than those in phonology, owing to the wide diffusion of dialectal words and to the complete freedom of selection which Spenser allowed himself. *Witch* (ash) appears to have been particularly common in the north, *cosset* (a lamb without dam) in East Anglia (? Cambridge); but other pregnant

Diction

archaisms—*dapper, eftsones, greete, wimble, whilome, listneth,* etc.—might have been gleaned from diverse sources and localities. Complication is further increased by the recurrence of cognates— *sithence* besides *since, her* and *theyr, lope* and *lepped, han* and *have, wae* and *woe,* both forms sometimes appearing in the same eclogue. Lastly there are spurious archaisms, some authorised by sixteenth-century usage, others invented for the occasion. *Musicall* does duty for *music* in order to save the rhyme. *Unkempt* and *adaw* were recent innovations, *forehaile, overgrast, dreeriment* new coinages. *Upryst,* as a past participle, comes from a mistranslation of the third singular present that persisted up to *The Ancient Mariner, kidst* from the confusion of two distinct Middle English verbs, *can* from *gan* (did), *yede* (infinitive) from the Middle English past tense of *go. Derringdoe*—subsequently borrowed from Spenser by Sir Walter Scott, who glosses it "desperate courage"—arises from a misunderstanding of "derring do", "daring to do", which occurs in a passage of Lydgate (*Chronicle of Troy,* II, xvi) closely modelled on Chaucer (*Troilus,* v, 834 ff.).

But a courtly maker seeking to extend the flexibility of his instrument needed other strings besides that of "natural rudeness". The tradition of polite poetry from Chaucer downwards sufficed to dispel any delusion as to the superiority of pure Saxon vocabulary and of monosyllables over foreign additions, whether ancient or modern. The language of the *Calender* is as varied in texture as its forms and subject-matter. "Those rough and harsh termes enlumine, and make more clearly to appeare, the brightnesse of brave and glorious words." Through the warp of native speech runs the woof of foreign importation, a "gallymaufray" of Latinism, Gallicism and Italianisation. Contemporary practice authorised such coinages as *crumenall, coronall* and the English Italianate *stanck. Overture,* as E.K. properly notes, is "borrowed of the French and used in good writers". *Francke shepheard* translates Marot's *franc pasteur. Availe* (lower) occurs in Surrey and other sixteenth-century poets, *chamfred* comes from a technical term of architecture. To these special cases must be added the much larger group of pure romance words like *jouissance, sovenance, surquedrie, encheason*, etc., common property to the whole school of polite poetry from Chaucer downwards. In "April" the pretty word *chevisaunce*, apparently without any authority, is divested of its regular prosaic meaning to appear within a catalogue of flowers.

Outside the *Calender* the relative importance of archaism to other anomalies in vocabulary considerably diminishes. Elizabethan freedom of usage allowed such adaptations as *gladed, deaded, kynded, gulphing, falsers. Abrayd* is a spurious present analogous to *yede. Abject, aemuling, aggrate, caerule, caprifole, daedale, gust* (taste), *miniments, reaedify, sacrament* (oath), *singults, wade* (go), *extract* (past participle) are but a few witnesses to the wholesale process of Latinisation in which Spenser ventured as far as any of his contemporaries; and the protagonists of pure English might well have looked askance at *capuccio, gondolay, battailous, belaccoyle, capitayne, dortours, devoyr, malengin, rosiere*. The change of instrument from "oaten reed" to "trumpet stern" allows a much larger proportion of "brave and glorious" words like *accoutrement, aumayl, beauperes, debonayr, grammercy*, together with the technical vocabulary of ancient usage as represented in *amis, camis, checklaton, complyne, feutre, hacqueton, limitours, replevie, umbriere*. Such "terms aureate" tend to enforce the native vigour of "honest plain words" that accompany them—*algate, cleep, dernely, gastful, groveling, hawberk, luskishnesse, mucky pelfe*—of compounds like *basen-wide, halfendeale, lusty-hed*. In diction, as in fable, Spenser flatly defies the unities of time and place. *Seisin, gree, duress, conge, belamy* bespeak the age and habit of chivalry; but *harrow, housling, leachcraft, star-read*, the *folke-mote* of competitors for Florimell and the *handsell* threatened by Pastorella's abductor carry us straight back to *Beowulf* and *The Battle of Maldon*.

Diction

The rich and flexible language compounded from so diverse sources adapts itself to subject-matter under the ruling of decorum. The *Complaints* alone admit several distinct types—the decorative word-play of *Virgils Gnat* and *Muiopotmos*, the sententious rhetoric of *The Ruines of Time* and the *Visions*, the colloquialism of *Mother Hubberds Tale*, broken by the burlesque canonical jargon of the "formal priest" and the grand style of the plea for "poor suitors". At the opposite pole to *Mother Hubberds Tale* is *Amoretti*, couched in the *lingua cortese* of the Petrarchans. The "middle style" of urbanity between the two extremes is represented in *Colin Clouts Come Home Againe*, a courtly piece admitting popular features to accord with its bucolic setting. In *Epithalamion* the resources of ornamental speech are squandered with all the prodigality proper to the choric ode. *Prothalamion*, on the other hand, impersonal and unimpassioned, contains hardly a word or figure beyond the range of current usage. Yet another kind of diction is peculiar to the didactic *Hymnes*, which include few archaisms but an exceptional number of abstract words like *wit, fantasy, influence, disposition, idees, intelligences, speculation, extasy*.

With good reason, therefore, Edward Bolton, discussing diction in his *Hypercritica* (1616), prefers the *Hymnes* to Spenser's other writings "as for practick English"; for generally with Spenser "practick", logical significance counts for less than outward appearance, euphony and tone. His archaisms, quaint spelling and childish onomatopœia betoken a language designed to catch the eye and ear rather than to stir the mind, the language of a decorative artist in words.

The same may be said of his syntax and style. A century before Milton took occasion to denounce the "swelling epithets, thick laid as varnish on a harlot's cheek" over the pages of ancient poetry the same mannerism had been criticised as a defect of contemporary "vulgar writers" by the author of *The Arte of English Poesie* (1589). Among such "vulgar writers" the critic might properly have included Spenser, who consistently embellishes each item of his descriptive catalogues with ornamental "attribution":

> Coole Violets, and Orpine growing still,
> Embathed Balme, and chearfull Galingale,
> Fresh Costmarie, and breathfull Camomill,
> Dull Poppie, and drink-quickning Setuale,
> Veyne-healing Verven, and hed-purging Dill,
> Sound Savorie, and Bazil hartie-hale,
> Fat Colworts, and comforting Perseline,
> Colde Lettuce, and refreshing Rosmarine.[8]

The value of such distributed epithets may be rhetorical rather than descriptive:

> High towers, faire temples, goodly theaters,
> Strong walls, rich porches, princelie pallaces,
> Large streetes, brave houses, sacred sepulchers,
> Sure gates, sweete gardens, stately galleries,
> Wrought with faire pillours and fine imageries.[9]

Accumulated epithets almost invariably constitute a rhetorical figure, conveying only a general impression of the object described:

> Faynt, wearie, sore, emboyled, grieved, brent.

> He seemed breathlesse, hartlesse, faint, and wan.

> On that bright shynie round still moving Masse.[10]

These are favourable specimens of their kind. But all too often Spenser falls into the snare of excessive "attribution". The worst line in *An Hymne of Heavenly Love*, one of his least successful efforts, is damned on this account alone:

> O huge and most unspeakable impression.[11]

Though fortunately such lapses are rare, overweighting by epithets, either expletive or at best more pretty than forceful, tends to hamper mobility of thought and to encourage prolixity:

> After all these there marcht a most faire Dame,
> Led of two grysie Villeins, th'one Despight,
> The other cleped Cruelty by name:
> She, doleful Lady, like a dreary Spright
> Cald by strong charmes out of eternall night,
> Had Deathes owne ymage figurd in her face,
> Full of sad signes, fearfull to living sight;
> Yet in that horror shewd a seemely grace,
> And with her feeble feete did move a comely pace.
>
> A stately Pallace built of squared bricke,
> Which cunningly was without morter laid,
> Whose wals were high, but nothing strong nor thick,
> And golden foile all over them displaid,
> That purest skye with brightnesse they dismaid:
> High lifted up were many loftie towres,
> And goodly galleries far over laid,
> Full of faire windowes and delightful bowres:
> And on the top a Diall told the timely howres.[12]

The heaviness of the expletive epithet may serve a dramatic purpose in expressing the temper of speech or soliloquy:

> Ye dreary instruments of doleful sight,
> That doe this deadly spectacle behold,
> Why doe ye lenger feed on loathed light,
> Or liking find to gaze on earthly mould,
> Sith cruell fates the carefull threds unfould,
> The which my life and love together tyde?
> Now let the stony dart of sencelesse cold
> Perce to my hart, and pas through everie side,
> And let eternall night so sad sight fro me hyde.[13]

But many of Spenser's most characteristic epithets have intrinsic value apart from their context. The rugged strength of colloquialisms like *dumpish, lumpish, despairefull, dislikeful* is unmistakable. "Dapper ditties", "pale and wan" are pure Elizabethan, "middle smale", "so blessed and so blythe" savour of ballad and folk-song. The common note connecting "gyrlonds trim", "their trim consort", "trim array",

> A little gondolay, bedecked trim

is the very essence of Spenserian grace and harmony. *Jolly* and *merry* are both favourites, the latter extended in application from the traditional "mery England", "mery moneth of May" to "mery oaten pipe", "mery London", "merry Cuckou", "Bacchus merry fruit". *Sweet* hovers between sense and sentiment in "sweete sight", "sweete home", "sweete poets", "sweete eventide", "sweete diversity", "sweet Alarmes" (of love) and the conventional "sweete sugred speaches", "sweete wordes like dropping hony"; in the very luscious *Virgils Gnat* it occurs about a dozen times, generally as a translator's addition but also as a rendering of both *dulcis* and *iucundus*. An even more adaptable epithet is *greedy*, which Spenser applies to each of the senses and to the mind, as instanced in "greedie mouths", "greedie eares", "greedie eye", "greedy lust", "greedy fancy", "greedy rage", "greedy speede", "greedy vengeance", "greedy t'understand". The fine sensuousness of "dim eielids", "cool violets", "smooth fields", the vivid image of "creeping deadly cold" are random specimens which might be multiplied indefinitely. Night is half personified through association with *silent, lingring, drouping, griesly, drery*. Prominent characters are denoted by their attributes: Gloriana is simply *great*; Amoret *fayre, lovely, gentle*; Florimell *famous, sorry, goodly*; Britomart *fayre, famous, noble, bold, blameless, stout*.

Spenser's free use of the compound epithet tends to restrain his natural diffuseness. The compression of familiar rhetorical conceits into vivid images like "harts close-bleeding book", "soule-enchaunting might", "hart-thrilling eies" adds speed and vigour by enforcing economy of words; and epic energy, Virgilian if not Homeric, animates "bitter-breathing windes", "long-wandring woe", "Spring-headed Hydres; and sea-shouldring Whales". No less effective is the static power of "blood-frosen hart", "self-pleasing pride", "cold congealed feare", "eye glutting gaine", "foolehappie oversight", "faint-heart fooles". The figures of "stoop gallant Age", "self-consuming care", of "hell-dreaded" magic and "light-shonning" theft supply notable instances of concrete symbolism admitted through compounding. The fine sensuousness of Ovid and his Elizabethan imitators appears in "milk-dropping goats", "bees-alluring thime", "lilly handed Liagore", "aire-cutting wings", "fayre pouldred skin", "Junoes Bird in her ey-spotted traine". "Yvie-winding trayle" and the Homeric "rosy fingred Morning" are commonplaces of the picturesque mode, *sunshyny*, *brass-scaly*, *golden fleecy* inventions in the new style of naïve rusticity. The force and distinction imparted to familiar attributes when compounded are sufficiently illustrated in "sweete slumbring deaw", "sweete-breathing Zephyrus", "the Mirrhe sweete-bleeding", "dead-living swayne", "dead-doing might", "dead-sleeping Poppy".

While Spenser's vocabulary preserves an even balance between polite and popular usage, in his syntax courtliness predominates. E.K. collates the ancient words of the *Calender* with "the knitting of them so short and intricate, and the whole Periode and compasse of speache so delight-some for the roundnesse, and so grave for the straunge-nesse". His further remarks upon the subject clarify this summary estimate:

For the knitting of sentences, whych they call the joynts and members therof, and for al the compasse of the speach, it is round without roughnesse, and learned without hardnes, such indeede as may be perceived of the leaste, understoode of the moste, but judged only of the learned. For what in most English wryters useth to be loose, and as it were ungyrt, in this Authour is well grounded, finely framed, and strongly trussed up together.

To confirm this last statement it is only necessary to contrast the crudity of Gascoigne, Tusser or other early Elizabethans with the ease and maturity of the New Poet. The "round-ness" or directness of the new style, as E.K. justly affirms, strikes the simplest intelligence but is properly appreciated only by those who understand its purport, the particular effect which it is designed to induce. For with Spenser the first consideration is tone and effect; the very object of his "rough and harsh terms" would have been defeated had they been accompanied by syntax likewise "rough and harsh", "heaps of huge wordes uphoorded hideously" after the manner of contemporary poetasters.

As a rule, therefore, Spenser admits such vagaries as ellipsis, syncope or apheresis only when pressed by the exigencies of verse or when deliberately affecting the "round" terms of colloquialism. Within these limits examples are numerous:

> They wont in the wind wagge their wrigle tayles.

> Seest howe brag yond Bullocke beares.

> That name of native syre did fowle upbrayd.

> Selfe have I worne out thrise threttie yeares.

> As carefull Nourse her child from falling oft does reare.[14]

The same rule would also cover a characteristic Spenserian idiom, the use of adjective for substantive:

> And mightie strong was turnd to feeble frayle.

> Gay without good is good hearts greatest loathing.[15]

Juggling with syntax is a more dangerous pastime than word coinage. Tradition would sanction the prolepses in

> And evill men, now dead, his deeds upbraid:

> That mote enlarge her living prayses, dead;[16]

but it is another matter when compression wrecks the whole grammatical structure:

> The Geaunt strooke so maynly mercilesse,
> That could have overthrowne a stony towre:
> And, were not hevenly grace that did him blesse,
> He had bene pouldred all as thin as flowre.[17]

Such lapses on the part of the New Poet into the old style are sufficiently rare to demand only passing notice. It is more profitable to study him in his natural element, as courtly maker of "lively hyperbolical amplification".

The aureate terms of the troubadours had been transmitted to the Elizabethans through the schools of both Chaucer and Petrarch, but with a difference. While the elder "Gothic" poets show little discrimination in their use of ornament, the Petrarchans seek to relate the part with the whole by expanding verbal into rhetorical figure. The oxymoron in Spenser's *dearest dread, deare foe, faire cruel, sad joy, false Fidessa faire, luckelesse lucky* can be paralleled in *Troilus and Criseyde* and other polite poetry of the same period. But by habitually inflating term to phrase or sentence he proves himself a true son of his age, subject to its limitations. Thus if the gnomic tag

> A dram of sweete is worth a pound of sowre

is saved through its wit, where the turn of thought is less distinctive the antithesis is liable to collapse into flat verbiage:

> The cruell worker of your kindly smarts.

> My chearefull day is turnd to chearelesse night.

> With mourning pyne I: you with pyning mourne.[18]

The same may be said of other rhetorical devices such as *epanorthosis*, or "correction", the happy use of which is noted by E.K. to the special credit of the New Poet:

> Nowe dead he is, and lyeth wrapt in lead,
> (O! why should Death on hym such outrage showe?)

> Why doe we longer live, (ah! why live we so long?)

> Was (O! what now availeth that I was?)
> Borne the sole daughter of an Emperour.

> "I love thilke lasse (alas! why doe I love?)
> And am forlorne, (alas! why am I lorne?)"

> Donwallo dyde, (for what may live for ay?)

> And verses vaine, (yet verses are not vaine.)[19]

In the last example the figure exposes its inherent weakness by reducing itself to absurdity. Such qualification, or reversal of argument, however serviceable to the orator, in poetry betrays itself as pleonasm of the most frigid and mechanical kind.

But rhetorical figure, judiciously selected and properly set, is a legitimate and effective poetic ornament, inseparable from the florid style of the courtly makers. This would generally apply to simple repetition, a favourite device with Spenser, who can invest it with a dramatic significance beyond the range of its traditional usage as elegiac convention:

> Then woe, and woe, and everlasting woe: (catastrophe).
> All full of love, and love, and love my deare: (irony).[20]

Anaphora—the recurrent phrase at the opening of successive lines,—used to excess throughout *Daphnaida*, is only to be expected of the plaintive Colin:

> And yet, alas! but now my spring begonne,
> And yet, alas! yt is already donne.
>
> Waile we the wight whose presence was our pryde;
> Waile we the wight whose absence is our carke.
>
> Thus is my sommer worne away and wasted,
> Thus is my harvest hastened all to rathe.[21]

But this likewise is not confined to elegy, serving also to mark the subdivision of verse periods, as in sonnet lvi and in lines 492–583 of *Colin Clouts Come Home Againe*, where each "nymph" is introduced by the same formula. Anaphora of this kind may be linked with antithesis to produce a quaint, prosaic effect not altogether unpleasing:

> Both were full loth to leave that needfull tent,
> And both full loth in darkenesse to debate;
> Yet both full liefe him lodging to have lent,
> And both full liefe his boasting to abate.[22]

A development from verbal repetition is the "turn", which, in Dryden's opinion, Spenser uses more happily than any other English poet. Two striking instances are sonnet lxxxi, a cycle of images revolving round the pivot word "fair", and lines 63–103 of *An Hymne of Heavenly Beautie*, where the argument is enforced by the regular interplay of "fair" with "far". A less artful form of the same figure is the simple pun or "traductio", the "translacing" of a word into "many shapes":

> Till then give leave to me, in pleasant mew
> To sport my muse, and sing my loves sweet praise.
>
> He onely fayre, and what he fayre hath made;
> All other fayre, lyke flowres, untymely fade.
>
> "Colin, my liefe, my life, how great a losse."
>
> We deeme of Death as doome of ill desert.
>
> Her doubtfull words made that reboubted knight
> Suspect her truth: yet since no'untruth he knew.[23]

To the decorative artist in words fine phrasing offers resources second only to those of vocabulary, but without the same freedom of invention. For whereas words are the image of the individual mind figures of composition are as borrowed plumes that become a personal possession only after long usage and considerable trimming. In two pieces— *Daphnaida* and *Astrophel*—Spenser has allowed convention to override poetic fury and the result is frigid and unsatisfactory. But it would be unreasonable on this ground generally to condemn the figurative style which is his normal mode of poetic expression. Many of the *Amoretti* are little more than amplifications of rhetorical figures: xxvi and the opening of xliii turn entirely upon antithesis, ix upon negative simile, xv, xviii, etc., upon balance of clause. But they are none the less choice specimens of their own kind, pretty fancies on a conventional framework. The same principle of decorum governs the speech of *The Faerie Queene*. The reader might well be struck with the singularly dramatic effect of

Mammon's hypercritical rhetoric or of Duessa's frigidity in addressing her paramour,

> Ah deare Sansjoy, next dearest to Sansfoy,
> Cause of my new griefe, cause of my new joy;
> Joyous to see his ymage in mine eye,
> And greevd to thinke how foe did him destroy,[24]

until he discovers that "Arcadianism" is the normal idiom of this artificial Faeryland, in which finely fashioned soliloquy or stichomythia affords welcome diversion from the noise of war:

> "O, but," (quoth she) "great griefe will not be tould,
> And can more easily be thought then said."
> "Right so," (quoth he) "but he that never would
> Could never: will to might gives greatest aid."
> "But griefe," (quoth she) "does greater grow displaid,
> If then it find not helpe, and breeds despaire."
> "Despaire breeds not," (quoth he) "where faith is staid."
> "No faith so fast," (quoth she) "but flesh does paire."
> "Flesh may empaire," (quoth he) "but reason can repaire."
>
> "But mine is not" (quoth she) "like other wownd;
> For which no reason can finde remedy."
> "Was never such, but mote the like be fownd,"
> (Said she) "and though no reason may apply
> Salve to your sore, yet love can higher stye
> Then reasons reach, and oft hath wonders donne."
> "But neither God of love nor God of skye
> Can doe" (saith she) "that which cannot be donne."
> "Things ofte impossible" (quoth she) "seeme, ere begonne."[25]

Poetic ornament, says the author of *The Arte of English Poesie* (1589), is of two sorts,

one to satisfie and delight th' eare onely by a goodly outward shew set upon the matter with wordes and speaches smothly and tunably running, another by certaine intendments or sence of such wordes and speaches inwardly working a stirre to the mynde. That first qualitie the Greeks called *Enargia*, of this word *argos*, because it geveth a glorious lustre and light. This latter they called *Energia*, of *ergon*, because it wrought with a strong and vertuous operation.[26]

Diction

The prevailing tone and character of Spenser's diction reflects the *enargia* of the poet who looks upon fine phrases as a lover, loads every rift with ore and never scruples to "abate the sternenesse" of his style,

> Mongst these sterne stounds to mingle soft delights.

In depicting the sensuous abandon of Clarion he has almost literally described the several stages of his own workmanship:

> There he arriving round about doth flie,
> From bed to bed, from one to other border,
> And takes survey, with curious busie eye,
> Of every flowre and herbe there set in order:
> Now this, now that, he tasteth tenderly,
> Yet none of them he rudely doth disorder,
> Ne with his feete their silken leaves deface,
> But pastures on the pleasures of each place.
>
> And evermore, with most varietie
> And change of sweetnesse, (for all change is sweete)
> He casts his glutton sense to satisfie,
> Now sucking of the sap of herbe most meete,
> Or of the deaw which yet on them does lie,
> Now in the same bathing his tender feete;
> And then he pearcheth on some braunch thereby,
> To weather him, and his moyst wings to dry.[27]

In like manner Spenser amasses words and phrases with the sole object of adding "lustre and Light" to his theme. His mistress' smile provides material for two sonnets (xxxix and xl), the ruddiness of Belphœbe's cheeks for a complete stanza, the introduction of Prince Arthur for nearly a hundred lines. In many cases such circumlocution is saved through its rhetorical force:

> At last, when fayling breath began to faint,
> And saw no meanes to scape, of shame affrayd,
> She set her downe to weepe for sore constraint;
> And to Diana calling lowd for ayde,
> Her deare besought to let her die a mayd.

Edmund Spenser

The goddesse heard; and suddeine, where she sate
Welling out streames of teares, and quite dismayd
With stony feare of that rude rustick mate,
Transformd her to a stone from stedfast virgins state.[28]

But the lure of "wordes and speaches tunably running" is a
dangerous snare, encouraging the prolixity and ornate redundance of polite poetry handsomely parodied by Chaucer
in *Troilus*; for no useful purpose, beyond the replenishment
of lacunae in verse, is served by such tags as "dearest dear",
"sweetest sweet", "I wot", or the artless verbiage of

Doth weepe full sore, and sheddeth tender teares:

Shewing us mercie (miserable crew!):

(Those trouts and pikes all others doo excell.):

That quite his hart from Guendolene remov'd,
From Guendolene his wife, though alwaies faithful prov'd.[29]

The length of Spenser's stanza and the eclectic nature of
his vocabulary increases this tendency to diffuseness, the
common characteristic of the school to which he belonged.
He never outgrew his Elizabethan taste for the cloying
luxuriance bequeathed by Virgil, Ovid and the Italian poets
to the authors of "sugared sonnets" or idylls such as *Venus
and Adonis*:

His palled face, impictured with death,
She bathed oft with teares, and dried oft:
And with sweet kisses suckt the wasting breath
Out of his lips like lilies pale and soft.

Yet would not let just vengeance on her light;
But rather let, instead thereof, to fall
Few perling drops from her faire lampes of light.[30]

In formal tributes like "November" or *Daphnaida*, written in
the interests of patrons, frigidity is to be expected; but this
would scarcely account for Spenser's complete failure to rise
to the occasion in *Astrophel*, which suggests either lack of
feeling or incapacity to express it. The wealth of intricate

figure and ornament that embroiders a simple percept even in his most effective pieces points to the same conclusion, implying a temperament acutely sensitive rather than profoundly emotional. At the same time it must be remembered that flamboyance, to an Elizabethan, was as natural a poetic idiom as epigram to an Augustan and colloquialism to a modernist. Where Spenser is most self-expressive often he is most ornate. The inner experiences that inspired the greater number of *Amoretti* are covered and concealed by layers of fine conceit and curious invention; the maker of *Epithalamion* reveals himself unmistakably in the treasures squandered upon his "endless moniment".

Nor is Spenser lacking in that other kind of "energy" (*energia*), without which his influence as poet's poet would inevitably have been much restricted. E.K. praises his style as "well grounded, finely framed, and strongly trussed up together". Both Sir Walter Raleigh and Sir Kenelm Digby considered him "the English Virgil" while Edward Phillips, prompted, perhaps, by his uncle John Milton, cites *The Faerie Queene* as a supreme exemplar of "Poetic *Energie*...which shines through the roughest, most unpolish't, and antiquated Language, and may happly be wanting in the most polite and reformed".[31] Sometimes it flashes from a single word or phrase pregnant with epic or dramatic vitality:

> Thunder, and lightning, and tempestuous fyre,
> The instruments of his avenging yre.
>
> Beside a bubling fountaine low she lay,
> Which shee increased with her bleeding hart.
>
> Pounching me with the butt end of his speare.
>
> How mortgaging their lives to Covetise.
>
> Pay to her usury of long delight.
>
> The cradle of her own creation.[32]

But as a rule the Spenserian idiom extends over a verse period and cannot adequately be represented by detached lines. In the vigorous colloquialism of *Mother Hubberds Tale* the "lustre and light" of "wordes and speaches tunably running" is entirely subordinate to the "strong and vertuous operation" of those "working a stirre to the mynde", a process that reaches its climax in the lines upon the pitiful state of poor suitors. The same may be said of many an epic passage in *The Faerie Queene*:

> As when that divelish yron Engin, wrought
> In deepest Hell, and framd by Furies skill,
> With windy Nitre and quick Sulphur fraught,
> And ramd with bollet rownd, ordaind to kill,
> Conceiveth fyre, the heavens it doth fill
> With thundring noyse, and all the ayre doth choke,
> That none can breath, nor see, nor heare at will,
> Through smouldry cloud of duskish stincking smoke;
> That th' only breath him daunts, who hath escapt the stroke.33

Such pieces carry more than a suggestion of Miltonic might, untempered by Milton's discrimination and secured chiefly through the massing of vivid and powerful imagery. And since might implies movement, where the action demands brevity the pace quickens:

> But the bold knight no whit thereat dismayd,
> But catching up in hand a ragged stone
> Which lay thereby (so fortune him did ayde)
> Upon him ran, and thrust it all attone
> Into his gaping throte, that made him grone
> And gaspe for breath, that he nigh choked was,
> Being unable to digest that bone;
> Ne could it upward come, nor downward passe,
> Ne could he brooke the coldnesse of the stony masse.34

On the other hand, energy "working a stir to the mind" may be equally evident in the slow march of accumulative figure:

> The gnawing envie, the hart-fretting feare,
> The vaine surmizes, the distrustfull showes,
> The false reports that flying tales doe beare,
> The doubts, the daungers, the delayes, the woes,
> The fayned friends, the unassured foes,
> With thousands more then any tongue can tell,
> Doe make a lovers life a wretches hell.35

Diction

This "potential energy" is particularly effective when sense is echoed by an abrupt change of speed, rapidity giving place to ponderous deliberation:

> Which well perceiving, that imperious boy
> Doth therwith tip his sharp empoisned darts,
> Which glancing through the eyes with countenance coy
> Rest not till they have pierst the trembling harts,
> And kindled flame in all their inner parts,
> Which suckes the blood, and drinketh up the lyfe,
> Of carefull wretches with consuming griefe.

> Thenceforth they playne, and make ful piteous mone
> Unto the author of their balefull bane:
> The daies they waste, the nights they grieve and grone,
> Their lives they loath, and heavens light disdaine;
> No light but that, whose lampe doth yet remaine
> Fresh burning in the image of their eye,
> That deigne to see, and seeing it still dye.[36]

The language of Spenser is the supreme achievement of Elizabethan poetic invention. Swayed by no law save that of decorum it supplies a perfect instrument for his theme, a make-believe vernacular for a make-believe world. "His delicious diction transports us to a fairy region whose inhabitants, we may imagine, eat cakes instead of bread. The language of the streets is not for such unearthly beings."[37] The peculiar effectiveness of this newly invented instrument lies in its range and flexibility. Between the *vox humana* of the more realistic passages in the *Calender*, *Mother Hubberds Tale* or *The Faerie Queene* and the *vox angelica* of *Epithalamion*, the *Hymnes* or the cantos of Mutability is almost every grade of tone and idiom. When rhapsody gives place to heroic argument the singing robe is doffed for a stage costume, set off by a language no less brilliant or vigorous but more mannered and distinguished by brave and glorious words that figure the semblance of antique usage. Only in the "very grave and profitable" sententiousness of *Complaints* and of certain episodes in other pieces where Spenser has attempted to express abstract thought without the aid of concrete allegory, does his grand style degenerate into bombast. Once he can find a pretext for description, words follow as naturally as the leaves from the tree and as varied in shape and colour. The nine hundred odd verses of *Colin Clouts Come Home Againe* combine all the different modes of the *Calender*— burlesque colloquialism, easy urbanity, fine rhapsody, courtly address. The ornate structure of *Prothalamion* is balanced by a pure, compact diction, familiar but by no means vulgar; the style of *Amoretti* changes perceptibly from number lx onwards, becoming simpler, more natural and more intense with the growing predominance of the personal note. In *The Faerie Queene* speech is as varied as subject-matter, ranging between the high heroics of the invocations that precede each book and the pure prose of "So ended he his tale, where I this canto end", between ornate hyperbole and the unobtrusive colloquialism of stanzas that hardly infringe the law of poetic diction propounded by the author of *Lyrical Ballads*:

> During the while that Guyon did abide
> In Mamons house, the Palmer, whom whyleare
> That wanton Mayd of passage had denide,
> By further search had passage found elsewhere;
> And, being on his way, approached neare
> Where Guyon lay in traunce; when suddeinly
> He heard a voyce that called lowd and cleare,
> "Come hither! hither! O, come hastily!"
> That all the fields resounded with the ruefull cry.[38]

In the stream of standard English and of semantic the work of Spenser is no more than a backwater, effecting little influence upon meaning and contributing but a single word, *blatant*, to the regular vocabulary. But from another aspect he may be said to have achieved his object, restoring "such good and natural English words as have been long time out of use and almost clean disherited"; for his influence upon English poetic diction, upon the vocabulary and usage that form the poet's peculiar monopoly, has proved greater than that of any single author, with the possible exception of Shakespeare and Milton. The outstanding characteristic of Shakespeare's diction is the dramatic energy of thought bursting into unexpected spontaneous expression. That of Milton conveys rather a sense of triumph in achievement as vast erudition reaches final and finished utterance. Spenser is more smooth, more equable, more monotonous than either. His diction is decorative rather than composite or associative, differing from Milton's as the music of Schubert from that of Bach, appealing through spontaneity and inherent suggestiveness, independent of source or application. It is this surface lustre that has made Spenser the poet's poet.

The anomalies in his language, wrested from their context, fail to satisfy any sort of analysis; and this defect has induced some purists to take their stand by Ben Jonson in denouncing such violation of established usage. Their case was fairly stated by Sir Thomas Culpepper:

> Some have thought to honour Antiquity by using such (words) as were obsolete, as hath been done by our famous *Spencer* and others, though the times past are no more respected by an unnecessary continuing of their words then if wee wore constantly the same trimming to our Cloaths as they did; for it is not Speech, but things which render antiquity venerable, besides the danger of expressing no Language, if as *Spencer* made use of *Chaucers*, we should likewise introduce his.[39]

Two hundred years later A. J. Ellis, in his classic treatise on English pronunciation, wrote in much stronger terms:

> The contrast between the genuine old tongue of Chaucer, or modern tongue of Shakespere, and the trumped up tongue of Spenser, which could never have been spoken at any time, is painful....It is sad that so great a poet should have put on such motley.[40]

Sad and painful it well may be to the grammarian, dismayed at the spurious forms, syntactical anomalies and distorted spelling that occur upon every page. But the vast majority of readers has been content to leave these curiosities in their proper place as inseparable from the fantastic device to which they belong. "His much frequenting of Chaucer's ancient words", wrote Francis Beaumont to Speght, "with his excellent imitation of diverse places in him, is not the least help that hath made him reach so high as many learned men do think that no poet, either French or Italian, deserves a second place under him". The association of Spenser's diction with that of Chaucer, despite the advertisement of E.K., is misleading, in view of the fundamental difference between an imitative, artificial vocabulary and one that is natural and current. But Beaumont's uncritical adulation hits nearer the mark than the hypercritical aspersions of Ellis, or the even less judicious statement of T. R. Lounsbury to the effect that, in contradistinction to Chaucer, Spenser "has never been able to make his vocabulary live, so far as it differed from the common vocabulary of his time".[41] For the diction of Spenser must be appraised as a whole, by the effectiveness with which it expresses the poetry of refuge to which it belongs. From this aspect his archaisms will appear, in the words of Henry Bradley, "the only fitting vehicle for his tone of thought and feeling".[42]

It was, above all, this perfect equipoise between thought and expression in Spenser that supplied a grammar of poetic art throughout the formative period of English poetry that extended from the Renaissance to the Romantic Revival. The language of his immediate successors was sufficiently near to his own to allow the free incorporation of his peculiarities without any general violation of customary usage. His influence upon Milton shows itself in the assimilation of odd phrases and images rather than in conscious imitation. Cases in point are "adamantine chains", "devilish engines", the adaptation of two lines from *Daphnaida*,

> O that so faire a flower so soone should fade,
> And through untimely tempest fall away,

at the opening of *On the Death of a Fair Infant*, verbal echoes from the *Hymnes* in Books I and II of *Paradise Lost* and numerous reminiscences from romantic episodes of *The Faerie Queene*. With the rapid development of language during the Augustan age Spenser receded into the obsolete past as the giant of a semi-barbarous age, and his diction, accordingly, ceased to be operative except as a source of artificiality, which appears first in clichés of the pastoral school and subsequently in larger imitations by "Spenserians". It was left to the romantics, with Chatterton at their head, to rediscover Spenser as not simply a source of amusement and pattern for trickery, but as the supreme artificer in words.

His daring experiment was justified in its results. The influence of his vocabulary comprises but a small part of his total contribution to the subsequent development of English poetry; yet in this alone he ranks with the highest. Several of his inventions have passed into the common property of English poetry. *Undersong*, for instance, was taken up by the pastoralists of the seventeenth and eighteenth centuries to be subsequently adopted by Coleridge, Keats and their successors. *Elphin* has been incorporated into the standard vocabulary. *Vermeil*, as a noun, was handed on from Giles Fletcher to Shenstone and thence to the romantics, the Lucretian "daedale earth" to Thomas Warton and Wordsworth. Far more numerous than these are Spenser's borrowings from older authors, words like *perceant, needments, lout, languorous, shallop*, which might easily have been lost but for this timely resuscitation, and through which his influence upon English poetic diction has proved most effective and enduring. The Spenserian echoes in Wordsworth's poems of 1807 are symptomatic of the change that led to the abandonment of the theories propounded in the preface of 1800. The archaic element in Shelley, represented in such words as *eyne, treen, glode, griding, swink, crudded, strook*, is derived mainly from Spenser. Keats' youthful excitement at the image "sea-shouldering whales" led to a close and exhaustive study of its inventor. But Spenser's diction as a whole is inseparable from the work for which it was created, and his experiment would not bear repetition. Even the best poems "in the manner of Spenser" like *The Castle of Indolence* or *The Schoolmistress* are no better than pretty travesties. His invention was copyright; like the girdle of Florimell it exposes the charlatan, fitting no one but its first and rightful owner.

CHAPTER VII

Imagery

A CONTINUOUS succession of authorities from Sir
William Davenant to M. Emile Legouis has endorsed
the view of the old lady who, after hearing Pope read
a canto of *The Faerie Queene*, remarked that he had been con-
ducting her through a picture gallery. Leigh Hunt went so
far as to catalogue the collection, assigning each exhibit to an
appropriate master in schools that range from Michael Angelo
to Claude Lorraine. In their enthusiasm for the principle
"Ut pictura poesis" some of the earlier critics undoubtedly
exaggerated this aspect of Spenser's descriptive art, which is
often too literary or too conventional to fall within the scope
of true picturesque. But the fact remains that many of his
pieces are composed largely of images or concepts open to
criticism in terms of visual art. The formality of *Amoretti*
from time to time gives place to vivid illustrations like that of
the hunter in number lxvii, and the feeling which inspired
Epithalamion finds expression through visual rather than
emotional imagery. The puppet figures of the *Calender* are
characterised through their setting, while the continuous
allegory of *The Faerie Queene* falls into a series of moving
pageants like the House of Pride, the Bower of Bliss or
"Epithalamion Thamesis".

But Spenser never squanders word-painting for its own
sake, confining its usage to the illustration of some larger
objective. The predominance of allegory throughout his
scenes and portraits would probably account for the comparison frequently drawn between his art and that of Rubens,
with whom, in other respects, he has little in common. The
pictures of Una, of the Seasons or the Seven Deadly Sins are

nothing if not symbolical and allegory alone could justify the
admission of figures so monstrous and repellant as Error and
the Blatant Beast. If Spenser ever approaches the megalo-
mania of Rubens this must be attributed to the same cause.
Whether his subject be pageantry or portraiture every particular is conditioned by the symbolic purport of the whole.
The vulgar luxuriance of the House of Pride as contrasted
with the austere simplicity of the House of Holiness spells a
corresponding difference in temper and disposition. Glory,
the prime motif of *The Faerie Queene*, requires a setting in
broad daylight, with bold outlines and colours radiant in the
splendour of the sun. Night pieces almost invariably spell
mischief—bad dreams, illicit traffic with the underworld,
treacherous intrigue against unsuspecting guests; and Prince
Arthur speaks for all law-abiding subjects of Gloriana in his
bitter apostrophe to

> Night! thou foule Mother of annoyaunce sad,
> Sister of heavie death, and nourse of woe.[1]

Even the wedded lovers of *Epithalamion* who might be
expected to desire "secret dark" for their "sweet snatches of
delight" welcome the cheerful beams of Cynthia,

> she that never sleepes,
> But walkes about high heaven al the night.[2]

Spenser is the poet of daylight as Chapman of darkness. To
the one, night is a portent of evil, "baleful", "drery", "sad",
only endurable at the thought of approaching day; to the
other, it is a liberator, "loosing his waking soul". In either
case, as in *L'Allegro* and *Il Penseroso*, the impression is mental
and figurative rather than visual.

In his care for "general properties and large appearances"
Spenser differs from the old romancers as the grand style of
the Renaissance from the piecemeal art of the mediæval
window or fresco. The instinct for pure description that

prevails throughout such pieces as *Virgils Gnat* or *Muiopotmos* is everywhere controlled by a sense of proportion and an eye for total effect. The success of Spenser's draftsmanship, as compared with that of all his English predecessors, including Chaucer, may be partly attributed to the recent development of painting, sculpture and stagecraft. Chaucer excels in his use of the odd and unexpected—sly touches of personality, passing comments, minute strokes of detail like the inscription on Madame Eglantine's ring or the widow's one sheep called Malle. Formality in the design or structure of a word-portrait would be foreign to his purpose. His larger pieces, like those of his original William de Lorris, are catalogues of massed particulars in which he runs breathlessly from item to item, linked only by the formula "I saw"; and even the figures of his foregrounds—Venus in *The Parliament of Fowls* or Alcestis in *The Legend of Good Women*—are little more than summary sketches:

> Her gilte heres with a golden thred
> Y-bounden were, untrussed as she lay,
> And naked from the breste unto the hed
> Men might hir seen; and sothly for to say,
> The remenaunt was well kevered to my pay,
> Right with a subtil kerchef of Valence,
> Ther nas no thikker cloth of no defence.
>
> And she was clad in real habite grene;
> A fret of gold she hadde next her heer,
> And upon that a white crowne she beer,
> With flourouns smale, and I shal not lye,
> For al the worlde ryght as a daysye
> Y-corouned is with white leves lyte,
> So were the flourouns of hire coroune white;
> For of o perle, fyne, oriental,
> Hire white coroune was i-maked al,
> For which the white coroune above the grene
> Made hire lyke a daysie for to sene,
> Considered eke hir fret of golde above.[3]

Edmund Spenser

Very different is Spenser's study of Acrasia:

> Upon a bed of roses she was layd,
> As faint through heat, or dight to pleasant sin;
> And was arayd, or rather disarayd,
> All in a vele of silke and silver thin,
> That hid no whit her alablaster skin,
> But rather shewd more white, if more might bee:
> More subtile web Arachne cannot spin;
> Nor the fine nets, which oft we woven see
> Of scorched deaw, do not in th' ayre more lightly flee.
>
> Her snowy brest was bare to ready spoyle
> Of hungry eies, which n'ote therewith be fild;
> And yet, through languour of her late sweet toyle,
> Few drops, more cleare then Nectar, forth distild,
> That like pure Orient perles adowne it trild;
> And her faire eyes, sweet smyling in delight,
> Moystened their fierie beames, with which she thrild
> Fraile harts, yet quenched not: like starry light,
> Which, sparckling on the silent waves, does seeme
> more bright.[4]

Chaucer's portraits serve their purpose. Alcestis enters as leader to the chorus of Cupid's saints, Venus as a principal in the festive pageant; but it is needless to waste words upon them, so they are dismissed with the few plain strokes of the mediæval draftsman. Spenser, on the other hand, develops his study with the utmost care and deliberation, correlating every stroke, every figure, verbal or visual, in the execution of the whole.

His word-pictures emanate from a larger poetic concept, rooted in allegory or convention; the most graphic are similes that serve to illustrate some action or state of mind. For Spenser has far too profound an understanding of his art to seek to usurp the function of the painter and accordingly he admits only such detail as is requisite for the poetic effect. The impression of variegated brilliance in Clarion's wings is conveyed with the minimum of specific word-painting:

> Lastly his shinie wings as silver bright,
> Painted with thousand colours, passing farre

Imagery

All Painter's skill, he did about him dight:
Not halfe so manie sundrie colours arre
In Iris bowe; ne heaven doth shine so bright,
Distinguished with manie a twinckling starre;
Nor Iunoes Bird in her ey-spotted traine
So many goodly colours doth containe.[5]

Marlowe, Keats or Morris devote far more attention to the exact details of colour. Spenser subordinates it to light and shade, noting the detail only as an incidental after the complete picture has already shaped itself in his imagination. The gold and silver that invariably adorn his pageantry are illuminants rather than pigments and none the less dazzling when they scintillate from an untinted surface:

His seahorses did seeme to snort amayne,
And from their nosethrilles blow the brynie streame,
That made the sparckling waves to smoke agayne,
And flame with gold; but the white fomy creame
Did shine with silver, and shoot forth his beame.[6]

Their associative meanings—gold as a symbol of worth, silver as suggestive of sound—are commonplaces of Petrarchan poetry, which supplies numberless parallels to the golden armour of Gloriana's knights, the silver fringe and hemming of their garments, ladies' locks "like wyrie gold", "silver-streaming rivers", the silver voice of Belphœbe breaking "twixt the perles and rubies". Where Spenser does specify colours it is often merely to enforce the contrast between them:

the pure snow, with goodly vermill stayne.

deckt with blossoms dyde in white and red.

The greene shield dyde in dolorous vermell.

in his silver shield
He bore a bloodie Crosse.

Seest how fresh my flowers bene spredde,
Dyed in Lilly white and Cremsin redde,
With leaves engrained in lusty greene;
Colours meete to clothe a mayden Queene?[7]

They are always "meet", blended with the decorum proper to allegory or convention. Red, crimson and scarlet cover a wide range of usage, from purely expletive association with "roses", "cheekes", "blood", "berries" to the finer discrimination of "cremosin coronet", "cremosin ray", "a red floodgate", "the rose engrained in pure scarlet die". "Purple", translating *purpureus*, "bright", in "purple wings", "purple hair" (of morn) is symbolical in "purple pall", purely visual in "purple blood". Green, the prevailing colour of the *Calender* and of many episodes in *The Faerie Queene*, bears figurative value in "yeares greene", "greene wounds" and the "green hair" of the Naiads at the marriage of Thames and Medway. Custom and tradition supply Spring and Autumn with their green and yellow garments, Duessa with her scarlet robe, Una with her white lamb, Tristram with a jacket of Lincoln green. Speranza's symbolical blue dress, the ape's blue jacket in *Mother Hubberds Tale* and the "blew silk riband" that binds the lover's garland in *Amoretti* are likewise articles of uniform rather than personal possessions.

The sense of harmony, of relation between part and whole, already noted as a characteristic of Spenser's imagery is no less conspicuous in its assemblage. The progressive episodes of *Prothalamion*, the ornate figures of "April" compose a single allegory at unity with itself, the vignettes of *Epithalamion* revolve in perfect equipoise around a single basic emotion. The studies of Acrasia amid her paramours, of Amoret in the lap of Womanhood encircled by Graces have the firm outline and statuesque rhythm of sculpture. Other pieces, falling into successive scenes of a common pattern and texture, approximate more to the art of tapestry, which directly inspires two passages in *Muiopotmos* (277–336) and *The Faerie Queene*, III, xi (29–46). Theatrical episodes like the fight between George and the dragon, the capture of Serena, the dance of the Graces, the contention for the belt of Florimell are executed with all the skill of a master producer in balancing gesture, figure and spectacle. A typical instance of Spenser's word-pageantry, presenting features in common with those of all the visual arts, is the interlude of Una's sojourn with the satyrs, which can be lifted from its context undamaged, as an episode complete in itself. The sensational prelude—an attempted rape—occasions the antimasque of fauns and satyrs "dauncing in a rownd" and rushing to the rescue. Tragedy now gives way to comedy as they persuade the apprehensive heroine to follow them and conduct her "as Queene with olive girlond cround" in triumphal procession to the accompaniment of a shepherd's song:

> And all the way their merry pipes they sound,
> That all the woods with doubled Eccho ring;
> And with their horned feet doe weare the ground,
> Leaping like wanton kids in pleasant Spring.
> So towards old Sylvanus they her bring;
> Who, with the noyse awaked, commeth out
> To weet the cause, his weake steps governing
> And aged limbs on cypresse stadle stout,
> And with an yvie twyne his waste is girt about.[8]

But Sylvanus can make nothing of the fair stranger, whereupon they all forsake their old loves the Hamadryads and fall worshipping her as goddess of the wood. In rhythmic grace, movement and design the whole piece is flawless.

Lavish imagery, verbal or conventional as well as visual, is Spenser's natural mode of poetic utterance. He cannot dispense with figure in representing even so simple a natural phenomenon as the time of day:

> fayre Aurora from the deawy bed
> Of aged Tithone gan herselfe to reare
> With rosy cheekes, for shame as blushing red.

> Hyperion, throwing foorth his beames full hott,
> Into the highest top of heaven gan clime,
> And, the world parting by an equall lott,
> Did shed his whirling flames on either side.

> now the golden Hesperus
> Was mounted high in top of heaven sheene,
> And warnd his other brethren joyeous
> To light their blessed lamps in Joves eternall hous.

>   Aldeboran was mounted hye
> Above the shinie Cassiopeias chaire,
> And all in deadly sleepe did drowned lye.[9]

This decorative art, together with the leisureness of his verse
and the lure of fine phrases, constantly impedes the progress
of his argument. The allusive circumlocution of "The son of
Thetis", "the bird that may the sun endure" often extends
over several lines. At nightfall Una and her lover feel
sleepy:

> The drouping night thus creepeth on them fast;
> And the sad humor loading their eyeliddes,
> As messenger of Morpheus, on them cast
> Sweet slombring deaw, the which to sleep them biddes.[10]

Drinking from an enchanted fountain, the Red Cross Knight
turns faint:

> Eftsoones his manly forces gan to fayle,
> And mightie strong was turnd to feeble frayle.
> His chaunged powres at first them selves not felt;
> Till crudled cold his corage gan assayle,
> And cheareful bloud in fayntnes chill did melt,
> Which like a fever fit through al his bodie swelt.[11]

Such embellishment of a simple idea with a tissue of elaborate
imagery, which no other poet has employed so successfully, is
often the means of imparting new vitality to conventional
figure, as may be seen by contrasting the frigidity of the first
two following specimens with the Spenserian animation of
the last:

> Thrise he assayd it from his foote to draw,
> And thrise in vaine to draw it did assay.

> And thrise his hand to kill her did upreare,
> And thrise he drew it backe; so did at last forbeare.

Imagery

He, tombling downe, with gnashing teeth did bite
The bitter earth, and bad to lett him in
Into the baleful house of endlesse night,
Where wicked ghosts doe waile their former sin.[12]

Frequently, however, Spenser has been content to reproduce the commonplaces of poetic ornament. Many of the sonnets consist of little more than excerpts from the open text-book of figure and conceit. The lover is a captive, a ship adrift in the storm, a victim smitten with the fiery dart of affection. His mistress is cold as ice, a tyrant, a panther or tiger, more cruel than lion to the helpless lamb, yet more to be desired than costly jewels. Such refurbishing of familiar devices was the pastime of an age that recognised no patent law protective of poetic invention; and most of the imagery of *Amoretti* has been tracked to its sources in Ronsard or Desportes, Petrarch or Tasso, the last of whom supplied the whole material of sonnet lxxxiii. Within these confines individual talent can but give new turns to old conceits, like that of the golden hair-net entrapping the lover, of the graces seated on Belphœbe's eyelids, of the angels peeping from around the altar at the nuptial ceremony. Set amid such a paradise of dainty devices as *Amoretti*, such a riot of gorgeous pageantry as *Epithalamion*, the central character is barely distinguishable. Sensuality is rendered innocuous through analysis and sublimation into metaphor. Despite the objective representation of "unquiet thought" in sonnet ii, *Amoretti* as a whole hardly come within the category of metaphysical poetry, their interest centering not so much upon the flux of mind or emotion as on the images suggested by the lover's state. Even in the *Hymnes* the abstract themes of love and beauty give place from the outset to concrete myth, metaphor and allegory.

For Spenser's use of metaphor is not merely conventional. It springs from the inner recesses of a poetic consciousness that instinctively transforms all perception to symbolic representation. It extends from simple verbal figure—"But now

weake age had dimd his candle light"—to complex visual
imagery. In the universal game of make-believe the rôle of
poet is abandoned for one livelier and more picturesque. He
is a ploughman resting his team or turning them back to a
neglected furrow, a mariner gladly beholding the port,
striking sail, landing his passengers and leaving his ship in
harbour for repair. In like strain Britomart, lamenting the
hopelessness of her quest, consoles herself by weaving a
tissue of metaphor, a supplication for rescue from the tempest
that tosses her "feeble bark":

> For els my feeble vessell, crazd and crackt
> Through thy strong buffets and outrageous blowes,
> Cannot endure, but needes it must be wrackt
> On the rough rocks, or on the sandy shallowes,
> The whiles that love it steres, and fortune rowes:
> Love, my lewd Pilott, hath a restlesse minde;
> And fortune, Boteswaine, no assurance knowes;
> But saile withouten starres gainst tyde and winde:
> How can they other doe, sith both are bold and blinde?[13]

Elaborated to this degree the verbal figure of metaphor approaches the larger concept of allegory and the one merges
imperceptibly into the other. Cupid bridling and bestriding
Marinell is hardly less vital than "bitter Penance with an iron
whip". Scudamour, at the House of Care, occupies a veritable no-man's land between fancy and imagination:

> For they for nought would from their worke refraine,
> Ne let his speeches come unto their eare,
> And eke the breathfull bellowes blew amaine,
> Like to the Northern winde, that none could heare:
> These Pensifenesse did move; and Sighes the bellows
>   weare.[14]

Even without the aid of such personification, which belongs
strictly to allegory, the effect of prolonged metaphor is often
exceedingly powerful and graphic, as shown in two passages
from the tragic history of Malbecco:

The sight whereof in his congealed flesh
Infixt such secrete sting of greedy lust,
That the drie withered stocke it gan refresh,
And kindled heat that soone in flame forth brust,
The driest wood is soonest burnt to dust.

He from that deadly throw made no defence,
But to the wound his weake heart opened wyde:
The wicked engine through false influence
Past through his eies, and secretly did glyde
Into his heart, which it did sorely gryde.[15]

The whole moral of Book II is enforced by the concluding stanza, which shows the complete process of metaphor crystallising into symbol:

Saide Guyon; "See the mind of beastly man
That hath so soone forgot the excellence
Of his creation, when he life began,
That now he chooseth with vile difference
To be a beast, and lacke intelligence!"
To whom the Palmer thus: "The donghill kinde
Delightes in filth and fowle incontinence.
Let Gryll be Gryll, and have his hoggish minde!"[16]

Whilst metaphor serves Spenser as a way of approach to allegory, simile offers him a means of escape. In their simpler and less subtle usage the two figures are closely related, both supplying favourite spices to the banquets of Ovid and Petrarch; and as such Spenser is often content to employ them. Yellow hair is like "wyrie gold", "snowy lockes" like hoar frost bespangling the mossy branches of the oak, Irena revives as a withered rose at the first drops of rain, Britomart is "trew in love as Turtle to her mate", the lover in *Amoretti* "lyke a young fawne, that late hath lost the hynd". Sugared comparisons fall thick and fast throughout the four stanzas to Cynthia dovetailed in *Colin Clouts Come Home Againe*:

Her words were like a streame of honny fleeting,
The which doth softly trickle from the hive,
Hable to melt the hearers heart unweeting,
And eke to make the dead againe alive.

> Her deeds were like great clusters of ripe grapes,
> Which load the braunches of the fruitfull vine;
> Offring to fall into each mouth that gapes,
> And fill the same with store of timely wine.
> Her lookes were like beames of the morning Sun,
> Forth looking through the windowes of the East,
> When first the fleecie cattell have begun
> Upon the perled grasse to make their feast.
> Her thoughts are like the fume of Frankincence,
> Which from a golden Censer forth doth rise,
> And throwing forth sweet odours mounts fro thence
> In rolling globes up to the vauted skies.[17]

For the delectable process of loading rift with ore the resources of simile are boundless. Its proximity and appropriateness to allegory are sufficiently indicated by the comparison of "idle thoughtes and fantasies" that buzz around Phantaste's chamber with

> many swarmes of Bees assembled round,
> After their hives with honny do abound,[18]

or the dreadful portrayal of Jealousy, adapted from Ariosto—allegory, metaphor and simile in one:

> Which when Malbecco saw, out of the bush
> Upon his handes and feete he crept full light,
> And like a Gote emongst the Gotes did rush;
> That, through the helpe of his faire hornes on hight,
> And misty dampe of misconceyving night,
> And eke through likenesse of his gotish beard,
> He did the better counterfeite aright:
> So home he marcht emongst the horned heard,
> That none of all the Satyres him espyde or heard.[19]

Simile admits within the phantom walls of faerie the whole range of human experience. The vivid suggestiveness of Envy's lips,   Like raw lether, pale and blew,

of Geryoneo's teeth,

> Like to a rancke of piles that pitched are awry,

of Arthur, wrapt in "silver slomber",

> Like to the Evening starre adorn'd with deawy ray,[20]

strike as the gleam of daylight through a broken stained glass window or as open air after the dankness of an ancient interior. With the same sense of relief we recognise Spenser the gentleman farmer in the figure of Calidore withstanding the minions of Crudor as a steer beats at the flies with his tail, of Slander backbiting Arthur as a cur snaps at the pebble thrown by a passing stranger, of Scudamour dumbfounded,

> like to a mazed steare
> That yet of mortall stroke the stound doth beare,[21]

of gold "lurking privily" within the arras at the House of Busirane,

Like a discolourd Snake, whose hidden snares
Through the greene gras his long bright burnisht back declares.[22]

But the most distinctive of all Spenser's pictorial devices is the extended epic simile which, under the influence of the classical poets and their Italian imitators, he was the first to naturalise in English poetry. Originally inherited from an age when war and its accompaniments were an everyday affair, in the more sophisticated epic of later times this figure still serves to maintain at least the semblance of relation between ideal and actual by reducing the demi-gods of high heroic argument to the level of common clay. In Homer the process is unnecessary. A primitive people, with whom war is inseparable from domestic life, would see nothing violent in the transition from the wounded Menelaus to the Mæonian ivory-stainer. Dante, who first introduced the epic simile into modern poetry, stands in line with Homer, since the strength and very essence of his cosmogony lies in his assurance of its actuality and of the exact correspondence, in every detail, between the two worlds on either side of the grave. But Spenser and Milton belong to a different category. Their arguments, of "painted forgery rather than matter of just memory", of "things unattempted yet in prose or rhyme" can be related with the things of this world only indirectly. To both, accordingly, the simile offers a means of escape from shadow to substance and of fitful awakening from the poet's dream to the realities of work-a-day existence. The opening stanzas of *The Faerie Queene* transport us to a time and region utterly remote from human experience. We know not where we are nor whither we are bound. We have met no one but an outlandish knight, with a mysterious veiled mistress, and a loathly monster, with her more loathly brood. But suddenly the phantasmagoria is lifted, when an unexpected glimpse of "old Father Nilus", of "gentle shepherd in sweete eventide" gives to airy nothings a local habitation and a name. The myth of Diana and Faunus, encircled by the even less substantial pageant of cosmic beings preparing for the trial of Mutability, is forgotten at the sight of a housewife catching a beast in the act of despoiling her pans of cream. The whole fabric of Faerie momentarily collapses at the poignant figure of

> The loving mother, that nine monethes did beare
> In the deare closett of her painefull syde
> Her tender babe, it seeing safe appeare,[23]

or at the telling home touch from Kilcolman in 1595:

> Like as a wayward childe, whose sounder sleepe
> Is broken with some fearefull dreames affright,
> With froward will doth set him selfe to weepe,
> Ne can be stild for all his nurses might,
> But kicks, and squals, and shriekes for fell despight;
> Now scratching her, and her loose locks misusing,
> Now seeking darkenesse, and now seeking light,
> Then craving sucke, and then the sucke refusing.[24]

Milton makes heavier demands. Hell with its fallen angels is a tougher proposition than Faeryland with its knights and bogeys, and the huge Leviathan of the first simile is little nearer our reach than the Prince of Darkness. But very soon afterwards we begin to recognise our bearings in the portrayal of the Tuscan artist on the slopes of Fiesole and of the autumnal leaves in Vallombrosa; and at a later stage, as Sir Walter Raleigh well remarked, how gladly we escape from Eden to rest "among the pleasant villages and farms".

For the simile allows a directness of self-expression denied to the poet so long as he pursues his flight above the Aonian mount. The Spenserian landscape is too fanciful and idealised to admit any distinctive features beyond the vague impression of woods and plains and flowers unfading in a temperate clime, of fountains and rivers that sweetly echo the fall of the verse. For more minute particulars we must look to the word-pictures of interspersed similes, which cover so wide a range as to supply specimens for almost every section of *England's Parnassus*. One feature common to them all is extreme susceptibility to light and shade. After the continued intrusion of mythological figures for dawn and sunset it is startling to read of Britomart's golden hair,

> Like as the shining skie in summers night,
> What time the dayes with scorching heat abound,
> Is creasted all with lines of firie light,
> That it prodigious seemes in common peoples sight.[25]

Such brevity is exceptional. As a rule the strokes are more delicate and the impression is evolved with greater deliberation, gradually spreading itself over a long verse period. False Florimell fades

> As when the daughter of Thaumantes faire
> Hath in the watry cloud displayed wide
> Her goodly bow, which paints the liquid ayre,
> That all men wonder at her colours pride;
> All suddenly, ere one can looke aside,
> The glorious picture vanisheth away
> Ne any token doth thereof abide.[26]

Touches of local colour impart new distinction and individuality to familiar objects. The Homeric figure of gnats rising at dusk becomes an impression from the Bog of Allen,

and many other pieces are minute records of atmospheric
effects typical of Kilcolman:

> As, when a foggy mist hath overcast
> The face of heven, and the cleare ayre engroste,
> The world in darkenes dwels; till that at last
> The watry Southwinde, from the seabord coaste
> Upblowing, doth disperse the vapour lo'ste,
> And poures it selfe forth in a stormy showre.[27]

Nothing short of direct observation could have inspired the
following graphic study of summer drought:

> Like as in sommers day, when raging heat
> Doth burne the earth and boyled rivers drie,
> That all brute beasts, forst to refraine fro meat,
> Doe hunt for shade, where shrowded they may lie,
> And, missing it, faine from themselves to flie;
> All travellers tormented are with paine:
> A watry cloud doth overcast the skie,
> And poureth forth a sudden shoure of raine,
> That all the wretched world recomforteth againe.[28]

Such accuracy over detail is especially evident in similes
drawn from animal life. The "cruell, craftie Crocodile" that
beguiles unwary travellers is a commonplace of fictitious
natural history, and Homer, Virgil or Ovid may have suggested the comparison between the stricken Marinell and the
sacrificial ox. But the first-hand knowledge of the husbandman appears in the sketches of a steer bound down by the
ploughman, of a mad bitch raving and snapping at everything in her way, of two rams stunned at a charge and "for-
getfull of the hanging victory", of a bull, driven frantic by
mastiffs and by the cur at his heels,

> bellowing disdaine,
> That all the forest quakes to heare him rore.[29]

The landowner in a hostile country surrounded by marauders
must certainly have known the value of dogs; but in heroic
poetry the dog is ever the oppressor and no match for his

victim, whom he can withstand only when placed at an unfair
advantage. Two similes are drawn from the popular sport
of bear baiting, another depicts a pack of watch-dogs chasing
a bear from the hives. Envy and detraction gird at Artegall
like sheep-dogs chasing a wolf; Atin reviles Guyon

> As Shepheardes curre, that in darke eveninges shade
> Hath tracted forth some salvage beastes trade;[30]

six knights of Malecasta attack one opponent

> Like dastard Curres that, having at a bay
> The salvage beast embost in wearie chace,
> Dare not adventure on the stubborne pray,
> Ne byte before, but rome from place to place
> To get a snatch when turned is his face.[31]

On the ways and habits of birds Spenser is as well informed
as his own Tristram, whose interest in falconry is all that
might be expected of an Elizabethan courtier:

> Ne is there hauke which mantleth her on pearch,
> Whether high towring or accoasting low,
> But I the measure of her flight doe search,
> And all her pray and all her diet know.[32]

He notes, by simile, the spectacle of the buzzard attacking a
bird too heavy for it, compelled to descend and fight with its
victim, of the hawk freed from bells and jesses, delighting in
her unaccustomed liberty, of a falcon on the remount after
"failing of her souse full neare". With close attention he has
watched the falcon as it swoops upon a brood of ducks in the
flags, the partridge escaping from the hawk only to be de-
voured by spaniels awaiting it below, the wild bird pruning
its feathers as it ventures forth from the cave that long has
sheltered it. Only a poet with his eye on his object could
have written:

> As when a cast of Faulcons make their flight
> At an Herneshaw, that lyes aloft on wing,
> The whyles they strike at him with heedlesse might,
> The warie foule his bill doth backward wring;
> On which the first, whose force her first doth bring,

Edmund Spenser

Her selfe quite through the bodie doth engore,
And falleth downe to ground like senselesse thing;
But th'other, not so swift as she before,
Fayles of her souse, and passing by doth hurt no more.33

Lastly the eagle, symbol of majesty, "soring through his wide
Empire of the aire", suggests several notable figures, in-
cluding the magnificent simile echoed by Shakespeare in
Henry IV, Part 1:

As Eagle, fresh out of the ocean wave,
Where he hath lefte his plumes all hory gray,
And deckt himself with fethers youthly gay,
Like Eyas hauke up mounts unto the skies,
His newly-budded pineons to assay,
And marveiles at himselfe stil as he flies.34

The sea and its associations inspire Spenser, as they have
inspired all the greater English poets, but with something of
the mingled terror and fascination expressed by Colin at his
home-coming. It is the symbol of elemental nature at war
with man, and familiar analogies, old as poetry, between
mortal combat and a mast blown down by the tempest, a ship
breasting the waves or hurled upon the rocks offer a special
appeal to an age when

Bold men, presuming life for gaine to sell,
Dare tempt that gulf, and in those wandring stremes
Seek waies unknowne, waies leading down to hell.35

The monotony of heroic argument from time to time is
broken by the interposition of graphic sea pieces, in which the
object of description becomes more vital than the individuals
with whom it is compared:

As a tall ship tossed in troublous seas,
Whom raging windes, threatning to make the pray
Of the rough rockes, doe diversly disease,
Meetes two contrarie billowes by the way,
That her on either side doe sore assay,
And boast to swallow her in greedy grave;
Shee, scorning both their spights, does make wide way,
And with her brest breaking the fomy wave,
Does ride on both their backs, and faire her self doth save.36

Imagery

The figures of "two warlike Brigandines" ramming and grappling bespeak their age, presenting scenes which their author must frequently have witnessed when engaged in active service. Others depict the mariner striking his sails, veering his mainsheet or consulting his card and compass, when the fog has "cover'd heaven with hideous dreriment". The joy of reunion after long parting suggests an animated picture derived, perhaps, from intercourse with the seamen who frequented the riverside within a few yards of East Smithfield:

> Much like, as when the beaten marinere,
> That long hath wandred in the Ocean wide,
> Ofte soust in swelling Tethys saltish teare;
> And long time having tand his tawney hide
> With blustring breath of Heaven, that none can bide,
> And scorching flames of fierce Orions hound;
> Soone as the port from far he has espide,
> His chearfull whistle merily doth sound,
> And Nereus crownes with cups; his mates him pledg around.[37]

It comes as something of a shock to recall that the occasion of this lively scene, even to the finishing stroke, is Una's meeting (as she supposes) with her long-lost love. But such freedom in the development of figure and imagery through a train of attendant associations is the special privilege of the pageant maker and all in keeping with the wayward conduct of romance.

Spenser's sound imagery is as varied and flexible as the pageantry which it accompanies. Faeryland is full of noises, not always so innocuous as those of Prospero's island. Would-be intruders might well be scared from Merlin's cave by the weird cacophony of clanking chains, rumbling cauldrons and groaning spirits that reverberates against the hollow rocks. At the House of Care Scudamour cannot sleep for the din of hammers and bellows, the howling of dogs, the shrieking of cocks and owls. The Blatant Beast, with his tongue of dogs, cats, tigers and detractors, is far more loathly to hear than to behold; on the other hand no word portrayal could so aptly denote the gentle instinct of the "wild man" as the "soft murmure and confused sound of senselesse wordes" that proceeds from his lips. The stronghold of Acrasia, reminiscent of Homer, Ovid and Tasso, abounds in wonders of every kind—mermaids, strange birds and beasts, flowery meads, wanton maids of ravishing beauty—calculated to startle and delight the beholder. But even to a Guyon sand-blind the experience of visiting these baleful quarters would have been memorable enough. He would still have heard the thunder of waves in the whirlpool of Decay, the roar of sea monsters, the screech of ill-boding birds, the bellowing of uncouth beasts; and after so harsh a prelude he might well have been enchanted by the Syren's song, the "straunge kinde of harmony" in the treble whistle of Zephyrus—which proves dangerously alluring, even as it is—the concord of "birdes, voices, instruments, windes, waters", modulating into a "lovely lay" on the text of "Carpe diem".

Sound emanating from unseen sources will often add to dramatic tension, especially when it precedes the rise of the curtain. Braggadochio and Trompart fleeing to the woods after robbing Malbecco are filled with terror on hearing the shrieks and bagpipes of the satyrs, and in the delectable episode of Colin and Calidore before any figures appear interest is aroused at the unexpected sound of the pipe and of "many feet fast thumping the hollow ground". Even when the source is visible the suggestion of confused noise—the "doleful shrieks" of the forsaken Muses, the wails of damned souls beside Phlegeton or the cries of the hungry cannibals at the sight of Serena—will often serve to convey what no visual image could depict. The entry of Canacee is greeted by a storm of enthusiasm suggesting a characteristic stroke of contemporary local colour:

> All suddenly they heard a troublous noyes,
> That seemd some perilous tumult to desine,
> Confusd with womens cries and shouts of boyes,
> Such as the troubled Theatres oftimes annoyes.[38]

Imagery

The sinister silence pervading the unholy House of Busirane is suddenly broken by a burst of thunder, an earthquake and a hurricane that rattles every door and shakes the whole edifice to its foundations. The hapless cry of an unseen captive is generally a prelude to enfranchisement and reconciliation. Belphœbe, rescuing Æmylia,

> Ne creature saw, but hearkned now and then
> Some litle whispering, and soft groning sound;[39]

Una suffers the torment of hearing the groans of her penitent lover, whom she can neither see nor aid; and Marinell at long last is won by the voice of Florimell as she bewails her woes within the confines of a cavern.

The frequent introduction of vocal and instrumental music into the poetic pageant bespeaks the age when a musical ear was an asset to an apprentice and when a tailor was not to be trusted who did not sing at his work. The shepherd's rustic quill is ever at hand for the making of eulogy, elegy or prize-song, and the most drastic symbol of dejection is the breaking of the pipe. In Faeryland singing is both a snare and a pastime. Britomart is as scandalised at the "trim consort" and wanton Lydian harmonies of Malecasta's love birds as Guyon at the Syren songs in Acrasia's bower. Paridell captivates the love of Hellenore with his voice, Celeno sitting before the gates of Pluto sings a heartrending song of bale, Pœana bewails her sorrow to the sound of the rote, and the harper Arion so enthrals the guests at the marriage of Thames and Medway that

> all the raging seas for joy forgot to rore.[40]

Continuous music accompanies the word-vignettes of *Epithalamion*, its cadence lingering in the refrain. Beginning, like Orpheus, with a solo to his love, the poet next invites participants—muses, nymphs of Mulla and all other streams, cheerful birds, Hours and Graces. The bride awakened, down the street moves the procession to the minstrels' song, the

merry note of pipe, tabor, fiddle and timbrel, the voices of
children,

>Crying aloud with strong confused noyce,
>As if it were one voice,
>Hymen, iö Hymen, Hymen, they do shout.[41]

The church re-echoes with pealing bells, roaring organs, the
choristers' anthem and the angels' answering song. Finally,
in contrast, the solemn stillness of the marriage night is
intensified by an exorcism of croaking frogs and ravens
whose dreary accents may disturb the lovers' rest.

In poetic description sound imagery is the natural accompaniment to word-painting. The clash of armour and the
noise of war gain impetus through comparison with any
object or phenomenon suggesting the double violence of
sound and movement—thunder, a hailstorm, the roar of wild
beasts, the rumble of a volcano. Here, as in other respects,
Spenser will often display his art by imparting new value to
a familiar figure:

>The ydle stroke, enforcing furious way,
>Missing the marke of his misaymed sight,
>Did fall to ground, and with his heavy sway
>So deepely dinted in the driven clay,
>That three yardes deepe a furrow up did throw.
>The sad earth, wounded with so sore assay,
>Did grone full grievous underneath the blow,
>And trembling with strange feare did like an erthquake
>   show.[42]

Orgoglio mortally wounded,

>—loudly brayd with beastly yelling sownd,
>That all the fields rebellowed againe,
>As great a noise, as when in Cymbrian plaine
>An heard of Bulles, whom kindly rage doth sting
>Doe for the milky mothers want complaine,
>And fill the fieldes with troublous bellowing:
>The neighbor woods arownd with hollow murmur ring.[43]

Guyon's dismay on discovering the corpse of Mortdant with

the luckless Amavia and their babe suggests a poignant touch of realism:

> At last his mighty ghost gan deepe to grone,
> As lion, grudging in his great disdaine,
> Mournes inwardly, and makes to him selfe mone.[44]

Birds' merry anthems greet the lovers of *Amoretti* and *Epithalamion*, their sweet consort blends with the seductive charm of Phædria's isle and Acrasia's bower:

> No tree whose braunches did not bravely spring;
> No braunch whereon a fine bird did not sitt;
> No bird but did her shrill notes sweetely sing;
> No song but did containe a lovely ditt.
> Trees, braunches, birds, and songs, were framed fitt
> For to allure fraile mind to carelesse ease.[45]

The disconsolate Timias abandoned by Belphœbe finds comfort in the "lamentable lay" of a dove bewailing the loss of her mate. The owl, the stork, the raven and the seamew invariably spell evil, sounding their baleful note in such eerie regions as the cave of Despair and the whirlpool of Decay. Night, bent upon the dark business of Duessa, arouses a dismal outcry from the creatures who are her fit companions:

> And, all the while she stood upon the ground,
> The wakefull dogs did never cease to bay,
> As giving warning of th' unwonted sound,
> With which her yron wheeles did them affray,
> And her darke griesly looke them much dismay:
> The messenger of death, the ghastly owle,
> With drery shriekes did also her bewray;
> And hungry wolves continually did howle
> At her abhorred face, so filthy and so fowle.[46]

Voice denotes mood or disposition. The speech of Cynthia, "like a streame of honny fleeting", is outmatched only by Belphœbe's: when she spake,

> Sweete wordes like dropping honny she did shed;
> And twixt the perles and rubins softly brake
> A silver sound, that heavenly musicke seemd to make.[47]

Each instrument has its symbolic overtones. The trumpet, with shawms and clarion, is to the epic as the pipe to the pastoral. Unknown to the Saturnine age of peace it proclaims the opening of combat, compelling the sometime shepherd

> For trumpets sterne to chaunge mine Oaten reeds.[48]

The horn likewise has ancient ancestry. Belphœbe and Tristram carry it as a proper accompaniment to the chase. Arthur's dates back to the earliest romances. But long usage has neither dulled its note nor impaired its utility. The dastards Braggadochio and Trompart have scarce recovered from their terror at the airy flight of Archimago when they hear a resounding trumpet-blast which preludes an even more startling apparition. The winding of the horn at Orgoglio's gates is an event of such consequence as to require two stanzas for the telling; for it announces the last act of the story, the long awaited respite to the hapless lovers. The Æolian harp, as introduced at the close of *The Ruines of Time,* is no more than a convention; but a distinctively Tudor note is struck by the porter ringing his alarum in the Barbican of Alma's castle, the Muses hymning Elisa with their violins and the lady of *Iambicum Trimetrum* "playing alone carelesse on hir heavenlie Virginals".

Spenser's imagery is conditioned by the taste and temper of an age which drew no rigid distinction between the functions of the several arts, in which every resource of music, painting and sculpture available for the process of ideal imitation was grist to the poet's mill. As a conscious device addressed to the senses rather than to the mind it is comparable with his diction, but less individual, more dependent upon custom and tradition. In the making of images his superiority to his contemporaries is one of degree, resulting from a finer sensitivity and a wider range of appeal which have strengthened his position as Poet's Poet. For these objective symbols of his poetic fancy, though ordered

i, i, 41) admits several onomatopœic words—*lull*, *twinkling*, *trickling*, *drizzling*, *murmuring*, *swarming*; but the onomato-pœia would be ineffectual without the aid of other artifices—protracted voice sibilants at rhyme close, avoidance of harsh consonantal combination, internal assonance (*soft–rock*, *noyse* *–annoy*), drowsy repetition of present participles, predomi-nance of short vowels, except in line 6 where the sense demands a slight *crescendo*. The significance of such features in the whole tonal effect appears unmistakably when these "sounds, and sweet airs, that give delight, and hurt not" are contrasted with others in different modes, for instance with the sinister bass monotone of Despair, luring his victim to the sleep from which there is no awakening:

> He there does now enjoy eternall rest,
> And happy ease, which thou doest want and crave,
> And further from it daily wanderest:
> What if some little payne the passage have,
> That makes frayle flesh to feare the bitter wave,
> Is not short payne well borne, that bringes long ease,
> And layes the soule to sleepe in quiet grave?
> Sleep after toyle, port after stormie seas,
> Ease after warre, death after life, does greatly please.[2]

Description has given place to argument, and the hollow accents bewray the man of darkness. Successive mono-syllables and long stressed vowels allow to every beat its full value, reducing the speed to *grave*. The rhetorical contrast drawn between the care of life and the peace of death is echoed in the cumulative consonants of the first five lines and the ensuing vocalic cadence, with sudden transition to trochaic rhythm and prolonged *rallentando*. A third specimen, equally distinct from either of the above, is the famous *allegro* stanza beginning

> At last, the golden Orientall gate
> Of greatest heaven gan to open fayre;
> And Phœbus, fresh as brydegrome to his mate,
> Came dauncing forth, shaking his deawie hayre,
> And hurld his glistring beams through gloomy ayre.[3]

The vivacious movement and brilliant tone colour of the verse matches the image. An alarum of rolling liquids and rounded vowels develops with steadily increasing resonance into the grand climax of the fourth and fifth lines, announcing the main subject with a clash of consonants and protracted vowels, like the burst of the full orchestra.

The *enargia* of "wordes and speaches smothly and tunably running" establishes in Spenser's poetry a predominance of the Lydian mode, "an easie running verse with tender feete", tuned to the waterfall like the songs of his nymphs and shepherds. Apart from the *Complaints*, all his poems begin and end quietly. At the limpid flow of words and verses the maker himself, like his own Morpheus, is "lulled in slomber of delight", charming his reader with "Spenserian vowels that elope with ease". But once the spell is induced the mode may be varied, on the principle that "dischord ofte in Musicke makes the sweeter lay". The fluent melody of the opening stanzas to *Virgils Gnat* is suddenly arrested by cacophony harsh and spiteful as the serpent's hiss:

> He, passing by with rolling wreathed pace,
> With brandisht tongue the emptie aire did gride,
> And wrapt his scalie boughts with fell despight,
> That all things seemd appalled at his sight.
>
> Fellie he hisseth, and doth fiercely stare,
> And hath his jawes with angrie spirits rent,
> That all his tract with bloudie drops is stained,
> And all his foldes are now in length outstrained.[4]

Foul deeds and spectacles are fitly echoed in strident notes and broken rhythms:

> That detestable sight him much amazde,
> To see th' unkindly Impes, of heaven accurst,
> Devoure their dam; on whom while so he gazd,
> Having all satisfide their bloudie thurst,
> Their bellies swolne he saw with fulnesse burst,
> And bowels gushing forth.

His face with smoke was tand, and eies were bleard,
His head and beard with sout were ill bedight,
His cole-blacke hands did seeme to have ben seard
In smythes fire-spitting forge, and nayles like clawes appeard.[5]

The divers motives of *Colin Clouts Come Home Againe* compose a suite of verbal music. Hobbinol's monosyllables divide the lilt of the introduction from Colin's song, with its play upon proper names. The *Intermezzo* of the voyage is marked by trochaic rhythm, with a torrential rush of strong vowels and surging polysyllables. The lavish use of glides and liquids throughout the pæan to the court adds speed and fluency, which gradually diminish as the singer approaches his solemn peroration. The two odes are set to two distinct accompaniments. *Prothalamion*, maintaining uniformity of tone and speed through each successive stanza, is as an air with variations, *Epithalamion* as a tone-picture or polychrome of diverse motives welded into an harmonious whole. "April" and "November", composed of similar texture, differ as the strain of the viol from the beat of the drum. Sudden contrast in tone or rhythmic phrasing will often convey effects beyond the reach of visual imagery. The choric melody of the *Hymnes* occasionally gives place to solemn monotone like that of the stanzas beginning

and

How vainely then doe ydle wits invent,

For love is a celestiall harmonie,[6]

while the polysyllabic fluency predominant throughout *The Faerie Queene* from time to time is interrupted by such verses as

Faynt, wearied, sore, emboyled, grieved, brent,
With heat, toyle, wounds, armes, smart, and inward fire.

And sayd "Ah sir, my liege lord, and my love."

Then woe, and woe, and everlasting woe,
Be to the Briton babe that shal be borne,
To live in thraldome of his fathers foe!
Late King, now captive; late lord, now forlorne.[7]

187

Edmund Spenser

The aspersions cast upon rhyme in the *Calender* and *The Teares of the Muses*, like the similar censures of Campion and Milton, are largely conventional and directed against the doggerel of poetasters. Taken literally they come ill from a poet who so obviously delights in the interlacing of verses by "concord", "proportion" and "staff" and who on occasions is quite as licentious as the rout of ragged rhymsters whom he attacks. For with rhyme, as with diction, Spenser is no purist but a law to himself. To meet the exigencies of strophic design he freely admits end-assonance (*disfigured–blubbered, discover–mother, emperisht–florisht*), eye-rhyme (*one –alone–gone, wrath–hat'th*), "cockneyism" (*gotten–soften–often*), unstressed and impure rhymes (*remora–away, Chryso-gonee–dree, hideous–monstruous*), anomalous pronunciation (*most–enforst, opprest–overkest*). Rhyme and assonance are as mortar to stanzaic structure, accentuating rhythm and inducing euphony; for this reason Spenser frequently duplicates the effect of end-rhyme through unobtrusive sound echo or medial assonance within the verse:

> Lo! now she is that stone; from whose two heads,
> As from two weeping eyes, fresh streames do flow,
> Yet colde through feare and old conceived dreads;
> And yet the stone her semblance seemes to show,
> Shapt like a maide, that such ye may her know.[8]

With the same object he pursues the traditional pastime of "playing with the letter". As might be expected, alliterative compounds—"passing perceant", "doleful dittie", "carefull cark"—are particularly common in early pieces after the style of older English poets, whose influence is unmistakable in verses retaining the catch letter throughout:

> His harmefull Hatchet he hent in hand.

> They setten to sale their shops of shame.

> Thus wildly to wander in the worlds eye.

> He chaffred Chayres in which Churchmen were set.

And teache the trees their trickling teares to shedde.

Heapes of huge wordes uphoorded hideously.[9]

A modification of this usage, in effect less mechanical and freely employed in later as in early works, is the division of the line into two hemistiches, each with its own catch letter:

Cover'd with cold, and wrapt in wretchednesse.

All deadly daungerous, all cruell keene.

With constancy and care, gainst daunger and dismay.

Lookte on them lovely, still in stedfast state.

Red as the Rose, thence gushed grievously.

Through thicke and thin, both over banck and bush.[10]

Here, as in Anglo-Saxon poetry, alliteration is a metrical device for punctuating rhythm. It may also serve to maintain strophic cohesion through a period of interlaced verses:

> But patience perforce, he must abie
> What fortune and his fate on him will lay;
> Fond is the feare that findes no remedie:
> Yet warily he watcheth every way,
> By which he feareth evill happen may;
> So th' evill thinkes by watching to prevent.

> Piers, I have pyped erst so long with payne,
> That all mine Oten reedes bene rent and wore,
> And my poore Muse hath spent her spared store,
> Yet little good hath got, and much lesse gayne.
> Such pleasaunce makes the Grashopper so poore,
> And ligge so layd, when Winter doth her straine.[11]

The frequent recurrence of metrical alliteration at the close of the Spenserian stanza, whilst tending to preserve the integrity of the verse, the balance between alexandrine and pentameter, is dangerously conducive to verbiage:

Then gan she wail and weepe to see that woeful stowre.

But she with blame would blot, and of due praise deprive.

Who taught his trampling steed with equall steps to tread.

He groveling fell, all gored in his gushing wound.

Whose bridle rung with golden bels and bosses brave.[12]

Though some of these specimens may savour of the lamentable comedy of Pyramus and Thisbe, they show the effectiveness of catch letters as a form of onomatopœia; the last line jingles as merrily as its "bells and bosses".

But with Spenser alliteration is not simply a trick or outward embellishment; he has fully exploited its more subtle usage as a continuous echo to meaning. It enforces the plaintive notes and formal periods of Colin's song in "January", expresses Cuddie's impatience at Thenot's "long tale", runs counter to the catchwords of the "August" sestina, intrudes as a light accompaniment to the "April" lay and marks the beat of the funeral procession in "November". Single lines like

And shields did share, and mailes did rash, and helmes did hew:

To ridd a wretched man from handes of hellish wight:

And into diverse doubt his wavering wonder clove:

Rapt with the rage of mine own ravisht thought[13]

show the rhetorical force of alliteration both in sententious and in descriptive verse. But as a means of echoing sense it is most effective when prolonged throughout a stanza and when least dependent upon tags or compounds:

> There was the Liffy rolling downe the lea,
> The sandy Slane, the stony Aubrian,
> The spacious Shenan spreading like a sea,
> The pleasant Boyne, the fishy fruitfull Ban,
> Swift Awniduff, which of the English man
> Is cal'de Blacke-water, and the Liffar deep,
> Sad Trowis, that once his people over-ran,
> Strong Allo tombling from Slewlogher steep
> And Mulla mine, whose waves I whilom taught to weep.

Eftsoones her shallow ship away did slide,
More swift then swallow sheres the liquid skye,
Withouten oare or Pilot it to guide,
Or winged canvas with the wind to fly:
Only she turnd a pin, and by and by
It cut away upon the yielding wave,
Ne cared she her course for to apply;
For it was taught the way which she would have,
And both from rocks and flats it selfe could wisely save.[14]

The ease and fluency of the second stanza are largely dependent upon unobtrusive alliteration with only a faint suggestion of recurrent sound, a device that frequently accompanies
sound imagery:

And in the midst a little river plaide
Emongst the pumy stones, which seemd to plaine
With gentle murmure that his cours they did restraine.[15]

Finally two passages may suffice to illustrate Spenser's mastery
over the more elusive rhythm of medial alliteration:

But her two other sisters, standing by,
Her lowd gainsaid, and both her champions bad
Pursew the end of their strong enmity,
As ever of their loves they would be glad:
Yet she with pitthy words, and counsell sad,
Still strove their stubborne rages to revoke;
That at the last, suppressing fury mad,
They gan abstaine from dint of direfull stroke,
And hearken to the sober speaches which she spoke.

They gathered some; the Violet, pallid blew,
The little Dazie, that at evening closes,
The virgin Lillie, and the Primrose trew,
With store of vermeil Roses.[16]

The fitful movement of catch sounds from initials to medials
in the first extract, the play upon -*v* and -*r* in the second
strike the ear almost unconsciously. Alliteration of this more
evasive kind, as an undertone heard intermittently but never
lost, lies at the very basis of Spenser's verbal music.

Edmund Spenser

It is significant that the one piece of prose criticism which has come down to us from the hand of Spenser should be concerned exclusively with the problem of verse. Seeking to naturalise a new poetry he is confronted at the outset with the task of regulating accent,

> whyche sometime gapeth, and as it were, yawneth ilfavouredly, comming shorte of that it should, and sometime exceeding the measure of the Number.... But it is to be wonne with Custome, and rough words must be subdued with Use. For, why a Gods name may not we, as else the Greekes, have the kingdome of oure owne Language, and measure oure Accentes by the sounde, reserving that Quantitie to the Verse?[7]

In short, until pronunciation becomes stabilised the poet may be allowed considerable licence so long as he duly respects his "numbers" or "quantities". Verse is conditioned by all the elements of sound, which include tone, stress, pitch and elision; but the unit of rhythm upon which it is grounded is temporal and not accentual. Thus, although the immediate concern of the poet is the luckless "English hexameter", the experiment focuses his attention upon a basic principle of his art.

The kinship between poetry and music during the Elizabethan period tended to emphasise the importance of this principle both in quantitative and in accentual verse. Sidney finds the former "more fit for Musick, both words and tune observing quantity, and more fit lively to express divers passions, by the low and loftie sounde of the well weyed silable." Campion, compelled as poet-musician constantly to weigh his "numbers", devotes his *Observations on the Art of English Poesie* to an examination of English prosody upon the sound premiss that "when we speake of a Poeme written in number, we consider not only the distinct number of the sillables, but also their value, which is contained in the length or shortnes of their sound". His failure to establish English prosody upon a strictly quantitative basis does not impair the validity of his statements upon the temporal element in verse and the relation between poetry and music. Neither Campion nor any considerable poet of his age submitted in practice to arbitrary laws of quantity. But with a natural sense of "numerosity" all alike, consciously or otherwise, measured their syllables.

The difficulty of adjusting verse to speech rhythm, which Spenser discusses at some length in the first of his letters to Harvey, is clearly evidenced in his earlier pieces. Staggering pentameters like

> The chapters Alablaster, the fryses cristall:
>
> Th'olde honour of the people gowned long:
>
> Seest thou not how all places quake and quiver [18]

are in a class apart from the "Chaucerian" lines of "February", from the free rhythms of the "April "ditty, from

> As the God of my life? why hath he me abhord? [19]

where the stress inversion is a deliberate rhetorical gesture, or

> Save Beares, Lyons, and Buls, which romed them arownd, [20]

where it could have been avoided through the interchange of "Beares" with "Lyons". On the whole, however, Spenser's Juvenilia reveal a conscientious, even laboured attempt to maintain metrical correctness, with "humdrum" installed as mistress of "harum-scarum". If Donne for not keeping of accent deserved hanging, the New Poet was determined to preserve it even at the cost of grammatical precision and clarity. The stresses and syllables of

> Which saw the messenger of tidings glad:
>
> Should able be so great an one to wring:
>
> For not to have been dipt in Lethe lake,
> Could save the sonne of Thetis from to die [21]

are fairly tortured into submission by means of expletives, elisions, inversions and syntactical anomalies. The unrhymed pentameters of the sonnets in *A Theatre of Worldlings* have little of the tonal and rhythmic subtlety that belongs to authentic blank verse. But the fusion of native with foreign elements in the *Calender* opened a way to emancipation from purist rigidity and monotony.

In this respect Spenser's diction and verse are inter-related. Boasting his native descent, he might well have been misled by a popular superstition adopted as a poetic axiom by George Gascoigne:

> Thrust as few wordes of many sillables into your verse as may be: and hereunto I might alledge many reasons. First, the most auncient English wordes are of one sillable, so that the more monosyllables that you use the truer Englishman you shall seeme, and the lesse you shall smell of the Inkehorne. Also wordes of many syllables do cloye a verse and make it unpleasant, whereas wordes of one syllable will more easily fall to be shorte or long as occasion requireth, or wil be adapted to become circumflexe or of an indifferent sounde.[22]

But like others who had "tasted the sweete and statelie measures and stile of the Italian Poesie" Spenser refused to be tied by so arbitrary a rule, freely admitting both mono-syllables and polysyllables as they serve his purpose. The preponderance of monosyllables and long vowels in

> Faire shields, gay steedes, bright armes be my delight[23]

has rhetorical significance, marking the final stroke of Guyon's rejoinder to Mammon. Elsewhere it is expressive of certain physical or emotional conditions such as weariness or timidity:

And sayd, "Ah Sir, my liege Lord, and my love":

Your owne deare sake forst me at first to leave:

Faynt, wearie, sore, emboyled, grieved, brent,
With heat, toyle, wounds, armes, smart, and inward fire:

Their hearts were sicke; their sides were sore; their feete were
   lame.[24]

Verbal Music, Verse

But the theory of Gascoigne is set at nought in

>Downe from the mountaines bordring Lombardie.
>
>Ambition is engendred easily.
>
>The Marigolde, and cherefull Rosmarie.
>
>Bring hether the Pincke and purple Cullambine,
>>With Gelliflowres;
>Bring Coronations, and Sops in wine,
>>Worne of Paramoures:
>Strowe me the ground with Daffadowndillies,
>And Cowslips, and Kingcups, and loved Lillies;
>>The pretie Pawnce,
>>And the Chevisaunce,
>Shall match with the fayre flowre Delice.²⁵

The predominant effect of Spenser's verse is polysyllabic; its prevailing ease and fluency is largely dependent upon the recurrence of light stressed vowels in polysyllabic groups and the counterpoint of this polysyllabic phrasing against an iambic norm. The opening lines of *The Shepheardes Calender* and of *The Faerie Queene*, in rhythm almost identical, and a stanza from *Muiopotmos* will serve as illustrations:

>A Shepheards boye, (no better doe him call).
>
>A Gentle Knight was pricking on the plaine.
>
>Not anie damzell, which her vaunteth most
>In skilfull knitting of soft silken twyne,
>Nor anie weaver, which his worke doth boast
>In dieper, in damaske, or in lyne,
>Nor anie skil'd in workmanship embost,
>Nor anie skil'd in loupes of fingring fine,
>Might in their divers cunning ever dare
>With this so curious networke to compare. ²⁶

The falling trisyllable, the rhythm of characteristic Spenserian names like Artegall, Britomart, Calidore, even Colin-et occurs continually in single lines and frequently extends throughout a complete stanza:

Oút of her dust líke to a worm arise.

Cháunting in shade their sundrie mélodie.

Áll as the Sheepe, súch was the shepeheards looke.

Pítifull spéctacle of deadly smart,
Beside a bubling fountaine low she lay,
Whích she increased with her bleeding hart,
And the cleane waves with purple gore did ray:
Áls in her lap a lovely babe did play
His cruell sport, in stead of sorrow dew;
Fór in her streaming blood he did embay
His little hands, and tender joints embrew;
Pítifull spéctacle, as ever eie did vew. [27]

The normal Spenserian line, in contradistinction to that of more forceful poets like Marlowe or Milton, does not contain more than three stressed long vowels; exception to this general rule is usually attributable to its context. The syllabic weight of Hobbinol's elegiac speech at the opening of *Colin Clouts Come Home Againe* sounds in marked contrast with the light, rapid movement of the poem as a whole:

Whilest thou wast hence, all dead in dole did lie:
The woods were heard to waile full many a sythe,
And all their birds with silence to complaine:
The fieldes with faded flowers did seem to mourne,
And all their flocks from feeding to refraine. [28]

In the first speech of Archimago the contrast between initial trisyllables and the uneven dissyllables that follow admirably expresses the counterfeit simplicity and timidity of the speaker:

Verbal Music, Verse

"Áh! my deare sonne," (quoth he), "how should, alas!
Sílly old man, that lives in idle cell,
Bídding his beades all day for his trespas,
Týdings of warre and worldly trouble tell?"[29]

Despite the allegations of Gascoigne and other critics
against inkhorn polysyllables, imitation from traditional
English verse forms fell almost inevitably into polysyllabic
rhythm. The last relic of the old alliterative verse was the
"tumbling measure" of *Flodden Field* and of Tusser's *Good
Husbandry*, a four-stress line of anapæsts with iambic substitution at the close; and although Spenser never adopts this
as a norm it appears sporadically in his imitations from
Chaucer ("February", "May" and "September"), which
admit all manner of licence in the poising of stress and
syllable. Misled by current pronunciation and by the practice
of fifteenth-century poets, particularly by Lydgate, he
evidently scanned Chaucer's pentameter as a four-stress line,
admitting an indefinite number of unstressed syllables
scattered at irregular intervals:

Whán that Áprille with his shoúres soóte,
The dróghte of Márch hath pérced to the roóte
And báthed every véyne in swích lícour
Of whích vertú engéndred is the flóur.

This arbitrary imposition of four stresses upon the pentameter is responsible for the ragged rhythm of

Áh for píttie! wil ráncke Winters ráge
These bítter blásts never gínne tasswáge?
The kéne cold blówes through my béaten hýde,
Áll as I were throúgh the bódy grýde.[30]

But with better luck it may result in dactylic "tumbling verse",
which is frequently emphasised by means of alliteration:

Clóthed with cóld, and hóary wyth fróst.
Lóvers of Lórdship, and tróublers of státes.
Sáy it out, Díggon, whatéver it híght.
Góod is no góod, but íf it be spénd.[31]

Spenser showed his good judgment in quickly abandoning this rhyme doggerel, which, like the corrupt measures of the fifteenth century, is no more than a travesty of its great original. But the licentious treatment of stresses and syllables here occasioned through misunderstanding of his predecessors gives promise of the flexibility that characterises all his later and more finished verse.

The sum of his achievement in sheer artistry of numbers is represented by the four odes—*Epithalamion*, *Prothalamion* and the "ditties" of "April" and "November". Here the dimeters or trimeters interspersed at regular intervals among pentameters are protracted by means of hiatus or syllabic weight to approximately the same duration, the change in speed reflecting a contrast in sense or tone. The rhythmic beauty of "April", the gem of the whole *Calender*, is entirely dependent upon this modulation within an intricate strophic pattern. In "November", which E.K. and possibly Spenser himself preferred to all the other eclogues, some of the freshness of "April" has been sacrificed to convention; but greater care has been bestowed upon the apportioning of time-values. The heavy beat of the funeral procession etched upon the wood-cut finds an echo in the sonorous verse with its long-drawn alexandrines and slow measured refrain:

> The fatall sisters eke repent
> Her vital threde so soone was spent.
>> O heavie herse!
> Morne now, my Muse, now morne with heavy cheare,
>> O carefull verse.[32]

The stanzas of *Epithalamion* and *Prothalamion*, far exceeding the limit of ten lines prescribed in *The Arte of English Poesie*, amount to "ditties of themselves, and no staffs". The rhyme system being too complex to be retained in memory, strophic balance and symmetry are preserved chiefly by means of recurrent trimeters and of closing refrain. The polysyllabic rhythm characteristic of Spenser, by accentuating the dis-

tinction between major and minor stresses, tends to super-
impose a trimetric structure upon his pentameters:

> Dáughter of Phœbus and of Mémorye:
> The whíles a most delítious hármony:
> He thénce them léd into his Hérmitage;33

and throughout the marriage odes, as in the *canzone* upon
which they are modelled, this relation between trimeter and
pentameter is organic. The syllabic weight and tonal breadth of

> Behóld, whíles shé befóre the áltar stánds:
> Thère vértue raýnes as Quéene in róyal thróne:
> In dréadful dárknesse lénd desíred líght,34

allowing almost equal intensity to major and minor stresses
are exceptional; the prevailing rhythm of the odes admits a
regular counterpoint of trimetric major stresses against the
pentameter base:

> Opén the temple gátes unto my love,
> Opén them wíde that she may énter in.
> How chéarefully thou lóokest from abóve.
> Wáke now, my love, awáke! for it is tíme.35

Under these conditions the trimeter can be introduced at
regular intervals without appreciable change either in rhythm
or in duration. The musical settings to other contemporary
pieces of the *canzone* type go to prove that constancy of
"numbers" is preserved by means of syllabic protraction and
rhetorical hiatus throughout the trimeter; and this distribu-
tion of time value over the trimeters of Spenser's marriage
odes is plainly indicated throughout *Prothalamion*, where the
continuity of the two trimeters—

> Which may your foes confound,
> And make your joyes redound—

allows of neither metrical nor grammatical interruption.

Spenser's English *canzoni* are perfect specimens of their
kind, beyond comparison with any others save Milton's *At a*

Solemn Music and *Upon the Circumcision*. But this triumph was not won without prolonged experiment in the manipulation of numbers, syllables and strophic design. His verse forms derive from sources as varied as those of his vocabulary. The "Chaucerian" couplets of "February", "May" and "September", the rime-couée of "March", the ballad measure of "July", the alternating tetrameters of "August" balance strophic forms of more recent importation like the *sizeine* of "January", Colin's *sestina* in "August" and the *ditties* of "April" and "November". The stanza of "June" is Chaucer's octave, modified by the reduction of rhymes from three to two. Chaucerian "rhyme royal", used throughout the *Hymnes* and *The Ruines of Time*, in *Daphnaida* is converted into a kind of strophic *terza rima*. *Virgils Gnat* and *Muiopotmos* are cast in the *ottava rima* of Ariosto. The sonnets fall into two main groups. The *Visions* of Bellay and Petrarch, *The Ruines of Rome* and the dedication to the *Historie of George Castriot* are composed of three distinct quatrains, concluded by a couplet. In the remainder the quatrains are linked by rhyme, the fourth verse rhyming with the fifth, the eighth with the ninth. The unwieldy structure of *The Ruines of Rome* and of *Visions of the Worlds Vanitie* shows little attempt at the correlation of content with form; but most of the *Amoretti* fall into rhetorical periods which correspond with the tripartite division of the verse.

In versification, as in diction, Spenser submits to the rule of decorum, "peyzing each sillable of each worde by just proportion according to the dignitie of the subject". His uncouth swains moralise their song in fable set to harsh "Chaucerian" couplets. The light rime-couée of "March" reflects that "pleasaunce which to spring time is most agreeable", the artless jingle of the competitors in "August" is silenced by Colin's "doolefull verse". For the ceremonial occasions of "April" and "August" the rustic quill is dropped, bucolic measures giving place to finely wrought "ditties". With two exceptions all poems subsequent to the *Calender* are written in stanzas based upon the iambic pentameter. The continuous quatrains of *Colin Clouts Come Home Againe* are designed to convey the effect of easy conversation. The heroic couplet, which Chaucer had perfected as an instrument adapted to all forms of narrative poetry, to Spenser, as to his contemporaries, is "merely riding rhyme", a crude measure befitting "base style" and "mean matter"; so he adopts it in *Mother Hubberds Tale*, a *tour de force* that "in heat of choller, forgetting the pure sanguine of her sweete Faery Queene, wilfully overshott her malcontented self". But in the pure sanguine of his natural element Spenser builds the lofty rhyme, embellishing and dignifying his theme by means of the well wrought stanza, the normal unit of his verse structure. He composes by staff, as may be gathered from *Colin Clouts Come Home Againe*, where from time to time the continuous quatrains assume a strophic character (308–27, 464–79, 596–615). He cannot adequately be represented by the citation of single lines or couplets, his purple patches usually extending to a complete stanza. But the discipline of a traditional pattern such as the sonnet is too rigid for the wayward temper of his Muse, and when thus enfettered he becomes stiff and artificial. In verse, as in speech, he needed an instrument of his own making; and seeking to satisfy this need he was led to the greatest of his inventions.

Largely as a result of the monosyllabic element in the English vocabulary, until comparatively recent times the hexameter has never proved a suitable norm for continuous English verse. During the sixteenth century, under the influence of Latin poetry, various attempts were made to naturalise it by means of quantitative hexameters, the "poulter's measure" of alternate alexandrines and fourteeners and the alexandrine couplet as used by Drayton in *Polyolbion*. But all alike failed, the hexameter generally collapsing into two unwieldy trimeters. Campion judiciously excepts it from the classical measures adapted to English poetry, pointing out that the English pentameter occupies the same average time as the Latin hexameter, both reaching the normal limit of duration. As a continuous measure the English alexandrine quickly palls. But recurring at intervals within a stanza of pentameters it is a highly effective variation, sounding as an overtone or a prolonged rhythmic phrase; and so Spenser introduces it at certain points of the *Calender* and in the *Epithalamion* refrain.

The Spenserian stanza, consisting of a Chaucerian octave (*a b a b b c b c*) amplified by means of a final alexandrine, was too unorthodox a medium for heroic poetry to escape censure. Zoilus, Momus and other disputants in Harington's *Metamorphosis of Ajax* (1596) complained "that the last verse disordered their mouths and was like a trick of seventeen in a sinkapace". Ben Jonson also disliked the stanza and Thomas Rymer, in his preface to Rapin's *Reflections on Aristotle's Treatise of Poesie*, blames the Italians for misleading Spenser by casting him on "the unlucky choice of the stanza, which in no wise is proper for our Language". On the other hand, Gabriel Harvey regarded the variation of the alexandrine as an added grace, and Edward Phillips, fired with the enthusiasm of his uncle John Milton for earlier Italian poetry, prefers the Spenserian stanza to the heroic measures favoured by his own generation: "How much more stately and Majestic in Epic Poems, especially of Heroic Argument, *Spencer's stanza*, which I take to be but an improvement upon *Tasso's Ottava Rima*, or the *Ottava Rima* it self, used by many of our once esteemed Poets, is above the way either of Couplet or Alternation of four Verses only, I am persuaded, were it revived, would soon be acknowledg'd".[36] Yet a century later Thomas Warton, one of the most ardent of Spenserians, admitting the appropriateness of Spenser's stanza to his descriptive manner of writing, criticised it as a source of circumlocution, redundance and puerility.

Such censures do not lack foundation. Spenser's stanza is the perfect accompaniment to his speech, and the two stand or fall together. The languorous note of recurrent rhyme with the long-drawn cadence of the close that enchants one reader will weary another. The alexandrine, at its worst, is a mere tag to the octave, a lure to prolixity or an occasion for nodding:

> Vaine is the arte that seekes it selfe for to deceive.

> Neither unseemly short, nor yet exceeding long.

> That oftentimes he quakt, and fainted oftentimes.

> So ended he his tale, where I this Canto end. [37]

But the general effect of the protracted cadence, flowing in an unbroken stream of rhythm and melody, is to transform the whole stanzaic structure, projecting its centre of gravity from the fourth line to the fifth or sixth. Thus proportioned, the stanza combines the flexibility of the octave with the distinction of the sonnet. Its organic unity is sustained through the echo of rhymes and the enjambment of sense "variously drawn out" not to a tag but to an inevitable climax or "dying fall":

> Till that they come unto a forest greene
> In which they shrowd themselves from causeles feare;
> Yet feare them followes still where so they beene.
> Each trembling leafe and whistling wind they heare,
> As ghastly bug, does greatly them affeare;
> Yet both doe strive their fearefulnesse to faine.
> At last they heard a horne that shrilled cleare
> Throughout the wood that ecchoed againe,
> And made the forrest ring, as it would rive in twaine.

> He ceast; and then gan all the quire of birdes
> Their diverse notes t'attune unto his lay,
> As in approvaunce of his pleasing wordes.
> The constant payre heard all that he did say,
> Yet swarved not, but kept their forward way
> Through many covert groves and thickets close,
> In which they creeping did at last display
> That wanton Lady with her lover lose,
> Whose sleepie head she in her lap did soft dispose. [38]

Though cast as a single piece, the Spenserian stanza is capable of subdivision into rhetorical verse periods:

> So downe he fell, and forth his life did breath,
> That vanisht into smoke and cloudes swift;
> So downe he fell, that th'earth him underneath
> Did grone, as feeble so great load to lift;
> So downe he fell, as an huge rocky clift,
> Whose false foundacion waves have washt away,
> With dreadfull poyse is from the mayneland rift,
> And rolling downe great Neptune doth dismay:
> So downe he fell, and like an heaped mountaine lay.

> His lovely wordes her seemd due recompence
> Of all her passed paines: one loving howre
> For many yeares of sorrow can dispence;
> A dram of sweete is worth a pound of sowre.
> Shee has forgott how many a woeful stowre
> For him she late endurd; she speaks no more
> Of past; true is, that true love hath no powre
> To looken backe; his eies be fixt before.
> Before her stands her knight, for whom she toyled
>   so sore. [39]

Interplay between metrical enjambment and rhetorical period imparts to the second passage an ease and fluency reflecting the implied sense of reconciliation. By way of contrast we may notice the halting rhythm of Guyon's embarrassed address to Shamefastnes, induced through manipulation of internal hiatus, and the end-stopt verses of a typical descriptive piece composed of detached particulars:

> "Fayre Damzell, seemeth by your troubled cheare,
> That either me too bold ye weene, this wise
> You to molest, or other ill to feare
> That in the secret of your hart close lyes,
> From whence it doth, as cloud from sea, aryse,
> If it be I, of pardon I you pray;
> But if ought else that I mote not devyse,
> I will, if please you it discure, assay
> To ease you of that ill, so wisely as I may."

After them went Displeasure and Pleasaunce,
He looking lompish and full sullein sad,
And hanging downe his heavy countenaunce;
She chearfull, fresh, and full of joyaunce glad,
As if no sorrow she ne felt ne drad;
That evill matched paire they seemd to bee:
An angry Waspe th'one in a viall had,
Th'other in hers a hony-laden Bee,
Thus marched these six couples forth in faire degree.[40]

The counterpoint between verse and speech rhythm, which endows Spenser's stanza with its characteristic freedom and flexibility, is most evident in his handling of the alexandrine. William Lisle, a translator of Du Bartas, defending the monotonous regularity of his "Bartassian" verses, an alexandrine bisected by a cæsura after the sixth syllable, affirms that "the neglect of this hath caused many a brave stanza in the *Faerie Queene* to end but harshly, which might have been at the first". Such regularity in division, a generally accepted principle of versification enjoined in *The Arte of English Poesie*, is admitted by Spenser as it serves his purpose—in tags, where it is almost inevitable, and also as a means of enforcing rhetorical parallelism or antithesis:

"Death is the end of woes; die soone, O faeries sonne."
They three be dead with shame, the Squire lives with renowne.
And prov'd himselfe most foole in what he seem'd most wise.
With fowle words tempring faire, soure gall with hony sweet.[41]

But the integrity of the alexandrine and its organic relation with the stanza requires variation rather than "Bartassian" uniformity; and this Spenser has allowed by placing the cæsura at almost every possible point:

O! who does know the bent of women's fantasy?
And bold, as ever Squyre that waited by knights side.
His slomber, yet so mazed that he nothing spake.
They tooke their steeds, and forth upon their journey went.
And antique praises unto present persons fitt.

He of his name Coylchester built of stone and lime.

The doughtiest knight that liv'd that day, and most of might.

"Where have ye all this while bin wandring, where bene
weft?"[42]

The verse may be so fluent or so firmly "trussed up" as to
admit no pause:

> But Britomart dissembled it with ignoraunce.

> Such as the troubled Theatres oftimes annoyes.

> Sweete is the love that comes alone with willingnesse.

> Who al this while lay bleding out his hart-blood neare.[43]

Or the pause may be duplicated, marking rhetorical emphasis:

> "Dy, if thou it gainesay: I will away her beare."

> Till then, for evermore she hated, never lov'd.[44]

Apart from pause manipulation the extended line offers endless possibilities for variation in speed, numbers and syllabic
grouping. Attached to the English octave, it is so bold a
licence as to become a law to itself, a mode of free verse with
speed and rhythm tempered to the context.

The most characteristic of these sense effects is the Spenserian "drowsyhed" which Thomson sought to recapture in
The Castle of Indolence, the spell of enchantment cast by the
"dying fall":

> "Sleepe after toyle, port after stormie seas,
> Ease after warre, death after life, does greatly please."

> Loosely displayd upon the grassie ground
> Possessed of sweete sleepe that luld him soft in swound.[45]

Pope's famous simile,

> A needless alexandrine ends the song
> That, like a wounded snake, drags its slow length along,

was probably borrowed from Spenser, who frequently emphasises this "slow length" by means of the accompanying figure:

> Each hour did seeme a moneth, and every moneth a yeare.

> That, as a Snake, still lurked in his wounded mynd.

> Like a discoloured Snake, whose hidden snares
> Through the greene gras his long bright burnisht back declares. [46]

The concluding *rallentando* is an effective means of conveying the sense of weariness or pathos, affording the poet occasion for weeping with his characters; at the close of the Lucretian hymn to Venus it voices all the lover's wistful aspiration towards the fulfilment of his ideal:

> Their hearts were sicke; their sides were sore; their
>   feete were lame.

> And sett her by to watch, and sett her by to weepe.

> Feele my hart perst with so great agony,
> When such I see, that all for pitty I could dy.

> "Great God of men and women, queene of th'ayre,
> Mother of laughter, and welspring of blisse,
> O graunt that of my love at last I may not misse." [47]

But sentiment is only incidental to epic poetry and the sensitivity of the Spenserian stanza renders it equally adaptable to the poetic representation of still life or heroic action. The alexandrine is sometimes a cadence following gradual diminution of speed, sometimes a coda or climax adding vigour and intensity; and whether the subject of the stanza be idyllic, epic or satiric the most vivid touch is generally reserved for the close:

>   he wearie sate
> To rest him selfe foreby a fountaine syde,
> Disarmed all of yron-coted Plate;
> And by his side his steed the grassy forage ate.

>   The same she followes, till at last she has
> A damzell spyde, slow footing her before,
> That on her shoulders sad a pot of water bore.

    Downe himselfe he layd
    Upon the grassy ground to sleepe a throw:
    The cold earth was his couch, the hard steele his pillow.

    For want whereof he weighed vanity,
    And fild his ballaunce full of idle toys:
    Yet was admired much of fooles, women, and boys. [48]

Spenser's verses, says Dryden, "are so numerous, so various, and so harmonious, that only Virgil, whom he profestly imitated, has surpassed him among the Romans; and only Mr Waller among the English".[49] His stanza was the instrument of a new poet speaking the language of an undiscovered world; and like his other inventions it quickly gained notice. The eldest of its large progeny are the stanzas of *Christ's Victory and Triumph, The Purple Island*, the introduction to Milton's *Nativity Ode* and other seventeenth-century imitations, composed of five or more pentameters with a concluding alexandrine. In the course of the eighteenth century the revival of the Spenserian stanza in its original form was cotemporaneous with a renewed interest in the poetry of Spenser as a whole; and the best of the Spenserians, such as Thomson and Shenstone, in artfully recapturing the style of their original, often give more than a suggestion of his verse effects. James Beattie, on the other hand, chose the Spenserian stanza for his *Minstrel* not as a form to burlesque but because it allows "both simplicity and magnificence of sound and of language beyond any other stanza that I am acquainted with...the sententiousness of the couplet, as well as the more complex modulation of blank verse". Striving to avoid obsolete expressions, Beattie found himself compelled to admit a certain number of archaic words; *Resolution and Independence* shows that even Wordsworth could not completely dissociate Spenserian verse from Spenserian diction. By the beginning of the nineteenth century, however, the stanza had become sufficiently elastic to fit many different modes and styles. Shelley adopted it in *The Revolt of Islam* as affording "better shelter for mediocrity" than Shakesperian or Miltonic blank verse, also on account of its "brilliancy and magnificence of sound". *Childe Harold's Pilgrimage* is simply Byron masquerading in Spenserian dress but bewrayed by an impetuosity of tone and speech clean contrary to the part he affects. At the opposite pole is *The Eve of St Agnes*, the work of a pure romantic instinctively recapturing the spirit of his original in the light of individual poetic consciousness. Similarly in *The Lotos Eaters* the verse alone suffices to convey the requisite atmosphere, without entailing any modification of Tennyson's natural idiom. In verse, as in diction, Spenser is the Poet's Poet. The stanza that he invented for a unique occasion, as the medium for expressing things unattempted either before or since, passed forthwith into the common heritage as of all verse forms the most purely English by nature and descent.

CHAPTER IX

Philosophical Ideas

BEN JONSON would have Spenser read for his matter,
Milton found in him "a better teacher than Scotus or
Aquinas", an equivocal designation but compatible
with its author's account of his early reading "among those
lofty fables and romances, which recount in solemn cantos
the deeds of knighthood". The humanist, Spenser, surpasses
the schoolman, Aquinas, in teaching not through dialectic,
but through example. His way is the way of poetry, which
subordinates argument to representation; the source of his
inspiration is neither Plato nor Aristotle, Tasso nor Ariosto,
but Apollo and the sacred Nine. He entices not by the
novelty of his doctrine, not by thoughts translated into the
language of poetry, but by the magic of winged words and
poetic thought. The dead matter of erudition has suffered a
sea-change into the new life of creative experience.

But Spenser set out to be a philosophical poet, never
doubting the high seriousness of his art. Granting him pre-
cedence as a poet, we cannot ignore that side of his achievement to which he himself attached supreme importance. His
contemporaries, who regarded all knowledge as the province
of the poet, would never have been guilty of such miscon-
ception. "It is not sufficient", writes Gabriel Harvey, "for
poets to be superficial humanists; but they must be exquisite
artists, and curious universal schollers".[1] In common with
the rest of his school Spenser consistently associated poetry
with philosophy, though he would doubtless have concurred
with Milton in appraising the former as more "simple, sensuous and passionate". If the moral value of *The Faerie
Queene* be negligible it is reduced to an epic of nonsense, the

very poetry of which must inevitably suffer from the author's persistent striving after the unattainable. To dissociate the poetry from the delectable teaching is to raise an artificial barrier between content and form.

Such a censure as that of M. Emile Legouis, who stigmatises the whole of Spenser's "philosophy", apart from his "borrowed Platonism", as "trite, tame, shallow, nerveless",[2] applies only to isolated excerpts and not to this philosophy as a whole. Living in an epoch of intellectual disruption and of second-hand scholarship Spenser showed himself peculiarly susceptible to the influence of the moment. His "philosophy", like that of Tennyson, temperamental rather than intellectual, finds expression through "short swallow-flights of song" that offer no final answer to the fundamental problems of existence. But neither plagiarism nor inconsistencies in argument disprove capacity for independent or discursive thought. The discovery of one age becomes the commonplace of the next, but in losing distinction it does not necessarily lose value. The originality of Spenser, both as poet and thinker, must be judged in the light of his times, which reveals him not as a mere mouthpiece of "borrowed Platonism" embellished with trite sentiment and shallow aphorism, but as a serious thinker striving earnestly, through reading and observation, to formulate a criticism of life.

Logical consistency and precision in reasoning were rendered impossible by the eclectic character of his scholarship, the diversity of his intentions and the form in which he chose to present his argument. His thought and beliefs betray the influence of authorities so widely different as Plato and Aristotle, the Bible and the Kabbala, Lucretius and Ovid, Latin Stoics and mediæval schoolmen, Italian Platonists and Protestant divines. His ideas are tinged with the scepticism of that obscure "Atheistic" school in which his patron Raleigh appears to have played a prominent part. So freely does he draw upon the commonplaces of contemporary thought that it is impossible to determine even approximately his immediate obligation to any single author. In the process of portraying ideal humanity he is diverted from the highway of ethics, from the rule of manners and conduct, to sidetracks of metaphysical speculation. The fashioning of the perfect life entails enquiry into the origin of life, but the moral and natural philosophy deduced therefrom is inconclusive, leaving a sense of dissatisfaction as with an unfathomable universe. To a mind thus at discord with itself allegory offers a means of reconciling abstract thought with concrete representation, at the same time affording a refuge from both; but in the shifting light of poetic fancy reasoning frequently becomes blurred or obliterated. This mental turmoil and confusion is particularly evident in Spenser's attitude towards Giordano Bruno, who seems at once to have interested and alarmed him. Mutability's case is advanced only to be rejected or explained away; nevertheless her defence remains as the finest and most effective piece of pure philosophic poetry throughout *The Faerie Queene*.

Spenser's few utterances upon matters of religion correspond broadly with the tenets of Low Church Anglicanism. *An Hymne of Heavenly Love* covers summarily the ground of *Paradise Lost* in recounting the story of the Creation, the revolt and overthrow of Lucifer, the Fall, the Incarnation and the Redemption. *An Hymne of Heavenly Beautie* embodies the commonplaces of Christian Platonism, possibly reinforced by Kabbalistic writings which, according to M. Saurat, suggested the figure of Sapience reposing in the bosom of the Eternal Father.[3] The legend of Holiness, portraying a pilgrimage towards perfection by the help of grace, follows familiar lines of mediæval allegory; and a strain of mysticism permeates the whole conception of ideal life as set forth in *The Faerie Queene*. Beyond this, religion counts for little in Spenser's moralising, and theology for even less. Only in the last extremity does he evoke a new world to redress the balance of the present.

The conflicting interests of his ethical thought may be

attributed largely to peculiarities of temperament and status. Lifelong distaste for his environment threw him back upon the resources of his inner being, strengthening an innate tendency towards introspection. The instinct of a humanist urged him to propound an objective criticism of life striking the balance between active and contemplative, adjusting "Nosce teipsum" to "Humani nihil a me alienum puto". Such ethic as may be deduced from the minor poems resolves itself into the pursuit of virtue through self-mastery, with a corresponding contempt for worldly vanities and vice. The same ideal, subjected to more minute analysis, supplies the allegorical motive of Books I and II of *The Faerie Queene*; throughout the remainder interest is fairly evenly divided between such private virtue and its practical demonstration in public service. Whilst duly enforcing the necessity of discipline Spenser never identifies it with repression and would probably have endorsed the Utopians' definition of virtue as "the life according to nature". "L'Allegro" and "Il Penseroso" play an equal part throughout his writings, from the *Calender* to the cantos of Mutability; the one is indispensable to the other.

When Bruno visited Oxford in 1583 he was dismayed to find the authorities of a university ostensibly devoted to philosophic studies still content with the dregs of Scholasticism; and although conditions may have been slightly better at Cambridge, as the result of recent humanistic influences, generally speaking, philosophy in England was reactionary, in no wise fulfilling the promise suggested by earlier protagonists like Colet and More. Probably Spenser owed most of his knowledge of Plato and Aristotle to recent Italian commentators; but even this second-hand philosophy impressed his friends in Dublin as a rare accomplishment, and by employing it as a didactic foundation to epic poetry he was breaking entirely new ground. Nearly a century earlier William Grocyn, a stalwart Aristotelian, had affirmed that between Aristotle and Plato lay all the difference dividing a world of fact from one of myth. But the poet and the allegorist could find in the Platonic myths the very basis of his metaphysic and an infinite store of suggestion for symbolic imagery. Whilst, therefore, the formal scheme of *The Faerie Queene* is Aristotelian, the life and soul of the allegory lies in Renaissance neo-Platonism, which enlarges Spenser's vision beyond the narrow horizon of formal ethic.

His starting-point is that of the orthodox sixteenth-century moralist as represented in Lodowick Bryskett's *Discourse of Civill Life* and in its original, the three dialogues of Giraldi Cinthio; and so close is the relation that, in many places, the *Discourse* reads as almost a commentary or prose paraphrase upon passages in *The Faerie Queene*. In his preface, Bryskett, like Spenser, proposes to treat of ethics, "which may move me to impart after unto thee another treating of the Politike part of Moral Philosophie, which I have likewise prepared to follow this, if I shall find the favourable acceptation hereof such as may encourage me thereunto". His "choice grafts and flowers" are "taken from the Greeke and Latine Philosophie, and ingrafted upon the stocke of our mother English-tongue", and his object, like that of his original, is "to frame a gentleman fit for civill conversation, and to set him in the direct way that leadeth him to his civill felicitie". Ethics he defines as that part of moral philosophy "which frameth men fittest for civill conservation, teaching them whatt morall vertues are,...and likewise what vice is, and how unseemly a thing, and how harmefull to a good mind the spot and contagion thereof is". The aim of life is felicity, civil and contemplative, "a perfection of all the good gifts of body and mind", attained through the exercise of reason, "ruling the disordinate affects". And here Dr Long is made to interpose an objection, borrowed from Giraldi, and echoed time and again by Spenser, to the effect that human felicity "is without, not your reach onely, but all mens, whiles they are here in this low and muddie world: for I wis that is no where to be found but above the stars: mans felicity is placed only in heaven, where God of his mercie hath appointed it for him to be found, and not here on earth".

Spenser was further indebted to Giraldi, or to his translator, for some of the details of his ethical scheme. According to the *Discourse* the magnanimous, or great-minded man, enjoying immunity from moral taint, "utterly despiseth all injuries, for that an ill man cannot by any injury he can do unto him, blemish those vertues wherewith he must be adorned to be truly magnanimous". The functions of human nature are divided into the Platonic categories vegetative, sensitive and intellective, the last of which shines most conspicuously in the man who "suppresseth all his passions, and abandoning all earthly cares, bendeth his studies and his thoughts wholly unto heavenly things; and kindled and inflamed with divine love, laboureth to enjoy that unspeakable beauty, which hath bin the cause to inflame him, and to raise his thoughts to so high a pitch". Reason, elevating man above brute creation, enables him to perceive "how all other things that grow and live on earth are corruptible, and do resolve into their first periods or beginnings, and cease any more to be, as soone as the soule of life departeth from them; but that our minds are immortal and incorruptible, whereby we may rest assured of an eternall life".[4] The last of the three dialogues presents many striking points of similarity to Spenser's legend of Friendship. In short, a close comparison of the *Discourse* with *The Faerie Queene* goes to prove that the former supplied a considerable body of raw material for the general design of fashioning a gentleman, for the attributes of principal personages and for such allegorical inventions as the House of Holiness, the Castle of Alma, or the Bower of Bliss.

But Spenser's criticism of life does not end with ethics and civil polity. The common motive that enables him to relate moral with natural philosophy is that of love, predominant in all his major works and presented under each of its three traditional aspects, conventional, physical and metaphysical. *The Faerie Queene*, *Amoretti* and the fugitive pieces addressed to the honour of Rosalind are among the latest English monuments to that chivalric code of devotion towards a mistress which, originally transmitted from Ovid by the troubadours, governs the whole ethic of mediæval romantic literature. In *Amoretti* sentiment provides little more than a basis to poetic figure and conceit. But throughout the later books of *The Faerie Queene* much space is devoted to the portrayal of various erotic types, smitten in divers ways by the common malady; and this large-scale extract from the general map of man affords occasion for inquiry into the nature of things, for progression from "the twelve moral virtues as Aristotle hath devised" to a metaphysic which, at different points, bears analogy with that of the pre-Platonics, Plato and his school, Lucretius, Ovid, Cicero and Plutarch.

The same subject is treated at considerable length in the four *Hymnes*. According to the first of these, in the beginning earth was a "moving mightie mass" of unruly elements warring within the wide womb of the world and imprisoned by

> An huge eternall Chaos, which supplyes
> The substaunces of natures fruitfull progenyes,[5]

a statement that would seem to corroborate Mutability's designation of earth as "Great Chaos child". To this universal discord and confusion Love brought peace and order, assigning to every creature its place in the cosmos, making unity of diversity and establishing the law of procreation. So Love becomes "the worlds great Parent", born of Venus, begot of Plenty and Penury, as Ficino, after Plato, represents it in his commentary upon the *Symposium*. All live unto Love, their heaven-born sovereign, who awakens in man desire for the best, operating through reason as opposed to appetite, the instrument of lust, whose feeble wings cannot fly above the dirty dross of earth. In *An Hymne of Heavenly Love* Spenser attempts to bring these Pagan notions into line with Christian theology. Love, here identified with "that eternall Powre", the Trinity, is uncreated, loving itself for all eternity; but

it is still the creative principle, proceeding from God first
to those "trinall triplicities", the Dionysian hierarchy of
angels, and, after the fall of Lucifer, to man. The witness
of divine love is the revelation of Christ through the Incarnation, the Redemption and the Sacrament. Its fruition is
universal brotherhood, the binding of the human race

> with an eternall band,
> Him first to love that us so dearely bought,
> And next our brethren, to his image wrought.[6]

Such commonplaces of Renaissance neo-Platonism might
have been gleaned from the treatises of Ficino, the more
practical illustrations of Castiglione or their many deriva-
tives. But Spenser has a great deal more to say on the subject
of love, which is a cardinal motive in all his poetry and which
elsewhere he treats under its physical aspects. At the opposite
pole to that of *An Hymne of Heavenly Love* stands the myth of
Amoret, curiously compounded of natural science and primitive religious cults; for Amoret is the adopted of Venus,
whose frank sensuality finds utterance in her speech to Diana:

> As you in woods and wanton wildernesse
> Your glory sett to chace the salvage beasts,
> So my delight is all in joyfulnesse,
> In beds, in bowres, in banckets, and in feasts;
> And ill beseemes you, with your lofty creasts,
> To scorne the joy that Jove is glad to seeke:
> We both are bownd to follow heavens beheasts,
> And tend our charges with obeisaunce meeke,
> Spare, gentle sister, with reproch my paine to eeke.[7]

Under the guidance of Psyche, Amoret learns "true feminity"
in the garden of Adonis, a very paradise of eternal spring and
harvest, peopled by lovers who freely enjoy the consummation of their bliss:

> Franckly each Paramor his leman knowes,
> Each bird his mate; ne any does envy
> Their goodly meriment and gay felicity.[8]

Their only law is that of love, here synonymous with pleasure in the act of union for the purpose of generation. The divine commission to be fruitful and multiply is fulfilled by a natural, physical process arising from the moisture in matter; and for this reason the birth of Belphœbe, "of the wombe of morning dew", is no miracle but capable of rational explanation. Genius, the porter of the garden, is continually letting forth those who desire a new terrestrial birth. After birth they return by the other gate to the garden, there to remain a thousand years before again assuming fleshly weeds. But although "infinite shapes of creatures there are bred", to be daily sent forth, this neither increases nor reduces the permanent unchanging substance in the "wide womb of the world", from which all creatures derive their being and to which, after successive changes in form, they return.

Such notions are nearer Ovid and Lucretius than Plato. The same theory of cyclic existence is expounded at length in the fifteenth book of the *Metamorphoses*, which ostensibly reproduces the philosophy of Pythagoras. The physical explanation of birth undoubtedly comes from Lucretius, who further supplies Spenser with details such as the simile of "fruitful Nile" and the walls of iron and gold encircling the garden, or the created universe. No gardener is needed to sow, plant or prune in a paradise where all things grow spontaneously, without divine intervention; and the solitary reference to the "Almighty Lord" who first established the law of generation amounts to little more than the formal tributes of Lucretius to the gods "who in tranquillity enjoy peace and an unruffled existence".[9] In the sequel to this episode, describing the abduction of Amoret by Scudamour, Spenser again stresses the physical origin of life and love. Though friendship between men who "on chaste vertue grounded their desire" stands on a higher plane than heterosexual passion, the latter is as innocent and immaculate as the conception of Amoret and Belphœbe. The Temple is set with

an hundred brasen caudrons bright
To bath in joy and amorous desire,[10]

whilst every object serves to stimulate passion and the instinct to reproduce, unchecked by moral or religious scruple. The one deity worshipped by all is Venus Genetrix, Mother of all, goddess of beauty and creation, whose praises are hymned in verses freely adapted from the opening of the *De Rerum Natura*:

> So all the world by thee at first was made,
> And dayly yet thou doest the same repayre;
> Ne ought on earth that merry is and glad,
> Ne ought on earth that lovely is and fayre,
> But thou the same for pleasure didst prepayre;
> Thou art the root of all that joyous is:
> Great god of men and women, queene of th' ayre,
> Mother of laughter, and welspring of blisse,
> O graunt that of my love at last I may not misse.[11]

The figures and machinery of Venus' Temple—Doubt, Delay, Danger, the shield of Cupid and the like—belong to mediæval erotic allegory. But Spenser has invested these familiar devices with a new metaphysical value. For Scudamour is the concrete representation of the lover whose abstract state forms the subject-matter of the first *Hymne*. To both love is a discipline refining character, the aspiration towards an ideal not lightly to be won. A connection, if not an identification, between the *Hymne* and Spenser's lost "Hell of Lovers, his Purgatorie" is rendered probable by the lines

> So thou thy folke, through paines of Purgatorie
> Dost beare unto thy blisse, and heavens glorie;[12]

in like manner Scudamour, before attaining his object, must endure the trials and setbacks of a lover's purgatory:

> Long were to tell the travell and long toile
> Through which this shield of love I late have wonne,
> And purchased this peerelesse beauties spoile,
> That harder may be ended then begonne.[13]

Thus, while his passion is more earthly than that of Arthur, Britomart or Artegall, whom love inspires to deeds and

honour beyond itself, Scudamour stands in the same position
as the lover of the *Hymne* and his ancient forbears, Leander,
Æneas, Achilles and Orpheus:

> Then forth he casts in his unquiet thought,
> What he may do, her favour to obtaine;
> What brave exploit, what perill hardly wrought
> What puissant conquest, what adventurous paine,
> May please her best, and grace unto him gaine;
> He dreads no danger, nor misfortune feares,
> His faith, his fortune, in his breast he beares.
>
> Thou art his god, thou art his mightie guyde,
> Thou, being blind, letst him not see his feares,
> But cariest him to that which he hath eyde,
> Through seas, through flames, through thousand
>   swords and speares.[14]

As the universal creative force, moving sun and stars and
inflaming the gentle heart with desire for the sovereign good,
love lies at the very foundation of Spenser's cosmos, and its
origin is appropriately related with the myth of Adonis.
Adonis is the Phœnician Thammuz, slain by the boar to be
born again, typifying sometimes day in conflict with night, at
others the seed lying buried through winter to burst forth
anew with the coming of spring. In the *Nativity Ode* and in
Paradise Lost Milton numbers him among the false gods on
account of the excesses associated with his worship, the
natural consequences of a phallic cult. But Spenser, unde-
terred by any such religious orthodoxy and recognising the
profound truth underlying the ancient tale, accords Adonis
honourable place in the natural mythology of *The Faerie
Queene*. The beloved of Venus, he holds his secret sanctuary
within the garden, confined, like Thammuz "the hidden one",
out of sight during his six months' rest underground:

> By her hid from the world, and from the skill
> Of Stygian Gods, which doe her love envy;
> But she her selfe, when ever that she will,
> Possesseth him, and of his sweetnesse takes her fill.

And sooth, it seemes, they say; for he may not
For ever dye, and ever buried bee
In balefull night where all thinges are forgot:
All be he subject to mortalitie,
Yet is eterne in mutabilitie,
And by succession made perpetuall,
Transformed oft, and chaunged diverslie:
For him the Father of all formes they call:
Therfore needs mote he live, that living gives to all.[15]

Alone he symbolises matter, from which all creation is derived and to which it ultimately returns; but by union with Venus, the divine and life-giving principle of form, he becomes the "Father of all forms", begetting an infinite progeny of living creatures. The sex symbolism is the reverse of that in the "House of Alma" episode, where the "immortal perfect mind" is masculine, the "imperfect mortal body" feminine. But both allegories are based upon the same conception of life as the imparting of form to matter, a theory originally derived from the *Timæus*.

The details of the Temple of Venus afford further evidence of Spenser's interest in old religious cults and comparative mythology. The priests of the goddess are damsels, "in soft linen dight", the feet and hands of her idol are entwined by a serpent, while the idol itself is covered with a veil for reasons not definitely known but perhaps because

she hath both kinds in one,
Both male and female, both under one name:
She syre and mother is herselfe alone,
Begets and eke conceives, ne needeth other none.[16]

This last attribute specially belongs to Venus Cypria, who is frequently represented as a Hermaphrodite. But Venus Cypria is identical with the Egyptian Isis, and Spenser is therefore justified in transferring to her some of the latter's attributes, in particular her linen-clad priests and her veil. In Book v, canto vii, of *The Faerie Queene* she reappears under her original Egyptian name. Britomart, on her way to rescue

Artegall, spends a night within the Temple of Isis, where she has a symbolic vision of her future union with Artegall and its consequence. The description of the appearance and ascetic habits of the priests who minister to the cult is drawn mainly from Plutarch's *Isis and Osiris*. But for the horrid vision which follows Spenser freely adapts ancient myth and symbol to his own allegory. Britomart dreams that she is sacrificing before the idol of the goddess, when suddenly a violent tempest kindles into flame the holy embers upon the altar, threatening to destroy the whole temple. At this the crocodile sleeping under the idol's feet suddenly awakes and, devouring both flames and tempest, grows big with pride and begins to threaten the stranger. But the goddess beats him back, whereupon his wrath turns to love, and throwing himself at Britomart's feet he offers her his embraces:

> Which she accepting, he so neare her drew
> That of his game she soone enwombed grew,
> And forth did bring a Lion of great might,
> That shortly did all other beasts subdew.[17]

In the morning she relates her dream to the chief priest, who is struck with amazement at this unexpected proof of her royal origin and tells her the interpretation. The crocodile is Osiris, sleeping under the feet of Isis as the symbol of justice ruled by clemency, his regular attribute in ancient mythology; so the union of Britomart with Osiris typifies her future marriage with Artegall, the knight of justice, while the lion represents their offspring, the royal ancestor of a noble progeny. Spenser's fable has, of course, many analogues, such as the traditional origin of Alexander the Great, Scipio Africanus and other heroes; but the myth with which he associates it greatly enhances its significance and romantic interest.

Spenser's notions concerning beauty, as the formative principle, owe more to authority and less to invention than his theory of love. In *An Hymne in honour of Beautie*, dedicated to the praise of Venus, we learn that beauty was born of heavenly race, serving as pattern to "this world's great workmaister", a conception drawn from the *Timæus*. The soul in its passage to earth from "that great immortal Spright" takes light from the sun, imparting this to the body which it assumes. Beauty of body, therefore, depends not upon the fusion "of colours faire and goodly temprament of pure complexions" but upon the celestial light within the soul, who has chosen a house meet for herself and whose beauty must therefore shine outwardly in the "comely corpse". This idea, which continually recurs in the *Amoretti*, as in other contemporary sonnet cycles, finds noblest expression in *Epithalamion*:

> But if ye saw that which no eyes can see,
> The inward beauty of her lively spright,
> Garnisht with heavenly guifts of high degree,
> Much more then would ye wonder at that sight,
> And stand astonisht lyke to those which red
> Medusaes mazeful hed.
> There dwels sweet love, and constant chastity,
> Unspotted fayth, and comely womanhood,
> Regard of honour, and mild modesty;
> There vertue raynes as Queene in royal throne,
> And giveth lawes alone,
> The which the base affections doe obay,
> And yeeld theyr services unto her will;
> Ne thought of thing uncomely ever may
> Thereto approch to tempt her mind to ill.
> Had ye once seene these her celestial threasures,
> And unrevealed pleasures,
> Then would ye wonder, and her prayses sing,
> That al the woods should answer, and your echo ring.[18]

Here is true Spenser and Spenser alone. But the adaptation of the familiar Platonic theme is not always so effective or so free from confusion. If beauty emanates from soul to body, how comes it

> That goodly beautie, albe heavenly borne,
> Is foule abusd,

or, on the other hand,

> that many a gentle mynd
> Dwels in deformed tabernacle drownd?[19]

Castiglione attributes the anomaly to man's defective vision
and judgment. But Spenser makes little or no attempt to
meet it. Moreover, in explaining the sense of beauty he
resorts to mysticism by representing it as a special gift of
heavenly Sapience to the initiate, instead of following Plato
and relating it to the theory of pre-existence figured in the
garden of Adonis. But it is not remarkable that Spenser
should have failed to penetrate very deeply into the metaphysics and psychology of beauty, for here reason and
argument necessarily give way to rhapsody, to the poet's
sheer physical delight in the joy of being, the glory of the
visible world and the mysterious loveliness of woman.

An Hymne of Heavenly Beautie presents a new interpretation
of the cosmos in the light of Christian theology. God has
imparted some measure of His own perfect beauty to the
created universe, grading it, on this basis, into the elements
of earth, water, air, fire and the empyrean heaven:

> By view whereof it plainly may appeare,
> That still as every thing doth upward tend,
> And further is from earth, so still more cleare
> And faire it grows, till to his perfect end
> Of purest beautie it at last ascend;
> Ayre more than water, fire much more than ayre,
> And heaven then fire, appeares more pure and fayre.[20]

Through the upper spheres beauty still progresses—from the
first heaven of blessed souls to the fairer realm of ideas and
intelligences, the ascending hierarchy of angels, finally to the
Primum Mobile itself. But this last perfection transcends the
power of human utterance. Man can behold only its image
as reflected in the visible world, thence eagle-like, with
"plumes of perfect speculation" mount from terrestrial
darkness to "that bright Sunne of Glorie". Through contemplation of beauty he may approach the footstool of the

"great Deity", enthroned upon the seat of Truth, bearing the Rod of Righteousness and cherishing His "soveraine dearling", Sapience,

> Clad like a Queene in royall robes, most fit
> For so great powre and peerelesse majesty,
> And all the gemmes and jewels gorgeously
> Adornd, that brighter then the starres appeare,
> And make her native brightnes seem more cleare.[21]

The whole poem is rooted in neo-Platonism, overlaid with the scholastic mysticism which distinguishes it from *An Hymne in honour of Beautie*. The replacement of Io, "Beauty's Queen" in the earlier poem, by Divine Sapience denotes a general transition from Pagan myth to Christian allegory. The conception of the soul's progress through successive stages of beauty towards the Beatific Vision resembles that of the *Paradiso*, and the metaphor representing it has as much in common with Dante's eagle of divine grace as with Plato's wings of the soul; nor is it difficult to recognise the affinity between Spenser's Sapience, portrayed as Queen of Heaven, and the figure of Our Lady in the mystical and apocalyptic literature of the Middle Ages.

In the second *Hymne* Spenser distinguishes between two orders or stages of beauty, the physical and the cosmic. The former is no more than the "pleasant grace" of outward appearance, gratifying sense alone; the latter, discerned by reason, reflects the divinity immanent in universal creation and in the individual soul, the "goodly Paterne" and

> perfect Beautie, which all men adore;
> Whose face and feature doth so much excell
> All mortall sence, that none the same may tell.[22]

But even this is only an image of "Heavenly" or "intellectual" beauty, the third and final stage which forms the subject of the fourth *Hymne*, the Divine Unity of Truth and Wisdom itself, fairer than Platonic ideas or angelic "trinal triplicities", and utterly beyond the grasp of human intelligence. Spenser's scheme is identical with that propounded by Giordano Bruno in *De gl' heroici furori*; and the inference that he was drawing directly upon Bruno is corroborated by his adoption of certain illustrations peculiar to Bruno as well as of the latter's cardinal principle of animism.[23] The same three orders of beauty have their respective symbols in *The Faerie Queene*. Adonis by union with Venus becomes the "father of all forms" and therefore of all concrete physical beauty throughout the natural world. Cosmic beauty is symbolised by Concord, who plays nature's part in maintaining the harmony of the universe :

> By her the heaven is in his course contained,
> And all the world in state unmoved stands,
> As their Almightie maker first ordained,
> And bound them with inviolable bands;
> Else would the waters overflow the lands,
> And fire devoure the ayre, and hell them quight,
> But that she holds them with her blessed hands.
> She is the nourse of pleasure and delight,
> And unto Venus grace the gate doth open right.[24]

Her attributes, though undoubtedly borrowed from Boethius,[25] also recall the theory of contraries, expounded by Bruno in the latter part of the *Causa, Principio et Uno*. Lastly, Una may be identified with Sapience, of the fourth *Hymne*, as personifying the mystical Unity of truth and wisdom, the idea of absolute beauty veiled from mortal eye. The differences dividing the didactic argument of the *Hymnes* from the symbolic representations of *The Faerie Queene* cover a common philosophy entailing the same conclusion:

> Then gin I thinke on that which Nature sayd,
> Of that same time when no more Change shall be,
> But stedfast rest of all things, firmely stayd
> Upon the pillours of Eternity,
> That is contrayr to Mutabilitie;
> For all that moveth doth in Change delight;
> But thence-forth all shall rest eternally
> With him that is the God of Sabaoth hight:
> O! that great Sabaoth God, grant me that Sabaoths sight.

And looke at last up to that Soveraine Light,
From whose pure beams al perfect beauty springs,
That kindleth love in every godly spright
Even the love of God; which loathing brings
Of this vile world and these gay-seeming things;
With whose sweete pleasures being so possest,
Thy straying thoughts henceforth for ever rest.[26]

From the frequency with which Spenser harks back to the foregoing sentiment it might appear that, failing to co-ordinate the one with the many, he was driven ultimately to the refuge of the contemplative ascetic, loathing "this state of life so tickle" and resolving to fix his thought upon eternity. The assumption could be supported by reference to his philosophy of the spirit, which is based largely upon the Christian doctrine of original sin—the root motive to *An Hymne of Heavenly Love,*—and the metaphysical conception of conflict between soul and body. Genius, granting a soul new fleshly weeds, "clothes it with sinfull mire" while the unique prerogative of Belphœbe is her immaculate conception,

> Pure and unspotted from all loathly crime
> That is ingenerate in fleshly slime.[27]

The dualism presented objectively and analysed at length under the figure of Alma suggests many a fugitive image pointing the same moral. The soul that should "rule the earthly masse" is more often frail and feeble, brought into captivity, fretted "with crosses and with cares", "soyld with fowl iniquity", dismayed by "the dart of sinfull guilt". At the moment of death she may "retaine her seat", returning "back to her home againe" or "flit from her cage", "unbodied of the burdenous corpse", either to be "assoyld from sinful fleshlinesse" or else descend "unto her place of punishment". Such figures are in complete accord with Christian eschatology, both Catholic and Protestant.

But Spenser's criticism of life may be viewed from quite another aspect. The envoy to *The Faerie Queene,* penned, perhaps, during those last unhappy days of January, 1599, and representing an obvious attempt to round off an unfinished work, sounds strangely discordant with the epic of Humanism and with the genius of an artist so alive to the joy of being and the beauties of physical creation. The retraction comes ill from a poet whose work composes one grand pæan to nature and to human achievement as intrinsically fair and laudable, not simply as the foretaste of an after-life, to which this is but a probation. Like the wayworn pilgrims of *The Earthly Paradise*, he would have his Elysium upon earth, clinging passionately to life and ever striving to dissolve present apprehensions in glamorous visions of the past. No moral law or religious inhibition mars the "sweete love" and "goodly meriment" of the Garden of Adonis, the "spotlesse pleasures" and unbridled Hedonism of Venus' Isle. For the "gay seeming things" of earth have too great a hold upon human nature to be easily abandoned, and the conception of beauty as the image of divine order throughout the cosmos opens the possibility of correlating metaphysics with natural philosophy. The creative principle moving all things in one celestial harmony is the God of Love; wherefore "All that's good is beautifull and faire", Spenser's version of "Beauty is truth, truth beauty". But the supreme authority invoked by Mutability and accepted by her opponents is Nature, "vicaire of the almyghty Lord", whose sergeant, Order, assigns to every creature his proper place within the whole design. The national pests disfiguring the land of Faerie—Error, Deceit, Tyranny, Anarchy, Lust, Detraction—all spring from the cardinal evil principle, Disorder. The golden age of antiquity, the long desired Millennium, is an age of concord, a reign of universal beauty emanating from the first designer, Who saw His work that it was very good.

Spenser's failure to reconcile the needs of the flesh with those of the spirit was symptomatic of contemporary intellectualism. The perfect logic of the scholastic system, which gave Dante his supremacy over all religious poets, would no longer serve in its entirety for minds questioning or discrediting the fundamental postulates upon which that system was based; nor, on the other hand, could a Christian poet rest satisfied with a Pagan Stoicism enjoining repression and the practice of virtue as more or less aimless ideals, unrelated to any ultimate purpose beyond the bounds of mortality. Between the Scylla and Charybdis of obscurantism and scepticism the only safe course was a correlation of ethics and metaphysics with the facts of nature, the course necessarily adopted by a poet devoting his greatest work to the broad and comprehensive interpretation of life.

Herein lies the peculiar interest attaching to the Garden of Adonis, the Temple of Venus and the case of Mutability. The garden is the source of physical generation,

> the first seminary
> Of all things that are borne to live and dye,
> According to their kynds.[28]

From the "huge eternall Chaos" situate in the "wide wombe of the world" issues a constant supply of substance, which is given "fleshly weeds" with "form and feature" by Genius, porter of the Garden, at the command of Fate. Death is no more than the dissolution and transformation of immortal substance which thereupon re-enters the garden, remaining within it for some thousand years before assuming another life on earth. So life consists in a cyclic process of continual change as unchanging substance revolves through successive re-incarnations. Adonis, or matter, quickened by life-giving Venus, or form, is

> eterne in mutabilitie,
> And by succession made perpetuall,
> Transformed oft, and chaunged diverslie.[29]

The innocent pleasures and frank intercourse of lovers and of mating birds accord with nature's universal law. So every inmate of the Garden enjoys eternal springtime and the satisfaction of desire, while at the Temple of "Venus Genetrix" every creature joins in hymning the Great Mother of generation, source of all life and pleasure. Yet over the whole picture broods a profound sense of pathos; for in the foreground is the figure of wicked Time with flaggy wings and cruel scythe, uprooting the young flowers, beating down the leaves and buds to wither in the dust. Substance is eternal, death but a transformation; but what of the beauty that dies, inherent in each successive form yet doomed to wane and vanish? Such is the universal ordinance,

> For formes are variable and decay
> By course of kind and by occasion,

but the pity of it yet remains,

> And that faire flowre of beautie fades away,
> As doth the lilly fresh before the sunny ray.[30]

And if beauty thus passes into nothingness, what of youth and vigour, brave paladins and fair women, the comely works of art and nature, what of all that graces the insubstantial land of Faerie? In spite of all that reason may allege, human sense recoils at the remorseless law of nature forbidding human survival and seemingly upholding the universal reign of Mutability.

The discrepancies in Spenser's natural philosophy arise partly from its eclectic character. Whilst his notions respecting birth, re-incarnation, the after-life and the cosmos undoubtedly owe something to the *Timæus*, the *Phædo* and the *Phædrus* of Plato, for the substance of the Garden of Adonis it was unnecessary for him to go far beyond the *Metamorphoses* of Ovid. Here he could find what purports to be a résumé of Pythagorean doctrine concerning the origin and incessant transformation of material life, the transmigration of souls without substantial annihilation by death, the mutability of elements, seasons and even of time itself, in short a sermon upon the text πάντα ῥεῖ, "omnia mutantur, nihil interit", much of which he has been content to reproduce. The contrast between Saturnine virtue and present degeneracy drawn by Pythagoras as a preface to this

imaginary discourse would likewise have infallibly appealed
to the author of *The Faerie Queene*. Moreover there was every
inducement for him to cull ideas and illustrations from the
favourite classic of the day, whose decorative style, romantic
fancy and passion for myth-making had so many features in
common with his own.

But when once we begin to compare the Ariosto of Latin
poetry with "our sage and serious Spenser" in genius, mood
and intention we immediately sense the gulf that divides a
compendium of popular science rounding off a miscellany
of monstrous fictions from a reasoned interpretation of
nature evolving from a comprehensive survey of human life
and character. Behind the surface features of Spenser's
nature-myths lies the nervous spirit of enquiry, a passionate
hold upon life, with a consequent sense of its pathos clean
contrary to Ovid's cheerful irresponsibility and more akin to
the stern conviction of Lucretius. Those mighty themes and
dark questions which Ovid cursorily surveys as matters of
common interest Lucretius subjects to long scrutiny and exhaustive analysis, investing them with all the majesty and
sublimity of "things unattempted yet in prose or rhyme".
So where the two Latin poets happen to touch common
ground—as in their discussion of universal change, the in-
destructibility of matter and the various phenomena of
animate creation—it is more than probable that Spenser
derived his main inspiration from the philosopher rather than
from the fabulist. Upon the ultimate facts of being—Divine
Providence, creation, the soul, immortality—and their outcome, religion, Spenser and Lucretius are, indeed, poles as-
under. In intellectual force, lucidity of exposition and breadth
of observation their several philosophic achievements are as
Monmouth to Macedon. But their opposing creeds often
drive them to a common conclusion. The lofty ideals of self-
control, of moderation in sensual pleasure, of indifference to
death and calamity deduced by Lucretius from the study of
Nature Spenser enjoins as the ordinance of man and of God.

Even the Platonic "House of Alma" may owe something to the observations of Lucretius concerning the mutual physical reactions of mind against body. Finally, within the confines of natural philosophy Spenser's admiration for Lucretius was sufficiently profound to induce him not only to adopt from the latter ideas, phrases and imagery but to incorporate within *The Faerie Queene* a free version of the whole invocation to the *De Rerum Natura*. To Spenser and his contemporaries, seekers after truth in an age of obstinate questioning, the poet of materialism had something to offer unsupplied by Plato or Aristotle, a theory of being reasoned out by the light of nature. Little as they might accept of his philosophy they could not but recognise and admire the Miltonic grandeur of his poetry, his sensuous and passionate response to the inexhaustible wonder and beauty of nature, his representation of life as a single visible process conforming with immutable laws; and many a passage from their works would seem to echo the magnificent close to the second book of the *De Rerum Natura*, where with remorseless logic the philosopher applies his own theory to enforce upon his readers the tragedy of existence.

The trend of Spenser's conclusions upon the nature of things is all in the direction of a fatalism, encouraged rather than averted through his reading of ancient writers. Probably it was the realisation of this fact that persuaded him, towards the end of his life, to tackle the problem afresh, at greater length than heretofore and in the light of more recent authority. In the first folio edition of *The Faerie Queene* (1609) there appeared for the first time two cantos of Mutability which, according to the editor, "appear to be parcell of some following booke of *The Faerie Queene*, under the Legend of Constancie". The hypothesis is unsubstantiated and not very ingenious, though the editor presumably had some authority for numbering the cantos as VI and VII. Apart from method and versification there is no internal evidence to connect them with the remainder of *The Faerie Queene* nor, apparently, was Constancy admitted in any current scheme of virtues. As they stand, the cantos constitute an independent allegorical poem representing Spenser's last and most systematic attempt to formulate a philosophy of nature, a theme so lofty and so unfamiliar as to demand a special invocation to his Muse.

The rebel Titaness, Mutability, having overthrown each of the lower planets in turn, finally challenges the supremacy of Jove himself, demanding trial at the bar of Nature. In support of her claim to sovereignty she cites the whole visible universe as all alike subject to incessant change. Day and night, light and darkness, time, hours and seasons, the four ages of man are never stable but ever moving. The elements are transmutable—earth becomes rarefied into water, air, and fire, fire feeds upon itself, reducing its prey to nought but barren ashes. Earth's surface continually shifts, land and sea encroaching upon one another. New creatures arise from the decay and death of their own kind, beasts are massacred as thralls to man's behest, man himself is never the same either in mind or body. Even time continually moves and changes. Nor is this universal mutability merely the lot of the sublunary world, as the gods would vainly allege. Luna, Mercury and Mars have run clean from their course, Jove himself is of terrestrial origin, born, according to different traditions, in Crete, Thebes and elsewhere, subject, therefore, to the law of change. The evidence embraces the entire range of physical creation, from its lowest strata to the empyrean heavens; and so passionate is the defence that none save Nature durst gainsay it. For though a rebel against the laws of the first Creator, Mutability is yet so fair to behold as to disarm the very gods and powers whom she threatens; nor is this remarkable, seeing that she symbolises the infinite variety and ever-changing beauty of the natural world, the insubstantial pageant of a poet's dream.

Despite the fundamental flaw which ultimately invalidates her defence, Mutability is expressing a point of view to which

Edmund Spenser

Spenser himself has often inclined and with which he has ample sympathy. The case which she defends with such enthusiasm and such wealth of illustration follows as a logical corollary from many passages in *The Faerie Queene*, more especially from the notions underlying the mythical Garden of Adonis. Spenser is deliberately confining himself to the domain of natural philosophy, without resort to mysticism, of which few traces are to be found in *The Faerie Queene* after the close of Book II. So the supreme arbiter in the case is neither Jove nor Jehovah but Nature, greater than gods or men, mother and impartial judge of all things in heaven and earth:

> This great Grandmother of all creatures bred,
> Great Nature, ever young, yet full of eld;
> Still mooving, yet unmoved from her sted;
> Unseene of any, yet of all beheld.[31]

So hard is it to describe her array that even Chaucer in his *Fowles Parley* durst not attempt it,

> But it transfered to Alane, who he thought
> Had in his *Plaint of kinde* describ'd it well:
> Which who will read set forth so as it ought,
> Go seek he out that Alane where he may be sought.[32]

"Alane" is Alain de l'Isle, whose *De Planctu Naturæ* supplied Chaucer with his information concerning the appointments and offices of Nature; and Spenser's reference is sufficiently guarded to suggest that he himself had not "sought out" the author in question, in spite of certain striking analogues to the *De Planctu Naturæ* in the House of Alma as well as in this episode of Mutability. But whether he knew Alain or not he must certainly have been struck by Chaucer's designation of Nature as "vicar of the Almighty Lord", culled direct from Alain but ultimately derived from their common source Boethius. For this is precisely the rôle of Nature at the trial of Mutability, as regent of the unseen Creator; and for Spenser the old mediæval notion acquired a new value by reason of its approximation to certain new phases of contemporary thought.

234

Philosophical Ideas

How Spenser became familiar with the ideas of Giordano Bruno, the most original philosopher of his time, we can only conjecture. Between 1583 and 1585 Bruno was in England, where he published five of his Italian works, dedicating two of them to Spenser's first patron, Sidney, and consorting with Sidney's circle. By this time Spenser had apparently been out of touch with Sidney for three years, and it is therefore equally probable that his attention was drawn to Bruno by some other means, especially as Sidney's own work shows no trace of Bruno's influence. In any case it can hardly be questioned that Spenser knew something of Bruno's philosophy and was impressed by it, though he may not have made this discovery before the closing years of his life. While most, if not all, of the parallels between Bruno's work and the *Hymnes* can be attributed to their common origin in neo-Platonic sources, the cantos of Mutability were undoubtedly written under the direct influence of Bruno, if not actually inspired by him.

Bruno's independence of mind and his enthusiastic acceptance of Copernican astronomy aroused in him an extreme contempt not merely for Scholasticism but also for much of both Plato and Aristotle. Refusing blind allegiance to any single authority he sought guidance from both pre-Platonic and neo-Platonic sources, from the nature philosophers of all ages, from the Arabian Peripatetics and even from certain of the despised schoolmen. His mobile intellect, his fervid imagination, the novelty of his doctrines and his peculiar modes of exposition were all calculated to appeal to Spenser, who was the first English writer, by nearly half a century, to show any traces of his influence in the domain of natural philosophy. To the familiar theme of universal change transmitted from Heraclitus and Pythagoras to Lucretius, Ovid and the Latin Stoics, allegorically figured by Spenser in his Garden of Adonis, Bruno added new and startling significance by connecting it with the results of recent scientific experiment and discovery; and here Spenser

235

was content to follow him, though only for a short space and at considerable distance.

Bruno regards the unity, or God, as a *causa immanens* operating throughout the universe, which thereby becomes a living cosmos for the fulfilment of the divine purpose; and the pantheistic trend of his thought, particularly apparent throughout the Italian dialogues published in England, would account for the importance which he attributes to nature as *deus in rebus*, the image and manifestation of God. To Spenser a cosmogony thus ordained not by accident but through divine immanence must assuredly have been preferable to the materialism of Lucretius or the Pagan myths of Ovid as an explanation of the law of change; and though his philosophy shows no trace of pantheism, one or two phrases reproduce ideas deduced by Bruno from his conception of a world soul. Thus Mutability contends that earth continually changes "in part and eke in generall", that the elements are interchangeable and incapable of isolation, that corruption is identical with generation, death but "a parting of the breath" and time only relative:

> For who sees not that Time on all doth pray?
> But Times do change and move continually;[33]

and though the germ of all these notions is to be found in both Lucretius and Ovid, the form in which they are expounded and the main argument which they substantiate relates them rather with the physical theories of Bruno, who, like Lucretius and Ovid, claimed that acceptance of his system would dispel the fear of death. The similarity both in thought and phrasing is sufficiently distinct to suggest that Spenser was acquainted with the two Italian dialogues, *La Cena de le ceneri* and *Della Causa, Principio et Uno*, in which Bruno develops his philosophy of nature.

Still more evident is the relation between the cantos of Mutability and Bruno's third dialogue, *Spaccio della Bestia*

Trionfante, which tells how the gods, disgusted at their own shortcomings, decide to remove their constellations from the heavens, enthroning in their place the moral Virtues, under the leadership of Truth. The allegory is a plea for intellectual freedom in matters of faith and for a right understanding of nature, which, according to Bruno, would lead to the rejection of anthropomorphic religion and to the worship not of individual gods but of the universal divinity in all things. The ethics and symbolism of this dialogue, as explained by the author in a prefatory letter to Sir Philip Sidney, are all of a character calculated to arrest the notice of Spenser. Jove stands for intellectual light, which orders the seats of virtue and vice in the architecture of man the microcosm. The expulsion of the Triumphant Beast signifies the divine nature in man re-asserting itself, purging the mind of error and sensuality and, inspired through love of beauty, resolving to follow the path of virtue and truth. Among the Muses, daughters of Mnemosyne, the highest place is accorded to the youngest born, *Ethica*, whose task is to institute religions, to make laws and execute justice after the manner of Gloriana's Knights, with prudence, wisdom and generosity, for the service of God and the profit of the community. Perhaps it is no more than a coincidence that practically every virtue listed by Bruno in his exceedingly complex scheme has a symbolical counterpart in *The Faerie Queene*; but this explanation could hardly account for the similarity in detail between the *Spaccio* and the cantos of Mutability. First there is the central situation—the superseding of ancient deities by a new power, in the one case through voluntary abdication, in the other through the usurpation of a pretender. In both a prominent place is assigned to the heavenly constellations as visibly betraying the characteristics of their divine patrons; and in citing them as evidence the rebel, Mutability, has only to repeat the arguments of Jove and his compeers, the self-accusers of the *Spaccio*, who even prompt her taunt against the father of the gods on the score of his dubious origin. Finally, her allusion to recent changes in the planetary courses which have extended so far

> That even these Star-gazers stonisht are
> At sight thereof, and damne their lying bookes,[34]

though probably glancing at recent corrections to the Ptolemaic cycles, hints also at the new astronomy, the foundation to Bruno's natural philosophy.

Between Bruno and Spenser lie all the differences dividing the philosopher from the poet, the active from the receptive intelligence, the born heretic from the instinctive conformist. We can hardly imagine our poet embracing or even understanding many of the theories put forward by the eccentric Nolan. As an orthodox product of the sixteenth-century schools he was certainly in no position to share Bruno's rationalism or his aversion for the abstract ideas of Aristotle and the Peripatetics, including Patrizi, whom Spenser would unquestionably have studied as a standard authority at Cambridge. For the same reason his theology, with its Protestant conception of divine transcendence, is totally incompatible with Bruno's pantheism. Finally, the whole romantic conception of *The Faerie Queene* turns upon the fable of the Golden Age, which is unconditionally condemned by Momus, the cynic of the *Spaccio*, on the ground that Saturnine virtues left men no better than brutes, that through the emulation of divinity difficulties had to be met by arts and inventions which opened the way to human progress. In his attitude to Bruno, as to all his originals, Chaucer included, Spenser is still the New Poet, ready to assimilate any odd motive or idea that may strike his imagination, without ceasing to be himself or to follow his own way. An interesting case of such casual borrowing is his figure of Concord, the intermediary between Love and Hate in the Temple of Venus, probably inspired by Bruno's theory of contraries. But where Bruno rendered Spenser the greatest service was in imparting a spiritual value to natural philosophy, thereby satisfying a need unmet

Philosophical Ideas

by Plato, Aristotle or Lucretius. For the ultimate truth which Bruno seeks to inculcate in the course of his dialogues is to the effect that through the exercise of understanding and the practice of virtue men may at length become "heroes", worthy to contemplate the eternal verities, a condition reserved for the blessed few whose aspirations are described in the last of the Italian dialogues, *De gl' heroici furori*; and this is precisely the moral of *The Faerie Queene*. Bruno, therefore, could supply Nature with her final retort to the allegations of Mutability:

> I well consider all that ye have said,
> And find that all things stedfastnesse do hate
> And changed be; yet, being rightly wayd,
> They are not changed from their first estate;
> But by their change their being do dilate,
> And turning to themselves at length againe,
> Do worke their own perfection so by fate:
> Then over them Change doth not rule and raigne,
> But they rayne over Change, and do their states maintaine.[35]

In the light of fresh discoveries old theories acquired a new value. The unchanging substance behind the changing exterior, the atom or monad is not simply material, as averred by Democritus and Lucretius, but spiritually partaking in the divinity of an infinite universe. Without necessarily realising the full implications of Bruno's philosophy Spenser had assimilated sufficient of it to abandon the materialism of the Garden of Adonis for a theory of life more compatible with his religious convictions. Change is not purposeless but an evolutionary dilation of being. The fallacy in Mutability's case arises from her exclusive reliance upon sense evidence at the expense of spiritual realities only to be apprehended through understanding. In seeking omnipotence she seeks her own ruin. For the time will come when "we shall all be changed"; but after this last supreme triumph Mutability will be dissolved in changeless Eternity.

In thus adapting to his own account the advanced and

novel ideas of a contemporary Spenser never committed himself to the principles upon which these ideas were based. He would probably have been alarmed rather than attracted by Bruno's science and by his insistence upon experiment as the only means of discovering truth. According to Harvey, Spenser regretted the inadequacy of his acquaintance with astronomy, which did not extend beyond the rules of the Astrolabe.[36] In *The Ruines of Time* and the cantos of Mutability he introduces the signs of the Zodiac as decorative and symbolical imagery. But the subject never fascinates him as it fascinated Chaucer, and in the introduction to *The Faerie Queene*, Book v, he can only compare the wayward courses of the planets with the universal degeneracy of mankind. Nor is this to be wondered at. To sage and poet of the Middle Ages the stars are beneficent images of Divine Providence, pledges of immortality and visible witnesses to the blessed truth that

The heavens declare the glory of God; and the firmament sheweth his handywork.

One day telleth another; and one night certifieth another.

There is neither speech nor language; but their voices are heard among them.

So long as men could retain so sublime a vision of a universe extolling its Creator in one glad harmonious song they could behold the friendly stars undismayed; and this spirit of assurance, together with the cosmogony upon which it is based, survives in *La Sepmaine* of Du Bartas, who, on theological ground, joins issue with ancient astronomers as well as with Copernicus. But by this time the progress of Humanism and the ever-changing interests of terrestrial life were drawing man's attention more and more from the heavens above to the world around him. With the loss of old beliefs star-gazing tended to excite feelings of despondency rather than exaltation, except with the professing astronomer. An interesting contrast with *La Sepmaine* is provided in the *Zodiacus Vitæ* of the Italian Marcellus Palingenius, translated into English

by Barnabe Googe, whose version was widely read throughout the later sixteenth century. The theology underlying this
curious farrago of satire and fantastic cosmography is a
bleak deism, irreconcilable with orthodox Christianity. But
the author's violent attacks upon the Catholic Church, which
ultimately occasioned his death at the stake, secured his poem
a hearing in Protestant countries, where he passed for a
martyr to the reformed faith. Gabriel Harvey's acquaintance,
Mr Thomas Digges, had "the whole Aquarius of Palingenius
bie hart", rating him "above all modern poets for a pregnant
introduction into Astronomie".[37]

Spenser was certainly an admirer of Du Bartas, esteeming
as "the proper profession of Urania" the fourth day of the
first week in *La Sepmaine*, which treats of the firmament,
celestial motions, the signs of the Zodiac and the changing
seasons. He was also probably acquainted with Palingenius,
whose outlook upon the universe is quite in accord with
the gloomy reflections upon transitory existence scattered
throughout *The Faerie Queene* and sustained as a ground bass
to the *Complaints*:

> All that is perfect, which th' heaven beautefies;
> All that's imperfect, borne belowe the Moone.
>
> .   .   .   .   .
>
> All is but fained, and with oaker dide,
> That everie shower will wash and wipe away;
> All things doo change that under heaven abide,
> And after death all friendship doth decaie.[38]

The lack of steadfastness throughout sublunary creation as
contrasted with the constancy of heaven was already a well-
tried theme, which Spenser might frequently have encountered in Boethius, Chaucer, Sackville or the Petrarchans,
not to mention their originals. But the familiar matter that
could evoke from Chaucer commonplaces little in accord
with his genial philosophy of life was now presenting an
acute problem to minds faced with the prospect of subversive
changes in religion and thought. The attempt to find unity in

variety was fraught with new difficulties to which accepted dogmas offered no solution, and the ever-present spectacle of change and corruption seemed but to mock the serious enquirer. Though the new astronomy as yet commanded no general acceptance, the old faith in the stars as media of destiny, radiating spiritual energy, was already on the wane. With an increased respect for his own individuality man was losing his sense of kinship to an inscrutable cosmos. The new learning had given him his desire but had brought leanness into his soul.

In an age of faith, or under the sway of a spiritual hierarchy Spenser's high seriousness and reverence for authority might have found utterance through religious poetry. But time and circumstance directed his energies towards another objective, to the exposition of a creed that is humanistic rather than Hebraic. Despite his preoccupation with human frailty and the instability of the material world he never displays the Puritan sense of man's utter worthlessness and self-contempt in the presence of his Maker, the conviction of sin that burdens the mind of such a writer as a Fulke Greville. Though Holiness stands first in his scheme of virtues, he dedicates his art not to the glory of God but to the praise of the godlike in man, grounding his ethic upon self-knowledge and self-mastery rather than upon abstract righteousness or fear of the Lord.

So his ideal is no Calvinistic theocracy, but a kingdom of this world, having little or nothing in common with a primitive Christian community. In the land of Faerie the rights of the individual are the last consideration while the notion of levelling, affected by certain Protestant sects, is unconditionally condemned. The spirit urging Gloriana's champions on errands of justice and mercy is not humanitarianism but the sense of discipline. The evil principle that opposes them is the spirit of lawlessness and disruption. Their foes must be exterminated partly because of their intrinsic wickedness, but chiefly as "caterpillars of the commonwealth". For the whole universe, "in part, and eeke in generall", is ruled not by unseen chance but by visible "law of kind"— this is the substance of Nature's retort to Mutability, the personification of all the grosser and undisciplined elements in cosmic and physical creation.

To aid the working of universal law is the high prerogative of man. Endowed with reason and free-will he is master of his fate, cleaving his way towards the highest good. If he fail, the fault is not in his stars nor in divine predestination, but in himself. If he succeed, virtue proves its own reward. The true hero who has gained the mastery over reason and appetite will pursue wisdom and beauty wherever they may be found. He will seize the occasion without venturing too far into spheres of existence beyond his own, confident that life will ultimately triumph over death, since the very thought of corruption and annihilation is unendurable. So Nature enjoins no blind acceptance of theological dogma nor the sacrifice of present reality to an unknown future, but a sense of responsibility, conformity with the law of self-development whereby every creature, fulfilling its destiny, may further the realisation of divine purpose.

In this humane philosophy, concerned with being rather than with knowledge, we may detect the reaction of a self-centred personality against the conflicting forces of the time. With Spenser the impetus to poetry was not the Faustic yearning after knowledge infinite, the zeal for discovery or new enlightenment, but a wise passiveness continually absorbing impressions from books, from nature, from life. The modesty of his intellectual endowment allowed free play to the genius that could fashion great poetry from familiar matter. But the matter could bear this transformation. Love and beauty, the knightly virtues of "trouthe, and honour, fredom and curteisie" are noble themes which custom has never staled or rendered unworthy of poetic usage; the philosophy to which Spenser has applied them bears a human interest, broad-based upon experience and of enduring value.

REFERENCES & NOTES

ABBREVIATIONS

F.Q.	The Faerie Queene	*C.C.*	Colin Clouts Come Home Againe
S.C.	The Shepheardes Calender	*As.*	Astrophel
R.T.	The Ruines of Time	*Am.*	Amoretti
T.M.	The Tears of the Muses	*Ep.*	Epithalamion
V.G.	Virgils Gnat	*H.L.*	Hymne in Honour of Love
M.H.	Mother Hubberds Tale	*H.B.*	Hymne in Honour of Beautie
R.R.	Ruines of Rome	*H.H.L.*	Hymne in Honour of Heavenly Love
Mu.	Muiopotmos		
V.W.V.	Visions of the Worlds Vanitie	*H.H.B.*	Hymne in Honour of Heavenly Beautie
V.B.	The Visions of Bellay		
V.P.	The Visions of Petrarch	*Pr.*	Prothalamion
Da.	Daphnaida		

CHAPTER I

1. Deduced from *Am.* lx.
2. William Oldys' notes on Winstanley in the Bodleian; J. Hunter, *Chorus Vatum*, B.M. Add. MS. 24490, IV. 450.
3. *Notes and Queries*, CLIV (1928), 69, 123.
4. *S.C.* "December", 37 ff.   5. *F.Q.* IV, xi, 34.
6. Peter Cunningham, *Extracts from the Accounts of the Revels*. London. Shakespeare Soc. 1842, xxx.
7. A. B. Grosart proposed to identify Vander Noodt with "Diggon Davie" ("September"), who "had bene long in forrain countryes, and there seene many disorders". *Works of Edmund Spenser*, 1882–4, I, 25 ff.
8. E. Koeppel, *Englische Studien*, xv (1891), 53 ff., XXVII (1900), 100 ff.; J. B. Fletcher, *Mod. Lang. Notes*, XIII (1898), 409 ff.
9. *Works*, ed. A. B. Grosart, Huth. Lib. 1884, I, 71, 73.
10. *Gabriel Harvey's Marginalia*, ed. G. C. Moore Smith, Stratford-upon-Avon, 22, 23; I. Gollancz, *Proc. Brit. Acad.* 1907–8, 99 ff.
11. *Works*, ed. cit. I, 111 ff., 126 ff.
12. Discussed at length by J. J. Higginson in *Spenser's Shepherd's Calender in Relation to Contemporary Affairs*, N.Y. 1912.
13. "January", Gloss., "April", Gloss.
14. *Lives*, Lond. 1813, II, 541.

15. For further discussion as to her identity see *Anglia*, XXXI (1908), 72 ff. and *Proc. Roy. Irish Acad.* IV (1850), 445 ff.
16. *H.B.* 211 ff.; *H.L.* 190 ff.; *H.H.B.* 295 ff.
17. *C.C.* 931 ff.   18. *F.Q.* VI, X, 12–16.
19. *S.C.* "June", 17 ff.
20. G. Harvey, *Works*, ed. cit. 1, 6.
21. T. Tanner describes Sir Philip Sidney as Spenser's "first Mæcenas", *Bibl. Brit. Hib.* Lond. 1748, 684.
22. *P.M.L.A.* XLI (1926), 568 ff.
23. *Works*, ed. cit. I, 26.   24. *Ib.* I, 38, 40, 107.
25. Mr Douglas Hamer (*Rev. of Eng. Stud.* VII (1931), 271) makes a good case for an early marriage of Spenser on the ground that Sylvanus Spenser must have attained his majority by 1605–6 and therefore could not have been the child of Elizabeth Boyle. Mr Mark Eccles, the discoverer of the Spenser-Chylde marriage register (*Times Lit. Supp.* 31.12.31), whilst concurring with this part of Mr Hamer's argument, judiciously refuses to accept his views as to the date of *Epithalamion*. Mr Hamer, in turn, declines to accept the Spenser-Chylde record as corroborative of his case. The witnesses do not agree, and the case must be regarded as still unproven, though worthy of consideration.
26. G. Harvey, *Works*, ed. cit. I, 37, 38.
27. Other references to Spenser's lost works are to be found in E.K.'s notes to the *Calender* and in Ponsonbie's advertisement to *Complaints*.
28. *Works*, ed. cit. I, 24, 93, 95. 31. "July", 81 ff, 41 ff.
29. Ll. 110 ff.   32. "May", 13, 14; "June", 26, 27.
30. *Works*, ed. cit. I, 95.   33. *Works*, ed. cit. I, 92, 37.
34. E. Greenlaw in *P.M.L.A.* XXV (1910), 535 ff.
35. *M.H.* 1118 ff.   36. *Works*, ed. cit. I, 141, 146 ff.
37. E. M. Albright in *Stud. Phil.* XXV (1928), 93 ff., XXVI (1929), 482 ff.; H. M. Belden, *ib.* XXVI (1929), 142 ff.; E. Greenlaw, *P.M.L.A.* XLV (1930), 684 ff.

CHAPTER II

1. *Cal. State Papers, Ireland*, 1574–85, 486.
2. *Works*, Globe Ed. Lond. 1910, 655, 617. According to Camden, Grey wept upon hearing of his troops' determination to massacre the garrison. *Annales*, 1717, II, 344.

References and Notes

3. *Works*, Globe Ed. 654.
4. Charles Smith, *The Ancient and Present State of the County and City of Cork*, 1774, I, 341.
5. *C.C.* 138 ff.
6. *Works*, Globe Ed. 616, 617.
7. *Ib.* 626, 623, 624, 679.
8. *Ib.* 641, 639, 635.
9. *F.Q.* III, vii, 6; II, ix, 13.
10. *Works*, Globe Ed. 677.
11. *C.C.* 181 ff.
12. *Ib.* 76 ff., 184 ff.
13. Raleigh, who probably accompanied Spenser to London, was at Lismore on September 26 and in London on November 12 (*Cal. Carew MSS.* 1589–1600, 12, 14).
14. H. E. Sandison in *P.M.L.A.* XLIII (1928), 645 ff.
15. P. W. Long propounded the theory that Spenser may have courted Lady Carey as a suitor, addressing to her some of the sonnets subsequently incorporated in *Amoretti*. *M.L.R.* III (1908), 257 ff.; IX (1914), 457 ff.
16. Thomas Fuller, *Worthies*, ed. J. Nichols, London, 1811, II, 80.
17. Gilfillan omitted *Ruines of Rome* from his edition of 1859 as spurious, and others have adopted the same view, but with little justification.
18. The title-page of *Muiopotmos* is dated 1590, so possibly this poem was set up in type before the remainder of the volume. There is no reason for supposing that it was intended for separate publication and its page signatures are in order.
19. The identification of "our pleasant Willy" with Shakespeare has little to support it; but the allusion might well apply to Richard Tarleton, the actor, who died in 1588. See B. E. C. Davis in *Notes and Queries*, ser. 12, XII (1923), 323 ff.
20. Harl. MS. 6910.
21. *Works*, ed. cit. I, 164.
22. *Works*, ed. R. B. McKerrow, London, 1903–10, I, 281.
23. VI, xii, 41.
24. W. H. Welply in *Notes and Queries*, CXLVI (1924), 445 ff.; cf. Aubrey's note on the Northants connections of "Rosalind" (*vide sup.* ch. I, n. 14). The identification of "Rosalind" with Elizabeth Boyle is rendered highly improbable by
    (*a*) the absence of all reference to the former in *Am.*:
    (*b*) the reference to the unsuccessful suit in *C.C.*:
    (*c*) E.K.'s description of "Rosalind" as a "widow's daughter", in 1579, when both the parents of Elizabeth were still alive.
25. I. Gollancz in *Proc. Brit. Acad.* 1907–8, 99 ff.

26. J. G. Scott in *M.L.R.* xxii (1927), 189 ff. shows that four of the sonnets are free translations from Tasso.

27. *Am.* lxxiv.   28. *Ep.* 167 ff.

29. *Cal. State Papers, Scotland*, ed. M. J. Thorpe, London, 1858, ii, 723, 747.

30. Ll. 5 ff.   32. *Works*, Globe Ed. 682.

31. *Ib.* 147 ff.   33. *Vide sup.* n. 24.

34. Preface to *The Historie of Ireland, collected by Three Learned Authors*. Dublin, 1633.

35. *Works*, ed. A. B. Grosart, 1882–4, i, 231.

36. *Works*, ed. Gifford and Cunningham, London, n.d. iii, 478.

37. *The Truth of Our Times*, 1638, 37, 38.

38. W. Warner, *Albions England*. London, 1612, in address "To the Reader".

39. The monument was restored in 1778.

CHAPTER III

1. J. Aubrey, *Brief Lives*, Oxford, 1898, ii, 233.

2. *Wits Miserie*, 1596, 57.

3. *F.Q.* ii, vii, 52; iv, Pr. 3.

4. *Positions*, ed. R. H. Quick, London, 1888, 11.

5. *English Works*, Cambridge, 1904, 265, 266.

6. *Works*, ed. cit. i, 282.   8. *T.M.* 559 ff.

7. Ll. 400 ff.   9. *S.C.* "October", 79 ff.

10. Jonson, *Works*, ed. cit. iii, 412. Milton, *Prose Works* (Bohn's St. Lib.), 1884, ii, 68.

11. *Ep.* 250 ff.

12. R. Robinson, *A Moral Methode of Civile Policie*, London, 1576, 2.

13. *F.Q.* iii, ii, 2.

14. The doctrine of "Divine Right" glanced at in the Mercilla episode was defended at some length by John Leslie in his *Treatise touching the Right of Mary Queen of Scotland* (1584) and by Thomas Bedingfield in his preface to the *Florentine Historie of Machiavelli* (1595).

15. *M.H.* 141 ff.   16. *F.Q.* v, ii, 39.

17. G. Harvey, *Works*, ed. cit. i, 139.

18. *Works*, Globe Ed. Lond. 1910, 612, 618, 650, 614.

19. *F.Q.* v, Pr. 1.   20. *Ib.* ii, Pr. 4.

21. *Ib.* ii, x, 69.

References and Notes

CHAPTER IV

1. Gregory Smith, *Elizabethan Critical Essays*, Oxford, 1904, I, 323.
2. *Le Morte Darthur*, x, ii; XVI, vi.
3. *F.Q.* II, viii, 36.   4. *Le Morte Darthur*, II, ii.
5. *Ib.* IX, xii.
6. T. Warton, *Observations on The Fairy Queen*. London, 1807, I, 272 ff.
7. *F.Q.* III, x, 47.
8. *Ib.* IV, iii, 45.   9. *Ib.* III, ii, 14.
10. The 1590 version of Book III closes with the reunion of Scudamour and Amoret; but in subsequent issues the five stanzas recording this were dropped and three others substituted, doubtless with the object of sustaining interest in the fortunes of the two lovers throughout the later books.
11. *F.Q.* IV, vi, 45.   12. *Ib.* v, vi, 7.
13. Chaucer, *Wife of Bath's Tale*, 3 ff.
14. Coleridge, *Lectures on Shakespeare*. London (Bohn's Standard Library), 1900, 67.
15. *The Works of Edmund Spenser*, ed. H. J. Todd, 1805, II, clxxi.
16. *F.Q.* VI, Pr. 1.
17. *S.C.* "January", 1 ff.; *F.Q.* I, i, 1.
18. *F.Q.* III, ii, 49, 50. The episode is adapted from the pseudo-Virgilian *Ceiris*.
19. *Ib.* I, xii, 10, 11.
20. *Ib.* III, xii, 8; II, xi, 26; L. Whitney in *Mod. Phil.* XIX (1921), 143 ff.

CHAPTER V

1. *F.Q.* I, i, 18; I, iii, 6.
2. Gregory Smith, *op. cit.* II, 201, 213.
3. E. M. Albright in *P.M.L.A.* XLI (1926), 497 ff.
4. *Inferno*, IX, 61.
5. Spenser's authorities probably included Melanchthon's *Enarrationes aliquot Librorum Ethicorum Aristotelis*. See F. M. Padelford in *Stud. in Phil.* XXI (1924), 367 ff.
6. *F.Q.* I, v, 1.   9. *Ib.* II, iv, 35.
7. *Works*, ed. cit. I, 94.   10. *Ib.* II, ix, 24.
8. *F.Q.* II, i, 58.   11. *Ib.* II, ix, 43.

12. Plutarch's *Moralia*, tr. Philemon Holland. London (Everyman's Lib.), 1911, 11 ff.

13. *F.Q.* III, i, 49.
14. *Ib.* III, v, 2.
15. *Ib.* III, iii, 1.
16. *Ib.* IV, Pr. 2.
17. *Ib.* IV, ii, 29.
18. *Ib.* IV, x, 52.
19. *Ib.* v, i, 8.

20. *Ib.* v, ii, 20.
21. *Ib.* v, vii, 45.
22. *Ib.* v, xi, 41.
23. *Ib.* VI, Pr. 4.
24. *Ib.* VI, ii, 1.
25. *Ib.* VI, vii, 18.
26. *Ib.* VI, v, 13.

27. *Ib.* VI, vi, 7.
28. Lytton Strachey, *Books and Characters*, London, 1924, 52.

CHAPTER VI

1. *Of Myself. Selected Works*, London, 1777, II, 266.
2. J. E. Spingarn, *Critical Essays of the Seventeenth Century*, Oxford, 1908, II, 167.
3. *S.C.* "October", 100 ff. 4. *C.C.* 823 ff.
5. Gregory Smith, *op. cit.* I, 160.
6. *Ib.* I, 47. 7. *Astrophel and Stella*, i.
8. *Mu.* 193. 9. *R.T.* 92 ff.
10. *F.Q.* I, xi, 28; II, vi, 41; *H.H.B.* 51.
11. *L.* 155. 12. *F.Q.* III, xii, 19; I, iv, 4.
13. *Ib.* I, vii, 22.
14. *S.C.* "February", 7, 71; *F.Q.* I, v, 48; *S.C.* "February", 17; *F.Q.* I, x, 35.
15. *F.Q.* I, vii, 6; *M.H.* 232.
16. *R.T.* 214; *Am.* xxxiii.
17. *F.Q.* I, vii, 12.
18. *Ib.* I, iii, 30; *H.L.* 32; *F.Q.* I, iii, 27; *S.C.* "January", 48.
19. *S.C.* "June", 89; "November", 73; *F.Q.* I, ii, 22; *S.C.* "January", 61; *F.Q.* II, x, 40; *As.* 68.
20. *F.Q.* III, iii, 42; *C.C.* 777.
21. *S.C.* "January", 29, 30; "November", 65, 66; "December", 97, 98.
22. *F.Q.* III, ix, 14.
23. *Am.* lxxx; *ib.* lxxix; *C.C.* 16; *S.C.* "November", 184; *F.Q.* I, i, 53.
24. *F.Q.* I, iv, 45.
25. *Ib.* I, vii, 41; III, ii, 36.
26. Gregory Smith, *op. cit.* II, 148.

References and Notes

27. *Mu.* 169 ff.   28. *F.Q.* II, ii, 8.
29. *Ib.* I, v, 18; *H.H.L.* 214; *Ep.* 59; *F.Q.* II, x, 17.
30. *As.* 163; *F.Q.* v, ix, 50.
31. Spingarn, *op. cit.* II, 271.
32. *H.H.B.* 181, 182; *F.Q.* II, i, 40; VI, ii, 22; I, v, 46; *Ep.* 33;
    C.C. 613.
33. *F.Q.* I, vii, 13.   35. *H.L.* 259 ff.
34. *Ib.* VI, iv, 21.   36. *Ib.* 120 ff.
37. G. H. Palmer, *Formative Types in English Poetry*, Boston and
    N.Y., 1918, 77.
38. *F.Q.* II, viii, 3.
39. *Essayes*, London, 1671, 118.
40. *Early English Pronunciation*, London, 1869–89, III, 862.
41. *Studies in Chaucer*, N.Y., 1892, III, 62.
42. *The Making of English*, London, 1904, 228.

CHAPTER VII

1. *F.Q.* III, iv, 55.   2. Ll. 374, 375.
3. *Parliament of Fowls*, 267 ff.; *Legend*, Prologue B, 214 ff.
4. *F.Q.* II, xii, 77, 78.   5. *Mu.* 89 ff.
6. *F.Q.* III, xi, 41.
7. *Ep.* 227; *F.Q.* II, xii, 12; *ib.* II, x, 24; *ib.* II, i, 18; *S.C.* "February", 129 ff.
8. *F.Q.* I, vi, 14.
9. *F.Q.* I, xi, 51; *V.G.* 156; *F.Q.* III, iv, 51; I, iii, 16.
10. *Ib.* I, i, 36.   11. *Ib.* I, vii, 6.
12. *Ib.* I, xi, 41; IV, i, 54; III, v, 22.
13. *Ib.* III, iv, 9.   14. *Ib.* IV, v, 38.
15. *Ib.* III, viii, 25; III, ix, 29.
16. *Ib.* II, xii, 87.   18. *F.Q.* II, ix, 51.
17. Ll. 596 ff.   19. *Ib.* III, x, 47.
20. *Ib.* v, xii, 29; v, xi, 9; VI, vii, 19.
21. *Ib.* IV, vi, 37.   29. *Ib.* II, viii, 42.
22. *Ib.* III, xi, 28.   30. *Ib.* II, vi, 39.
23. *Ib.* III, ii, xi.   31. *Ib.* III, i, 22.
24. *Ib.* v, vi, 14.   32. *Ib.* VI, ii, 32.
25. *Ib.* IV, i, 13.   33. *Ib.* VI, vii, 9.
26. *Ib.* v, iii, 25.   34. *Ib.* I, xi, 34.
27. *Ib.* III, iv, 13.   35. *C.C.*, 209 ff.
28. *Ib.* IV, iv, 47.   36. *F.Q.* II, 2, 24.

37. *F.Q.* I, iii, 31.
38. *Ib.* IV, iii, 37.
39. *Ib.* IV, vii, 33.
40. *Ib.* IV, xi, 23.
41. Ll. 138 ff.
42. *F.Q.* I, viii, 8.

43. *Ib.* I, viii, 11.
44. *Ib.* II, i, 42.
45. *Ib.* II, vi, 13.
46. *Ib.* I, v, 30.
47. *Ib.* II, iii, 24.
48. *Ib.* I, Pr. 1.

CHAPTER VIII

1. Gregory Smith, *op. cit.* I, 172.
2. *F.Q.* I, ix, 40.
3. *Ib.* I, v, 2.
4. Ll. 253 ff.
5. *F.Q.* I, i, 26; II, vii, 3.
6. *H.B.* 64 ff., 197 ff.
7. *F.Q.* I, xi, 28; I, i, 51; III, iii, 42.
8. *Ib.* II, ii, 9.
9. *S.C.* "February", 195; "September", 36; *M.H.* 185, 1159; *S.C.* "June", 96; *T.M.* 553.
10. *F.Q.* VI, iii, 44; II, xi, 21; II, xii, 38; II, xii, 51; II, viii, 39; III, i, 17.
11. *Ib.* III, x, 3; *S.C.* "October", 7.
12. *F.Q.* I, ii, 7; IV, viii, 25; II, i, 7; II, viii, 32; I, ii, 13.
13. *Ib.* IV, ii, 17; II, 5, 23; II, ii, 3; *H.H.B.* 1.
14. *F.Q.* IV, xi, 41; II, vi, 5.
15. *Ib.* III, v, 39.
16. *Ib.* II, ii, 28; *Pr.* 30 ff.
17. Letter to Harvey, April 2, 1580; Harvey, *Works*, ed. cit. I, 35.
18. *V.B.* iv, 3; *R.R.* xxxii, 14; *V.G.* 340.
19. *F.Q.* I, iii, 7.
20. *Ib.* III, i, 14.
21. *V.B.* xiv, 3; *V.W.V.* ix, 14; *R.T.* 428.
22. Gregory Smith, *op. cit.* I, 51.
23. *F.Q.* II, vii, 10.
24. *Ib.* I, i, 51; I, i, 52; I, xi, 28; VI, v, 40.
25. *V.B.* vi, 10; *R.R.* xxiii, 10; *V.G.* 668; *S.C.* "April", 136 ff.
26. *Mu.* 361 ff.
27. *V.B.* vii, 14; *V.P.* iii, 6; *S.C.* "January", 7; *F.Q.* II, i, 40.
28. Ll. 22 ff.
29. *F.Q.* I, i, 30.
30. *S.C.* "February", 1 ff.
31. *Ib.* "February", 79; "May", 123; "September", 172; "May", 71.
32. Ll. 148 ff.
33. *F.Q.* III, iii, 4; III, xii, 6; VI, v, 38.
34. *Ep.* 223, 194, 412.
35. *Ib.* 204, 291, 74.

36. Spingarn, *op. cit.* II, 265.
37. *F.Q.* IV, vi, 40; II, ix, 24; I, ix, 48; IV, x, 58.
38. *Ib.* II, iii, 20; II, xii, 76.
39. *Ib.* I, xi, 54; I, iii, 30.
40. *Ib.* II, ix, 42; III, xii, 18.
41. *Ib.* I, ix, 47; III, v, 25; IV, ii, 9; I, vii, 3.
42. *Ib.* I, iv, 24; III, v, 12; IV, i, 43; III, i, 67; III, Pr. 3; II, x, 58;
    IV, iv, 42; VI, v, 23.
43. *Ib.* III, i, 50; IV, iii, 37; IV, v, 25; III, v, 32.
44. *Ib.* III, viii, 12; I, v, 24.
45. *Ib.* I, ix, 40; VI, vii, 18.
46. *Ib.* v, vi, 5; III, x, 55; III, xi, 28.
47. *Ib.* VI, v, 40; III, ii, 47; I, iii, 1; IV, x, 47.
48. *Ib.* I, vii, 2; I, iii, 10; III, iv, 53; V, ii, 30.
49. *Essays*, ed. W. P. Ker, Oxford, 1926, II, 29.

CHAPTER IX

1. *Marginalia*, ed. cit. 161.
2. *Spenser*, London, 1926, 43.
3. *Literature and Occult Tradition*, London, 1930, 222 ff.
4. *Discourse*, 2, 5, 18, 21, 40, 41, 45, 76.
5. *F.Q.* III, vi, 36.   7. *F.Q.* III, vi, 22.
6. *H.H.L.* 187.   8. *Ib.* III, vi, 41.
9. For further details concerning Spenser's use of old religious
   cults and of Lucretius see E. A. Greenlaw in *Stud. in Phil.*
   XIV (1917), 196 ff.; XVII (1920), 320 ff., 439 ff. and XX (1923),
   216 ff.
10. *F.Q.* IV, x, 38.   16. *Ib.* IV, x, 41.
11. *Ib.* IV, x, 47.   17. *Ib.* v, vii, 16.
12. *H.L.* 278.   18. Ll. 185 ff.
13. *F.Q.* IV, x, 3.   19. *H.B.* 149, 141.
14. *H.L.* 218.   20. *H.H.B.* 43.
15. *F.Q.* III, vi, 46, 47.   21. *Ib.* 185 ff.
22. *H.B.* 40 ff.
23. See especially *H.H.B.* 113–133. Spenser's metaphor of the
    looking-glass may derive from Bruno's "non già in questo
    stato dove non possemo veder dio se non come in ombra et
    specchio". *Op. Ital.* Lagarde, Göttingen, 1888, 646.
24. *F.Q.* IV, x, 35.
25. *De Consolatione Philosophiæ*, II, Met. 8.

26. *F.Q.* VII, viii, 2; *H.H.B.*, 295.
27. *F.Q.* III, vi, 3.
28. *Ib.* III, vi, 30.
29. *Ib.* III, vi, 47.
30. *Ib.* III, vi, 38.
31. *Ib.* VII, vii, 13.
32. *Ib.* VII, vii, 9.
33. *Ib.* VII, vii, 47.
34. *Ib.* VII, vii, 52.
35. *Ib.* VII, vii, 58
36. *Marginalia,* ed. cit. 162.
37. *Ib.* 161.
38. R.R. xix, 1, 2; R.T. 204.

SUMMARY LIST OF PRINCIPAL EDITIONS AND OF BOOKS RECOMMENDED FOR FURTHER CONSULTATION

A Theatre...(of) *Voluptuous Worldlings*.... Devised by S. John vander Noodt. London. Henry Bynneman. 1569. Contains English versions of the *Visions* of Du Bellay and Petrarch suspiciously close to those afterwards included in Spenser's *Complaints*.

The Shepheardes Calender. London. Hugh Singleton. 1579. Other editions followed in 1581, 1586, 1591 and 1597.

Three proper, and wittie, familiar Letters: lately passed between two Universitie men....

Two other, very commendable Letters, of the same mens writing. London. H. Bynneman. 1580.

The Faerie Queene. Disposed into twelve books...London. William Ponsonbie, 1590. Books I–III.

Muiopotmos. London. 1590.
> Probably printed before the rest of *Complaints,* but not intended for separate publication.

Complaints. Containing sundrie small Poemes of the Worlds Vanitie...London. Imprinted for William Ponsonbie, 1591.

Daphnaida. An Elegie upon the death of the noble and vertuous Douglas Howard...London, for William Ponsonby, 1591. Another edition followed in 1596.

Foure Letters, by Gabriel Harvey, 1592.
> Contains Spenser's sonnet to Harvey, written in 1586.

Colin Clouts Come home againe, and *Astrophel,* London...for William Ponsonby, 1595.

Amoretti and *Epithalamion*...for William Ponsonby. 1595.

Fowre Hymnes and *Daphnaida,* London...for William Ponsonby. 1596.

Prothalamion or A Spousall Verse...London...for William Ponsonby, 1596.

The Faerie Queene. Disposed into twelve bookes, Fashioning XII Morall vertues. *With* The Second Part of the Faerie Queene, Containing the Fourth, Fifth and Sixth Bookes, by Ed. Spenser. Imprinted at London for William Ponsonby, 1596. 2 vols.

Summary List of Editions

The Faerie Queene...Printed by H. L. for Mathew Lownes, London. 1609.

> The first Folio edition and the first edition of the cantos of Mutability.

The Faerie Queene: The Shepheards Calendar: Together with the other Works of England's Arch-Poët, Edm. Spenser: Collected into one Volume; and carefully corrected. H.L. for M. Lownes, 1611.

> The first Folio Edition of collected works.

Prosopopoia, or Mother Hubberd's Tale...London. 1613.

> This poem is missing in several copies of the Folio edition up to 1617.

The Faerie Queen...with the other Works of England's Arch-Poët, Edm. Spenser...Matthew Lownes, 1617.

> The second Folio edition of collected works.

A View of the State of Ireland. In Sir James Ware's edition of *The Historie of Ireland, collected by Three Learned Authors.* Dublin, 1633.

> In the Preface it is stated that the *View* is printed from a MS. copy found in the Library of Archbishop Ussher. The *View* appears to have been issued separately in the same year.

The Works of that Famous English Poet, Mr Edmond Spenser... London, 1679, Folio.

> Containing a "Life", the *View*, the spurious *Brittain's Ida* and Theodore Bathurst's Latin version of *The Shepheardes Calender* (published in 1653).

Works, edited by John Hughes, London, 1715. 6 vols.

> Containing prefatory essays which extend to over a hundred pages, the works, with the additions of 1679, and the correspondence with Harvey.

Works, with the principal illustrations of the various commentators, ed. H. J. Todd. London, 1805. 8 vols.

> A variorum edition, which still remains the best of its kind; complete with life, prefatory essays and copious annotations.

Poetical Works...with notes, original and selected, by F. J. Child. Boston, 1855. 5 vols.

> Long the standard American edition; containing valuable new material.

Complete Works, ed. R. Morris and J. W. Hales. London, 1869. Globe Ed. Revised 1897.

Summary List of Editions

Complete Works in Verse and Prose, with Life by A. B. Grosart, essays and notes. Privately printed, 1882–4. 9 vols.

Useful, though unreliable; overladen with irrelevant detail and conjecture. Never completed.

Poetical Works, ed. with preface, introductions and notes by R. E. N. Dodge. Boston, 1908. Cambridge edition. One vol.

Poetical Works. Vols. I, II, *The Faerie Queene*, ed. J. C. Smith; vol. III, Minor Poems, ed. E. de Sélincourt. Oxford, 1909–10. Indispensable for textual study.

Poetical Works, ed. J. C. Smith and E. de Sélincourt. One vol. Oxford, 1912.

Works. Ed. W. L. Renwick. London (Scholartis Press), 1928 etc. In progress.

An authoritative edition, with full notes and commentaries.

Thomas Warton. *Observations on the Fairy Queen of Spenser*. London, 1807.

George L. Craik. *Spenser and his Poetry*. London, 1845. 3 vols.

C. H. Herford. *The Shepheards Calender*. London, 1895.

L. Winstanley. *The Fowre Hymnes*. Cambridge, 1907.

J. W. Mackail. *The Springs of Helicon*. London, 1909.

C. G. Osgood. *A Concordance to the Poems of Edmund Spenser*. Washington, 1915.

F. I. Carpenter. *A Reference Guide to Edmund Spenser*. Chicago, 1923.

W. L. Renwick. *Edmund Spenser: an essay in Renaissance Poetry*. London, 1925.

E. Legouis. *Spenser*. (Six lectures.) London, 1926.

P. Henley. *Spenser in Ireland*. Cork, 1928.

INDEX

Acrasia, 67, 68, 86, 91, 92, 94, 114, 117, 162, 164, 178, 179, 181

Adonis, 220, 221, 226; Garden of, 104, 217, 218, 224, 228–30, 234, 235, 239

Advancement of Learning, The, by Francis Bacon, 115

Æsop, 102

Alain de l'Isle, 84, 115, 234

Albright, E. M., 246, 249

Alençon, Duke of, 21, 22, 24

Allegory, 7, 8, 22, 23, 41, 42, 44, 51, 52, 53, 64, 68, 69, 81, 83, 84, 89, 91, 95, 100–28, 132, 154, 159, 160, 162, 164, 167–70, 212, 214, 217, 221, 222, 227, 233, 237, 238, 240

Alliteration, 188 ff.

Alma, 36, 67, 69, 101, 115, 116, 122, 182, 215, 221, 227, 232, 234

Althorpe, Spensers of, 2, 7, 43

Amadis of Gaul, 34, 79

Amoret, 51, 89, 94, 119, 121, 142, 164, 217, 218, 249

Amoretti, 10, 47–51 *passim,* 54, 120, 130, 139, 146, 147, 149, 151, 154, 159, 164, 167, 169, 181, 200, 215, 216, 223, 245, 247, 248, 250, 255

Anaphora, 146

Andrewes, Lancelot, 4

Antithesis, 145, 147

Apocalypse, *see under* Bible

Apollonius Rhodius, 91, 124

Apologie for Poetrie, see under Sidney, Philip

Aquinas, 64, 210

Arcadia, see under Sidney, Philip

"Arcadianism", 148

"Areopagus", The, 13, 58

Aretine (Aretino), Pietro, 16, 17

Argonautica, see under Apollonius Rhodius

Ariosto, L., 17, 18, 67, 74, 79, 81, 82, 84–9 *passim,* 97, 101, 170, 200, 210

Aristotle, 59, 60, 66, 69, 81, 99, 108–10, 114–16, 119–21, 124–8 *passim,* 134, 210–14 *passim,* 216, 232, 235, 238, 239, 249

L'Art de chevalerie selon Vegece, 110

Arte of English Poesie, The, see under Poetry

Artegall, 29, 30, 72, 73, 86, 89, 91, 92, 93, 100, 106, 122–6, 175, 195, 219, 222

Arthur, Prince, 68, 73, 75, 76, 82, 85, 86, 89, 91, 92, 104, 108, 121, 122, 123, 127, 149, 160, 170, 171, 182, 219

Arthur of Little Britain, 78, 82

Ascham, Roger, 3, 60, 61, 78, 81

Astronomy, 233–42 *passim*

Astrophel, 13, 31, 37, 51, 147, 150, 250, 251, 255

Aubrey, John, 9, 247, 248

Aylmer, John, Bishop of London ("Morrell"), 7, 19

Baltinglas, Viscount, 28

Bandello, M., 36

Bathurst, Theodore, 256

Battle of Maldon, The, 138

Beattie, James, 208

Beaumont, Francis, 156

Beauty, 222–8; *see also under* Hymnes

Bedingfield, Thomas, 248

Belden, H. M., 246

Belphœbe, 51, 71, 88, 90, 94, 101, 106, 119, 122, 149, 163, 167, 179, 181, 182, 218, 227

Beowulf, 138

Berosus, 33

Bibbiena, B., 17

Bible, 5, 8, 65, 102, 113, 115, 133, 211

Bion, 19

Blandamour, 35, 94, 120, 122

Blatant Beast, the, 65, 83, 95, 105, 125, 126, 127, 160, 177

Bliss, Bower of, 69, 86, 159, 215

Bodin, Jean, 25, 72

Boethius, 226, 234, 241

Boiardo, M. M., 79

Boke of the Governour, The, by T. Elyot, 68

Index

Bolton, E., 139
Book of the Duchess, The, see under Chaucer
Bowes, R., 52
Boy and the Mantle, The, 84
Boyle, Elizabeth (Elizabeth Spenser), 47, 54, 56, 246, 247
Boyle, family of, 47, 54, 55, 56
Bradford, John, 3
Bradley, Henry, 156
Braggadochio, 86, 94, 95, 178, 182
Britomart, 67, 69, 70, 73, 83, 85, 86, 88–93 passim, 106, 117, 118, 119, 122, 123, 142, 168, 169, 173, 179, 195, 219, 221, 222
Broken Heart, The, by John Ford, 66
Browning, Robert, 64
Bruno, Giordano, 76, 112, 212, 213, 226, 235–40 passim, 253
Bryskett, L., 31, 37–9, 41, 48, 58, 108, 110, 214, 215
Buchanan, George, 33
Buckhurst, Lord, Thomas Sackville, 41, 102, 241
Burleigh, Lord, 21–4 passim, 41, 44, 45, 46, 52, 55, 106
Busirane, 96, 97, 119, 171, 179
Byron, Lord, 209

Cæsar, Julius, 33
Calidore, 11, 47, 51, 72, 75, 89, 90, 92, 101, 106, 126, 127, 171, 178, 195
Calvin, John, 72
Cambel, Canacee, Triamond, 35, 83, 101, 120, 178
Cambridge, University of, 3–7, 21, 62, 72, 213, 238
Camden, William, 16, 56, 75, 246
Campion, Thomas, 103, 188, 192, 193, 201
Canticum Canticorum, see under Bible
Carey, Lady, 43, 44, 106, 247
Carlyle, Thomas, 36
Carpenter, F. I., 257
Cartwright, Thomas, 5, 6, 7
Castiglione, B., 22, 68, 132, 217, 224
Castle of Indolence, The, see under Thomson, James
Castle of Perseverance, The, 115
Caxton, William, 80, 81, 92, 110, 136
Cecil, Robert, 46

Chanson de Roland, 78
Chapman, George, 102, 160
Chastity, 67, 84, 105, 109, 117–19, 122, 128
Chatterton, Thomas, 135, 136, 157
Chaucer, Geoffrey ("Tityrus"), 19, 20, 23, 35, 43, 57, 58, 60, 85, 97, 102, 133, 135, 136, 137, 138, 145, 155, 156, 161, 162, 193, 197, 200, 201, 202, 238, 240, 241; Legend of Good Women, 251; Parliament of Fowls, 84, 234, 251; Squire's Tale, 83; Troilus, 76, 145, 150; Wife of Bath's Tale, 249
Cheke, John, 3, 133
Child, F. J., 256
Christ's Victory and Triumph, see under Fletcher, Giles
Chylde, Machabyas, 15, 246
Cicero, 8, 60, 110, 132, 216; Somnium Scipionis, 115
Claude Lorraine, 159
Clement VI, Pope, 70
Coleridge, Samuel Taylor, 157, 249; The Ancient Mariner, 137
Colet, John, 213
"Colin", see under Spenser, Edmund
Colin Clouts Come Home Againe, 5, 32, 36, 37, 40, 42, 44, 46, 47, 51, 139, 146, 154, 169, 187, 196, 201, 246, 247, 250, 251, 255
Colour, 163, 164
Complaints, 5, 13, 15, 22, 27, 44, 46, 102, 139, 153, 186, 241, 246, 255; see also under separate titles
Copernicus, see under Astronomy
Courtesy, 52, 68, 70, 81, 92, 109, 110, 111, 114, 125, 126
Courtier, The, see under Castiglione, B.
Cowley, Abraham, 129
Craik, G. L., 257
Cromwell, Oliver, 28, 29, 30, 36
Culpepper, Sir Thomas, 155
Cumberland, Margaret, Countess of, 54
Cunningham, Peter, 245

Daniel, Samuel, 51
"Danse Macabre", 102
Dante, 58, 105, 107, 111, 112, 113, 133, 171, 225, 228

260

Index

261

Index

Friendship, 68, 70, 108–13 *passim*, 119, 120, 122, 125, 215
Fuller, Thomas, 247

Gascoigne, George, 131, 132, 143, 194, 195, 197
Gawain and the Green Knight, 84, 135
Gentillet, I., 72
Geoffrey of Monmouth, 82, 83
George, St, *see under* Red Cross Knight
Gilfillan, G., 247
Gilford, Henry, 52
Giraldi, G. B. (Cinthio), 38, 39, 69, 214, 215
Gloriana, 30, 36, 42, 65, 68, 71, 72, 75, 82, 92, 94, 106, 121, 122, 124, 142, 160, 163, 237, 242
Golden Age, 25, 42, 74, 94, 228, 238
Golden Legend, The, 90
Gollancz, I., 245, 247
Googe, Barnabe, 37, 241
Gorges, Arthur ("Alcyon"), 43
Gosson, Stephen, 12
Greenlaw, E., 246, 253
Greville, Fulke, 242
Grey of Wilton, Lord, 12, 25, 27–30, 33, 36, 37, 39, 41, 51, 73, 74, 75, 92, 106, 122, 124, 126, 246
Grindal, Edmund, 4, 7, 21
Grocyn, William, 213
Grosart, A. B., 245, 248, 257
Grosseteste, Robert, 115
Guicciardini, F., 36
Guyon, 67, 70, 73, 84, 85, 86, 89–94 *passim*, 104, 114, 116, 117, 118, 122, 169, 175, 178, 179, 180, 194, 204

Hales, J. W., 256
Hall, Joseph, 100
Hamer, D., 246
Harington, Sir John, 101, 202
Harrison, John, 20
Harvey, Gabriel, 4–9 *passim*, 11–18 *passim*, 21, 24–7, 31, 41, 45, 46, 62, 72, 87, 113, 132, 193, 202, 210, 240, 241, 245, 246, 252, 255, 256; "Hobbinol", 4–11 *passim*, 19, 21, 40, 187, 196

Haryson, William, 16
Hawes, Stephen, 83; *The Pastime of Pleasure*, 111
Hazlitt, William, 100, 106
Heliodorus, 89
"Hell of Lovers, his Purgatorie, The", 219
Henley, P., 257
Henry VIII, King, 73, 94
Heraclitus, 235
Herford, C. H., 257
Herodotus, 17
Hexameters, English, *see under* Verse
Higginson, J. J., 245
Historie of George Castriot, sonnet prefixed to, 200
"Hobbinol", *see under* Harvey, Gabriel
Holiness, 66, 70, 92, 109, 111, 113, 122, 128, 212, 242; House of, 65, 69, 90, 102, 104, 107, 112, 116, 160, 215
Holinshed, Raphael, 16, 83
Holland, Philemon, 250
Homer, 41, 102, 114, 171, 174, 178
Howard, Douglas, 43, 255
"Howers of the Lord, The", 65
Howleglas, The, 6
Hughes, John, 129, 256
Humanism, humanists, 3, 42, 58–78, 98, 99, 106, 107, 115, 130, 183, 210–15 *passim*, 228, 237, 240, 242, 243
Hunt, Leigh, 159
Hunter, Joseph, 245
Huon of Bordeaux, 78, 84, 94, 124
Hymnes, 10, 54, 109, 118, 139, 153, 157, 167, 187, 200, 216, 226, 235, 255, 257; *of Love*, 216, 219, 220, 235, 246, 250, 251, 253; *of Beautie*, 222, 223, 225, 246, 252, 253;) *Heavenly Love*, 54, 65, 140, 212, 216, 217, 227, 251, 253; *of Heavenly Beautie*, 10, 54, 65, 147, 212, 224–7 *passim*, 246, 250–4 *passim*

Invention, 131, 132, 153
Irena, 30, 86, 106, 122, 123, 125, 169
Isis, 66, 221, 222

262

Index

Index

264

Index

Index

Spenser, Edmund: family and birth, 1, 2; education, 2–6; probable share in *A Theatre of Worldlings*, 5; friendship and correspondence with Gabriel Harvey, 4–7, 13–18, 25–7; secretary to John Young, 6; Puritan associations, 5–7; courtship of "Rosalind", 8–12; possible early visit to Ireland, 12; associations with the Earl of Leicester, Sir Philip Sidney and the "Areopagus", 12–16, 20–5; possible early marriage, 14–15; *The Shepheardes Calender*, 18–21; attacks Burleigh in *Mother Hubberds Tale*, 22–4; appointed secretary to Lord Grey, accompanying him to Ireland, 25–7; appointed Clerk for Faculties in Chancery and Commissioner for Musters in Kildare, 31; obtains manor of Enniscorthy, New Abbey and manor of Kilcolman, 31; visited by Raleigh at Kilcolman, 32, 36, 39, 40; associations with Lodowick Bryskett, 37–9; accompanies Raleigh to London, 40; *The Faerie Queene* (Books I–III), *Daphnaida*, *Complaints*, 40–6; returns to Ireland, 46–7; *Colin Clouts Come Home Againe*, 46, 47, 51; *Amoretti*, 47, 48, 51; marries Elizabeth Boyle, 48; *Epithalamion*, 49, 51; involved in suit against Lord Roche, 49, 50; re-visits London, 51; *The Faerie Queene* (Books IV–VI), 51, 52; *Prothalamion*, 52, 53; seeks patronage of the Earl of Essex, 53; *A View*, *Four Hymnes*, 53, 54; involved in suit on behalf of Elizabeth Spenser, 54, 55; the cantos of Mutability, 55; recommended for office as High Sheriff of Cork, 55; escapes to England from Kilcolman after Munster rebellion, 55; death, descendants, 55, 56; *see also under* separate titles and subject headings; "Colin", 4, 7, 8, 9, 11, 12, 19, 21, 32, 36, 41, 47, 59, 67, 126, 129, 130, 134, 136, 146, 176, 178, 187, 190, 195, 200

Spingarn, J. E., 250, 251, 253
Spondanus, 102
Squire of Dames, the, 86, 94, 117, 120
Squire's Tale, The, see under Chaucer
"Stemmata Dudleiana", 15, 24
Stichomythia, 148
Stoicism, Stoics, 14, 66, 68, 110, 117, 119, 211, 229, 235
Strabo, 33
Strachey, Lytton, 127, 250
Strafford, Thomas, Earl of, 28
Stubbes, John, 24
Sylvius, Æneas, 33
Symbolism, *see under* Allegory
Symposium, see under Plato
Syncope, 144
Synot, R., 31

Tacitus, 33
Talus, 86, 90, 91, 105, 123, 124, 125
Tamburlaine, see under Marlowe
Tanner, T., 246
Tarleton, Richard, 247
Tasso, Torquato, 39, 66, 67, 69, 79, 84, 87, 88, 89, 101, 114, 115, 167, 178, 202, 210, 248
Teares of the Muses, The, 8, 17, 43, 44, 63, 131, 188, 248, 252
Temperance, 70, 91, 108, 109, 110, 113, 118, 122, 128
Temple, William, 3
Tennyson, Alfred, Lord, 58, 209, 211
Theatre of Worldlings, A, see under Vander Noodt
Theocritus, 9, 19, 61
Thomson, James, 208; *The Castle of Indolence*, 158, 206
Throgmorton, Elizabeth, 51
Timæus, see under Plato
Timias, 51, 90, 101, 106, 122, 125, 126, 181
Tiptoft, John, Earl of Worcester, 71
Todd, H. J., 249, 256
Tom Jones, by Henry Fielding, 63
Trissino, G., 79, 87
Tristram, 78, 82, 92, 126, 164, 175, 182
Troilus and Criseyde, see under Chaucer
Truth, 71, 90, 92, 112, 113, 237

Index

Turler, H., 6
"Turns", 146, 147
Tusser, Thomas, 143, 197
Tynte, Robert, 56
Tyrone, Earl of, 55

Una, 71, 88, 103, 104, 106, 112, 159, 164, 165, 166, 177, 179, 226
Utopia, see under More

Vallans, William, 16
Vander Noodt, 5, 245, 255; *A Theatre of Worldlings*, 15, 104, 193
Venus, *and* Temple of, 94, 104, 119, 121, 207–29 *passim*, 238
Venus and Adonis, see under Shakespeare
Verse, 19, 192–209; hexameters, 14, 15, 16, 20, 60, 62, 192, 201; Spenserian stanza, 150, 189, 201–9; stanzaic forms, 200, 201
View of the present state of Ireland, A, 12, 29, 30, 33–6 *passim*, 50, 53, 54, 56, 66, 72–5 *passim*, 133, 136, 256
Vincentius, 33
Virgil, 19, 41, 61, 64, 89, 101, 129, 150, 151, 174, 208; *Ceiris*, 249
Virgils Gnat, 27, 36, 45, 139, 142, 161, 186, 200, 251, 252
Virtue, 38, 42, 66, 80, 81, 213–15, 229, 233, 237, 243; private and

politic, 68–77, 108–28 *passim*; theological, 104
Visions, of Bellay, of Petrarch, of the Worlds Vanitie, 5, 43, 44, 45, 104, 139, 200, 252
Vives, J. L., 78
Volsungasaga, 78
Voltaire, F. M. A. de, 101, 133

Waller, Edmund, 208
Walsingham, Sir Francis, 41, 52
Ware, Sir James, 55, 256
Warner, William, 248
Warton, Thomas, 113, 157, 202, 249, 257
Warwick, Anne, Countess of, 54
Webbe, William, 20
Weever, John, 45
Welply, W. H., 247
Whitgift, John, 6
Whitney, L., 249
William the Conqueror, 73
Wilson, Thomas, 3, 61, 133, 135
Winstanley, L., 257
Winstanley, W., 245
Wordsworth, William, 157, 208; *Lyrical Ballads*, 63, 154
Wright's Chaste Wife, The, 84
Wyatt, Sir Thomas, and Henry, Earl of Surrey, 62, 138

Young, John ("Roffy"), 4, 6, 7